Lecture Notes in Computer Science 12914

More information about this subseries at http://www.springer.com/series/7408

Una-May O'Reilly · Xavier Devroey (Eds.)

Search-Based Software Engineering

13th International Symposium, SSBSE 2021
Bari, Italy, October 11–12, 2021
Proceedings

 Springer

Editors
Una-May O'Reilly
Massachusetts Institute of Technology
Cambridge, MA, USA

Xavier Devroey 🄳
Delft University of Technology
Delft, The Netherlands

ISSN 0302-9743   ISSN 1611-3349   (electronic)
Lecture Notes in Computer Science
ISBN 978-3-030-88105-4   ISBN 978-3-030-88106-1   (eBook)
https://doi.org/10.1007/978-3-030-88106-1

LNCS Sublibrary: SL2 – Programming and Software Engineering

This Springer imprint is published by the registered company Springer Nature Switzerland AG
The registered company address is: Gewerbestrasse 11, 6330 Cham, Switzerland

Message from the General Chairs

Welcome to the 13th Symposium on Search-Based Software Engineering (SSBSE 2021). SSBSE is a premium venue dedicated to the discussion of novel ideas and applications of search-based software engineering, a research area focused on the formulation of software engineering problems as search problems. A wealth of engineering challenges can leverage the application of automated approaches and optimization techniques from AI and machine learning research.

This year, SSBSE was again organized as a virtual conference due to travel restrictions imposed by the COVID-19 pandemic. We would like to thank the members of the Organizing Committee for their effort in making the virtual event a success. We thank the track chairs for their great work in creating an exciting conference program: Una-May O'Reilly and Xavier Devroey (Research track), Tim Menzies (Journal First track), Ruchika Malhotra and Bruno Lima (New Ideas and Emerging Results track), Venera Arnaoudova and Gabriele Bavota (Replications and Negative Results track), and Gregory Gay and René Just (Challenge track). We thank Wesley K. G. Assunção, our publication chair, for their remarkable effort in coordinating the proceedings. We thank Marios Fokaefs for their support in organizing the virtual event. Last but not least, we thank our publicity chairs, Rebecca Moussa and Fiorella Zampetti, for their job in advertising SSBSE through mailing lists and social media, and Luigi Quaranta for setting up our website.

Finally, we would like to thank the University of Bari and Polytechnique Montreal and our sponsor Facebook for the generous support to SSBSE 2021 and the forthcoming 2022 installment.

Looking forward to seeing you all online!

August 2021   Giuliano Antoniol
                                                                     Nicole Novielli

Message from the Program Chairs

On behalf of the SSBSE 2021 Program Committee, it is our pleasure to present the proceedings of the 13th International Symposium on Search-Based Software Engineering.

The field of Search-Based Software Engineering (SBSE) has grown tremendously in the last few years, with research covering a wide range of topics in the intersection of software engineering and search algorithms. As in the previous years, and despite the deep impact of the COVID-19 pandemic which has been going on for over a year now, SSBSE 2021 continues to bring together the international SBSE community to present innovations, discuss new ideas, and celebrate progress in the field. This year we received 21 papers in total across four tracks: 14 full research papers, 3 challenge solutions, and 4 replications and negative results (RENE) papers. We would like to thank the authors for their submissions, and issue our appreciation for their efforts in advancing the SBSE field.

The success of SSBSE depends completely on the effort, talent, and energy of researchers in the field of search-based software engineering who have written and submitted papers on a variety of topics. Following a strict review process, where each submission received three reviews, we accepted 11 papers: 7 papers in the research track, 2 papers in the RENE track, and 2 papers in the challenge solutions track. The Program Committee members and external reviewers, who have invested significant time in assessing multiple papers, and who hold and maintain a high standard of quality for this conference, also deserve our appreciation. Their dedicated work and support makes this symposium possible and results in a stronger community.

In addition to a program full of research talks, SSBSE 2021 attendees had the opportunity to learn more about search-based system testing with EvoMaster in a tutorial given by Andrea Arcuri, Professor at Kristiania University College, Norway. Finally, SSBSE 2021 featured two outstanding keynotes from Aldeida Aleti, Associate Professor at Monash University, Australia, and Massimiliano Di Penta, Full Professor at the University of Sannio, Italy. We thank them for accepting our invitation and for their insightful talks!

We hope you enjoy the work contained in this volume and you can apply it to your own work. We are proud of the program assembled this year, and are thankful for the opportunity to present these proceedings to the SBSE research community.

July 2021

Una-May O'Reilly
Xavier Devroey

Organization

Organizers

General Chairs

Giuliano Antoniol   Polytechnique Montreal, Canada
Nicole Novielli   University of Bari, Italy

Program Chairs

Una-May O'Reilly   Massachusetts Institute of Technology, USA
Xavier Devroey   Delft University of Technology, The Netherlands

Journal First Chair

Tim Menzies   North Carolina State University, USA

RENE Track Chairs

Venera Arnaoudova   Washington State University, USA
Gabriele Bavota   Università della Svizzera italiana, Switzerland

NIER Track Chairs

Ruchika Malhotra   Delhi Technological University, India
Bruno Lima   University of Porto and INESC TEC, Portugal

Challenge Track Chairs

Gregory Gay   Chalmers University of Technology and the University
                           of Gothenburg, Sweden
René Just   University of Washington, USA

Publicity Chairs

Rebecca Moussa   University College London, UK
Fiorella Zampetti   University of Sannio, Italy

Virtualization Chair

Marios Fokaefs   École Polytechnique de Montréal, Canada

Web Chair

Luigi Quaranta   University of Bari, Italy

Publication Chair

Wesley K. G. Assunção   Pontifical Catholic University of Rio de Janeiro, Brazil

SSBSE Steering Committee

Federica Sarro   University College London, UK
Shaukat Ali   Simula Research Laboratory, Norway
Gregory Gay   Chalmers University of Technology and the University
                                    of Gothenburg, Sweden
Phil McMinn   University of Sheffield, UK
Mike Papadakis   University of Luxembourg, Luxembourg
Thomas Vogel   Humboldt University of Berlin, Germany
Shin Yoo   KAIST, South Korea

Technical Program Committee

Aldeida Aleti   Monash University, Australia
Shaukat Ali   Simula Research Laboratory, Norway
Paolo Arcaini   National Institute of Informatics, Japan
Andrea Arcuri   Kristiania University College and Oslo Metropolitan
                                    University, Norway
Betty H. C. Cheng   Michigan State University, USA
Thelma E. Colanzi Lopez   State University of Maringá, Brazil
Pouria Derakhshanfar   Delft University of Technology, The Netherlands
Massimiliano Di Penta   University of Sannio, Italy
Robert Feldt   Chalmers University of Technology, Sweden
Alessio Gambi   University of Passau, Germany
Lars Grunske   Humboldt University of Berlin, Germany
Erik Hemberg   Massachusetts Institute of Technology, USA
Hadi Hemmati   University of Calgary, Canada
Fuyuki Ishikawa   National Institute of Informatics, Japan
Fitsum Kifetew   Fondazione Bruno Kessler, Italy
Roberto E. Lopez-Herrejon   ETS Montreal - University of Quebec, Canada
Inmaculada Medina-Bulo   Universidad de Cádiz, Spain
Manuel Núñez   Universidad Complutense de Madrid, Spain

Annibale Panichella   Delft University of Technology, The Netherlands
Mike Papadakis   University of Luxembourg, Luxembourg
José Miguel Rojas   University of Leicester, UK
Federica Sarro   University College London, UK
Thomas Vogel   Humboldt-Universität zu Berlin, Germany
Shin Yoo   KAIST, South Korea

NIER Track Committee

Shaukat Ali   Simula Research Laboratory, Norway
Carlos Cetina   San Jorge University, Spain
Thelma E. Colanzi Lopez   State University of Maringá, Brazil
Gordon Fraser   University of Passau, Germany
Giovani Guizzo   University College London, UK
Pasqualina Potena   RISE Research Institutes of Sweden AB, Sweden
José Raúl Romero   University of Cordoba, Spain
Thomas Vogel   Humboldt-Universität zu Berlin, Germany
Fiorella Zampetti   University of Sannio, Italy

RENE Track Committee

Massimiliano Di Penta   University of Sannio, Italy
Gordon Fraser   University of Passau, Germany
Gregory Gay   Chalmers University of Technology and the University
                           of Gothenburg, Sweden
Kevin Moran   George Mason University, USA
Matheus Paixao   University of Fortaleza, Brazil
Fabio Palomba   University of Salerno, Italy
Sebastiano Panichella   Zurich University of Applied Sciences, Switzerland
Chaiyong Ragkhitwetsagul   Mahidol University, Thailand
Andrea Stocco   Università della Svizzera italiana, Switzerland
Sira Vegas   Universidad Politecnica de Madrid, Spain

Challenge Track Program Committee

Aldeida Aleti   Monash University, Australia
Jose Campos   University of Lisbon, Portugal
Junjie Chen   Tianjin University, China
Erik Fredericks   Grand Valley State University, USA
Gregory Kapfhammer   Allegheny College, USA
Inmaculada Medina-Bulo   Universidad de Cádiz, Spain
Manish Motwani   University of Massachusetts, USA

Pasqualina Potena	RISE Research Institutes of Sweden AB, Sweden
José Miguel Rojas	University of Leicester, UK
Silvia Regina Vergilio	Federal University of Paraná, Brazil

Sponsoring Institution

Facebook

SSBSE'21 Tutorial: Search-Based System Testing with EvoMaster (Tutorial Paper)[1]

Andrea Arcuri[1,2] (iD)

[1] Kristiania University College, Norway
[2] Oslo Metropolitan University, Norway
andrea.arcuri@kristiania.no

Abstract. In this tutorial, I will show how to use the open-source EVOMASTER tool to generate system-level test cases for different web services (e.g., RESTful APIs written in Java). The generated test cases can then be used to enable different kinds of research endeavors. I will also give an overview of the source code and architecture of EVOMASTER, to help researchers that need to extend it for their research work.

Keywords: REST API Testing · SBST · Fuzzing

1 Overview

EVOMASTER [1, 2] is an open source tool [8], under development since 2016. It is currently hosted on GitHub[2], with releases stored on Zenodo as well (e.g., [9]).

EVOMASTER aims at system-level test case generation for web and enterprise applications, using evolutionary techniques, such as the MIO algorithm [3]. It currently targets REST APIs [4], but can be extended for other domains (e.g., support for GraphQL APIs is in beta-version at the time of this writing). EVOMASTER supports both white-box and black-box testing [5]. Black-box testing is more general, and can be applied on any API regardless of the programming language they are written in. However, it lacks the advanced search-based heuristics like *testability transformations* [7] that can be used in the white-box version, as well as analyzing all interactions with SQL databases to improve the test generation even further [6].

The white-box testing is currently aimed at APIs running on the JVM, like the ones written in Java and Kotlin, where code-level search-based heuristics (e.g., the *branch distance*) are computed via bytecode instrumentation (which is fully automated). Furthermore, support for NodeJS (e.g., JavaScript) and .Net (e.g., C#) are currently under development.

EVOMASTER is divided in two main components: a core and a *driver*. The *core* is written in Kotlin, and it contains the implementations of different search algorithms

---

[1] This work is supported by the Research Council of Norway (project on Evolutionary Enterprise Testing, grant agreement No 274385).

[2] https://github.com/EMResearch/EvoMaster

(e.g., MIO [3]), and all the code to evaluate the fitness function via HTTP calls toward the system under test (SUT). It also includes the code to output the evolved test cases in different formats, such as JUnit in either Java or Kotlin, Jest for JavaScript and XUnit for C#. The core is released as an executable jar file, where we provide as well installers for the main operating systems[3] (e.g., MSI for Windows). On the other hand, the *driver* is responsible to start/stop/reset the SUT, as well as doing all the instrumentations needed to compute code-level search-based heuristics. For SUTs running on the JVM, the driver is written in Java, and released on Maven Central[4].

The *core* and the *driver* will run on two separated processes, where the driver exposes its functionality via a REST API. This architectural decision was purposely made to be able to support further programming languages, besides the original Java (e.g., JavaScript and C#).

This tutorial at SSBSE'21 is aimed mainly at researchers, and not practitioners in industry. The goal of this tutorial is to show how to use EvoMaster to generate test cases for REST APIs, which could be used in different research contexts. I will also go through and discuss some of the source-code of EvoMaster, for researchers that want to extend it to investigate different research questions.

References

1. Arcuri, A.: RESTful API automated test case generation. In: IEEE International Conference on Software Quality, Reliability and Security (QRS), pp. 9–20. IEEE (2017)
2. Arcuri, A.: EvoMaster: evolutionary multi-context automated system test generation. In: IEEE International Conference on Software Testing, Verification and Validation (ICST), pp. 394–397. IEEE (2018)
3. Arcuri, A.: Test suite generation with the Many Independent Objective (MIO) algorithm. Information and Software Technology. **104**, 195–206 (2018)
4. Arcuri, A.: RESTful API automated test case generation with EvoMaster. ACM Trans. Softw. Eng. Methodol. (TOSEM) **28**(1), 3 (2019)
5. Arcuri, A.: Automated black-and white-box testing of restful apis with EvoMaster. IEEE Softw. **38**(3), 72–78 (2020)
6. Arcuri, A., Galeotti, J.P.: Handling sql databases in automated system test generation. ACM Trans. Softw. Eng. Methodol. (TOSEM) **29**(4), 1–31 (2020)
7. Arcuri, A., Galeotti, J.P.: Testability transformations for existing APIs. In: 2020 IEEE 13th International Conference on Software Testing, Validation and Verification (ICST), pp. 153–163. IEEE (2020)
8. Arcuri, A., Galeotti, J.P., Marculescu, B., Zhang, M.: Evomaster: A search-based system test generation tool. J. Open Source Softw. **6**(57), 2153 (2021)
9. Arcuri, A., Galeotti, J.P., Marculescu, B., Zhang, M., Belhadi, A., Golmohammadi, A.: EvoMaster: A Search-Based System Test Generation Tool (Jun 2021). \DOIurl{https://doi.org/10.5281/zenodo.4896807}

---

[3] https://github.com/EMResearch/EvoMaster/releases
[4] https://search.maven.org/artifact/org.evomaster/evomaster

Contents

Challenge Solutions

Keynote

On the Effectiveness of SBSE Techniques
Through Instance Space Analysis

Aldeida Aleti[✉]

Faculty of Information Technology, Monash University, Melbourne, Australia
aldeida.aleti@monash.edu

Abstract. Search-Based Software Engineering is now a mature area with numerous techniques developed to tackle some of the most challenging software engineering problems, from requirements to design, testing, fault localisation, and automated program repair. SBSE techniques have shown promising results, giving us hope that one day it will be possible for the tedious and labour intensive parts of software development to be completely automated, or at least semi-automated. In this talk, I will focus on the problem of objective performance evaluation of SBSE techniques. To this end, I will introduce Instance Space Analysis (ISA), which is an approach to identify features of SBSE problems that explain why a particular instance is difficult for an SBSE technique. ISA can be used to examine the diversity and quality of the benchmark datasets used by most researchers, and analyse the strengths and weaknesses of existing SBSE techniques. The instance space is constructed to reveal areas of hard and easy problems, and enables the strengths and weaknesses of the different SBSE techniques to be identified. I will present on how ISA enabled us to identify the strengths and weaknesses of SBSE techniques in two areas: Search-Based Software Testing and Automated Program Repair. Finally, I will end my talk with potential future directions of the objective assessment of SBSE techniques.

Keywords: Search-based software engineering · Instance space analysis

1 Instance Space Analysis for SBSE

Instance Space Analysis (ISA) has two main goals:

- to help designers of SBSE techniques (SBSET) gain insight into why some techniques are more or less suited to solve certain SBSE problems, thus devising new and better techniques that address any challenging areas, and
- to help software developers select the most effective SBSET for their software system.

ISA provides a way for objective assessment of the effectiveness of SBSE techniques. It has been applied to Search-Based Software Testing [5,6], Search-Based

© Springer Nature Switzerland AG 2021
U.-M. O'Reilly and X. Devroey (Eds.): SSBSE 2021, LNCS 12914, pp. 3–6, 2021.
https://doi.org/10.1007/978-3-030-88106-1_1

Program Repair [1], machine learning [3], and optimisation [7]. The concept of instance space analysis was first introduced by Smith-Miles in her seminal work looking at the strengths and weaknesses of optimisation problems [7]. Understanding the effectiveness of an SBSE technique is critical for selecting the most suitable technique for a particular SBSE problem, thus avoiding trial and error application of SBSE techniques.

An overview of the ISA for SBSE is presented in Fig. 1. It starts with a set of problems $p \in P$ and a portfolio of SBSE techniques $t \in T$. For example, P can be a set of buggy programs and T can be a portfolio of Search-Based Program Repair techniques. The performance of each Search-Based Software Engineering Technique (SBSET) is measured for each problem instance as $y(t, p)$. For example, y can indicate whether a plausible patch has been found for a program p by the Search-Based Program Repair Technique t. The first step of ISA is to identify the significant features of problem instances $(f(p) \in F)$ that have an impact on how easy or hard they are for a particular SBSET. A feature can be the complexity of code, as measured by code-based complexity metrics. An example is the coupling between object classes, which is a count of the number of other classes to which the current class is coupled [2]. In Search-Based Program Repair, features may include those that are related to the prediction of source code transformations on buggy code [10] and detection of incorrect patches [9].

Next, ISA constructs the footprints $(g(f(P))) \in R^2$ which indicate the area of strength for each SBSET. Finally, ISA applies machine learning techniques on the most significant features to learn a model that can be used for SBSET selection for future application.

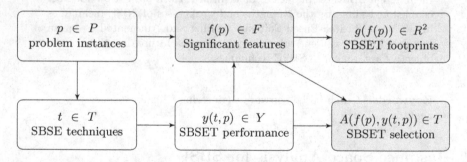

Fig. 1. An overview of instance space analysis for analysing the effectiveness of SBSE techqniques.

The features included in the feature space ($\mathcal{F}$) should be diverse and predictive of the performance of at least one algorithm. Hence, their selection requires careful consideration. They are domain specific and thus developing $\mathcal{F}$ requires significant domain knowledge. Features should be highly correlated with algorithm performance, not highly correlated with other features, and cheaper to compute compared to the runtime of the algorithm. Features should also be capable of explaining the similarities and differences between instances, and should be interpretable by humans [3,4].

The portfolio of SBSE Techniques is constructed by selecting a set of methods, each one with its unique biases, capable of solving the given problem. The more diverse the SBSETs, the higher the chance of finding the most suitable SBSET for a given instance.

The SBSET performance space $\mathcal{Y}$ includes the measures to report the performance of the SBSETs when solving the problem instances. Common performance measures for automated testing are coverage, length/size of the test suite and mutation score [8]. For Search Based Program Repair, a common measure is whether the techique produced a plausaible patch for a buggy program [1].

A critical step of ISA is identifying features of problem instances instances $f(p) \in F$ that have an impact on the effectiveness of SBSE techniques. Features are problem dependent and must be chosen such that the varying complexities of the buggy program instances are exposed, any known structural properties of the software systems are captured, and any known advantages and limitations of the different SBSETs are related to features.

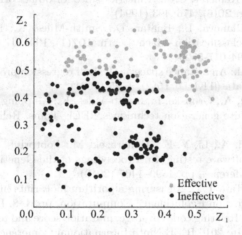

Fig. 2. SBSET footprint.

ISA applies a Genetic Algorithm to select the set of features which result in an instance space – as defined by the 2-dimensional projection of the subset of features through Principal Component Analysis – with problem instances that show similar performance of SBSETs closer to each other in this 2D space (as shown in Fig. 2). The best subset of features is the one that can best discriminate between easy and hard buggy program instances for SBSE techniques. The subset of features that have large coefficients and therefore contribute significantly to the variance of each Principal Component (PC), will be identified as the significant features. Rather than reporting algorithm performance averaged across a chosen set of problem instances, ISA reports the SBSET's footprint, which is the performance of a technique generalised across a diverse set of instances.

In the final step, ISA applies Machine Learning to predict the most effective SBSET for solving a particular SBSE problem. ISA uses the most significant features as an input to learn the relationship between the instance features and SBSET performance. A variety of machine learning algorithms can be used for this purpose, such as decision trees, or support vector machines for binary labels (effective/ineffective), or statistical prediction methods, such as regression algorithms or neural networks for continuous labels (e.g., time complexity of the approach). Previous work has reported Random Forest Classifier as the best performing method for Search-Based Program Repair [1], and Decisin Tree for Search-Based Software Testing [5].

References

1. Aleti, A., Martinez, M.: E-APR: mapping the effectiveness of automated program repair techniques. Empir. Softw. Eng. **26**(5), 1–30 (2021)
2. Chidamber, S.R., Kemerer, C.F.: A metrics suite for object oriented design. IEEE Trans. Softw. Eng. **20**(6), 476–493 (1994)
3. Muñoz, M.A., Villanova, L., Baatar, D., Smith-Miles, K.: Instance spaces for machine learning classification. Mach. Learn. **107**(1), 109–147 (2017). https://doi.org/10.1007/s10994-017-5629-5
4. Muñoz, M.A., et al.: An instance space analysis of regression problems. ACM Trans. Knowl. Discov. Data (TKDD) **15**(2), 1–25 (2021)
5. Oliveira, C., Aleti, A., Grunske, L., Smith-Miles, K.: Mapping the effectiveness of automated test suite generation techniques. IEEE Trans. Reliab. **67**(3), 771–785 (2018)
6. Oliveira, C., Aleti, A., Li, Y.-F., Abdelrazek, M.: Footprints of fitness functions in search-based software testing. In: Proceedings of the Genetic and Evolutionary Computation Conference, pp. 1399–1407 (2019)
7. Smith-Miles, K., Tan, T.T.: Measuring algorithm footprints in instance space. In: 2012 IEEE Congress on Evolutionary Computation, pp. 1–8. IEEE (2012)
8. Tengeri, D., et al.: Relating code coverage, mutation score and test suite reducibility to defect density. In: 2016 IEEE Ninth International Conference on Software Testing, Verification and Validation Workshops (ICSTW), pp. 174–179. IEEE (2016)
9. Ye, H., Gu, J., Martinez, M., Durieux, T., Monperrus, M.: Automated classification of overfitting patches with statically extracted code features. Technical report 1910.12057, arXiv (2019)
10. Yu, Z., Martinez, M., Bissyandé, T.F., Monperrus, M.: Learning the relation between code features and code transforms with structured prediction. Technical report 1907.09282, arXiv (2019)

Research Papers

Generating Failing Test Suites
for Quantum Programs With Search

Xinyi Wang[1]($\boxtimes$) , Paolo Arcaini[2] , Tao Yue[1,3] , and Shaukat Ali[3]

[1] Nanjing University of Aeronautics and Astronautics, Nanjing, China
wangxinyi125@nuaa.edu.cn
[2] National Institute of Informatics, Tokyo, Japan
[3] Simula Research Laboratory, Fornebu, Norway

Abstract. Testing quantum programs requires systematic, automated, and intelligent methods due to their inherent complexity, such as their superposition and entanglement. To this end, we present a search-based approach, called Quantum Search-Based Testing (QuSBT), for automatically generating test suites of a given size depending on available testing budget, with the aim of maximizing the number of failing test cases in the test suite. QuSBT consists of definitions of the problem encoding, failure types, test assessment with statistical tests, fitness function, and test case generation with a Genetic Algorithm (GA). To empirically evaluate QuSBT, we compared it with Random Search (RS) by testing six quantum programs. We assessed the effectiveness of QuSBT and RS with 30 carefully designed faulty versions of the six quantum programs. Results show that QuSBT provides a viable solution for testing quantum programs, and achieved a significant improvement over RS in 87% of the faulty programs, and no significant difference in the rest of 13% of the faulty programs.

Keywords: Quantum programs · Software testing · Genetic algorithms

1 Introduction

Testing quantum programs is essential for developing correct and reliable quantum applications. However, testing quantum programs is challenging due to their unique characteristics, as compared to classical programs, such as superposition and entanglement [11]. Thus, there is a need for the development of systematic, automated, and intelligent methods to find failures in quantum programs [11]. Such testing works have started to emerge, focusing on, e.g., coverage criteria [2], property-based testing [7], fuzz testing [12], and runtime assertions

QuSBT is supported by the National Natural Science Foundation of China under Grant No. 61872182 and Qu-Test (Project#299827) funded by Research Council of Norway. Paolo Arcaini is supported by ERATO HASUO Metamathematics for Systems Design Project (No. JPMJER1603), JST. Funding Reference number: 10.13039/501100009024 ERATO.

© Springer Nature Switzerland AG 2021
U.-M. O'Reilly and X. Devroey (Eds.): SSBSE 2021, LNCS 12914, pp. 9–25, 2021.
https://doi.org/10.1007/978-3-030-88106-1_2

(e.g., *Proq* [9]). In contrast to existing works, we propose an approach to automatically generate test suites of given sizes with search algorithms, which are dependent on available testing budgets, with the aim of maximizing the number of failing test cases in a test suite. We call our approach *Quantum Search-Based Testing* (QuSBT), where the generation of test suites is encoded as a search problem. We also identify two types of failures, devise statistical test-based test assessment criteria, and define the number of repetitions that are considered sufficient for test executions, by considering the inherent uncertainty of quantum programs.

QuSBT employs a Genetic Algorithm (GA) as its search strategy. To assess the cost-effectiveness of QuSBT, we compared it with Random Search (RS), the comparison baseline. We selected six quantum programs as the subject systems of the evaluation, and created 30 faulty versions of the programs (i.e., 30 benchmarks) to assess the cost-effectiveness of GA and RS in terms of finding test suites of given sizes and maximizing the number of failing tests. Results show that QuSBT performed significantly better than RS for testing 87% of the faulty programs, and there were no significant differences for the rest of 13% of the faulty programs.

Paper Structure. Section 2 reviews the related work. Section 3 presents the background. Section 4 introduces definitions necessary for formalizing the QuSBT approach, which is discussed in detail in Sect. 5. Sections 6 and 7 present our empirical evaluation. Then, Sect. 8 identifies threats that may affect the validity of QuSBT, and Sect. 9 concludes the paper.

2   Related Work

Ali et al. [2] proposed *Quito* – consisting of three coverage criteria defined on inputs and outputs of quantum programs, and two types of test oracles. Passing and failing of test suites were judged with one-sample Wilcoxon signed rank test, and mutation analysis was used to assess the effectiveness of coverage criteria. Results indicate that the least expensive coverage criterion, i.e., the input coverage, can manage to achieve high mutation scores, and the input-output coverage criterion (the most expensive one) could not increase mutation scores for most cases. As also acknowledged by the authors, the coverage criteria do not scale when handling quantum programs with more qubits, thus requiring the development of efficient quantum testing approaches such as QuSBT.

Huang and Martonosi [8] proposed a statistical assertion approach for finding bugs. They identified six bug types and their corresponding assertions. The chi-square test was used to test the hypothesis on the distributions of measurements, and determine a contingency coefficient with the confidence level of 95%. The approach tested three quantum programs followed by identifying bugs and their types in the programs.

Zhou and Byrd [10] proposed to enable runtime assertions, inspired by the quantum error correction, by introducing additional qubits to obtain information of qubits under test, without disrupting the execution of the program under test. The proposed approach was verified on a quantum simulator. Along the same lines, Li et al. [9] proposed *Proq*, a projection-based runtime assertion scheme for testing and debugging quantum software. Proq only needs to check the satisfaction of a projection (i.e., a closed subspace of the state space) on a small number of projection measurements, instead of repeated program executions. Proq defines several assertion transformation techniques to ensure the feasibility of executing assertions on quantum computers. Proq was compared with other two assertion mechanisms [8,10] and it showed stronger expressive power, more flexible assertion location, fewer executions, and lower implementation overhead. When comparing with QuSBT, 1) Proq is a white-box, whereas QuSBT is blackbox; 2) Proq requires the definition of projections and implements them as assertions, which requires expertise and effort, while QuSBT does not need to change the quantum program under test to include assertions; thereby reducing cost; and 3) Same as QuSBT, Proq also requires repeatedly executing assertions for a *sufficiently* large number of times in order to achieve the confidence level of 95%.

QSharpCheck [7] tests Q# programs. The paper presents a test property specification language for defining the number of tests to generate, statistical confidence level, the number of measurements, and experiments for obtaining data to perform statistical tests. Moreover, QSharpCheck defines property-based test case generation, execution and analysis, and five types of assertions. It was evaluated with two quantum programs, via mutation analysis. In comparison, we focus on finding the maximum number of failing test cases in test suites with a GA based on two types of failures.

QuanFuzz [12] focuses on increasing the branch coverage with a GA. It outperformed a random generator in terms of the effectiveness of triggering sensitive branches, and achieved a higher branch coverage than the traditional test input generation method. We, instead, focus on finding failing test suites based on two types of test oracles, whereas QuanFuzz focuses on searching inputs to cover branches. Thus, the search problems of QuanFuzz are different.

3   Background

Quantum programs operate on *quantum bits* (*qubits*). Similarly as in classical computers, a qubit can take value 0 or 1. However, in addition, a state of a qubit is described with its *amplitude* (α), which is a complex number and defines two elements: a *magnitude* and a *phase*. The magnitude indicates the probability of a quantum program being in a particular state, while the phase shows the angle of this complex number in polar form (it ranges from 0 to 2π radians). Taking a three-qubits quantum program as an example, we can represent all the possible states of the program in the Dirac notation:

$$\alpha_0 \left|000\right\rangle + \alpha_1 \left|001\right\rangle + \alpha_2 \left|010\right\rangle + \alpha_3 \left|011\right\rangle + \alpha_4 \left|100\right\rangle + \alpha_5 \left|101\right\rangle + \alpha_6 \left|110\right\rangle + \alpha_7 \left|111\right\rangle$$

$\alpha_0, \ldots, \alpha_7$ are the *amplitudes* associated to the eight program states. Note that each state is simply a permutation of the three qubits. The magnitude of a state, representing the probability of the program being in the state, is the square of the absolute value of its amplitude (α) (e.g., for $\left|100\right\rangle$, its magnitude is $|\alpha_4|^2$). Note that the sum of the magnitudes of all the states is equal to 1, i.e., $\sum_{i=0}^{7} |\alpha_i|^2 = 1$.

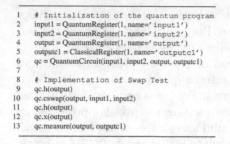

```
1    # Initialization of the quantum program
2    input1 = QuantumRegister(1, name='input1')
3    input2 = QuantumRegister(1, name='input2')
4    output = QuantumRegister(1, name='output')
5    outputc1 = ClassicalRegister(1, name='outputc1')
6    qc = QuantumCircuit(input1, input2, output, outputc1)
7
8    # Implementation of Swap Test
9    qc.h(output)
10   qc.cswap(output, input1, input2)
11   qc.h(output)
12   qc.x(output)
13   qc.measure(output, outputc1)
```

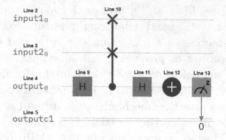

Fig. 1. Swap test – Qiskit code   **Fig. 2.** Swap test – circuit diagram

Figure 1 shows a three-qubits program (*Swap Test* [6]) in the Qiskit framework [13] in Python. Its equivalent circuit is shown in Fig. 2, which also shows which line number of the code matches to which part of the circuit. It compares two qubits: *input1* and *input2*. If they are equal in terms of their states, then the value of the measure qubit (i.e., *output*) becomes 1 (as it is initialized as 0 by default) with the 100% probability; otherwise, the probability decreases when the two inputs are increasingly different. Lines 2 and 3 initialize the two input qubits (i.e., *input1* and *input2*) that are to be compared. Line 4 initializes one output qubit (*output*) which is the condition qubit for controlling the swap gate. Line 5 initializes a classical register (*outputc1*) that stores the result of the comparison. Finally, Line 6 creates the quantum circuit. After the initialization (Lines 2–6), the state of the program will be *000* with amplitude of 1 (i.e., probability of 100%). In this execution of the program, we will compare *input1* initialized as 0 (by default) and *input2* initialized as 0 (by default). Line 9 applies the HAD gate [6] on *output* to put it in superposition. As a result, the state of the program will be 000 and 100 with amplitudes 0.707 (the 50% probability). Note that the *output* qubit is both 0 and 1 in this state of the program, whereas the other two qubits remain the same as initialized. Line 10 applies the CSWAP gate to swap the two input qubits (i.e., *input1* and *input2*). The swap only happens if the control qubit (i.e., *output*) has a value 1. Line 11 applies the second HAD gate on the *output* qubit. Due to the reversibility of the gates in quantum computing, another application of the HAD gate leads the program to its original state, i.e., *000*. Line 12 applies the NOT gate to the *output* qubit. As a result, the state in which the *output* qubit was 0 will become 1. Line 13 reads the *output* qubit and stores it in a classical register *outputc1*. The final state of the program is 1.

4   Definitions

Definition 1 (Inputs and outputs). Let Q be the set of qubits of the quantum program QP. A subset of qubits $I \subseteq Q$ defines the *input*, and a subset $O \subseteq Q$ identifies the *output*.[1] We define $D_I = \mathcal{B}^{|I|}$ as the input values, and $D_O = \mathcal{B}^{|O|}$ as the output values.

---

[1] Note that I and O do not need to be disjoint, i.e., an input qubit can also be an output qubit. Moreover, there could also be qubits that are neither inputs nor outputs, i.e., $I \cup O \subseteq Q$.

In the following, we will consider input and output values in their decimal representation. Note that input and output values are non-negative integers, i.e., $D_I = \{0, \ldots, 2^{|I|} - 1\}$, and $D_O = \{0, \ldots, 2^{|O|} - 1\}$.

Definition 2 (Quantum program). A quantum program QP can then be defined as a function QP: $D_I \rightarrow 2^{D_O}$.

Definition 2 shows that a quantum program, given the same input value, can return different output values. For each input, the possible output values occur by following a certain probability distribution. The program specification specifies the expected probabilities of occurrence of the output values.

Definition 3 (Program specification). Given a quantum program QP: $D_I \rightarrow 2^{D_O}$, we identify with PS the *program specification*, i.e., the expected behavior of the program. For a given input assignment $i \in D_I$, the program specification states the expected probabilities of occurrence of all the output values $o \in D_O$, i.e.,:

$$PS(i) = [p_0, \ldots, p_{|D_O|-1}]$$

where p_h is the expected probability (with $0 \leq p_h \leq 1$) that, given the input value i, the value h is returned as output. It holds $\sum_{h=0}^{|D_O|-1} p_h = 1$. We introduce the following notation for selecting probabilities that are different from 0, i.e., those of the outputs that can occur according to the program specification:

$$PS_{NZ}(i) = [p \in PS(i) \mid p \neq 0] = [p_{j_1}, \ldots, p_{j_k}] \qquad \text{with } j_1, \ldots, j_k \in D_O$$

We further write $PS(i, h) = p_h$ to specify the expected probability of occurrence of output value h for input value i.

Note that, for some programs, the specifications of the expected outputs may not exist, and thus our approach would not be applicable.

5 Quantum Search-Based Testing (QuSBT)

We first give definitions of failure, test, and test assessment for quantum programs in Sect. 5.1, and then propose a test generation approach in Sect. 5.2.

5.1 Failures Types, Test, and Test Assessment

Any testing approach (also for classical programs) tries to trigger failures of the program under test, to reveal the presence of faults. Therefore, we need to define what a *failure* is in a quantum program. In this work, we target two types of failures:

- *Unexpected Output Failure* (*uof*): the program, for a given input i, returns an output o that is not expected according to the program specification PS, i.e., $PS(i, o) = 0$;

– *Wrong Output Distribution Failure (wodf)*: the program, for multiple executions of a given input i, returns output values that follow a probability distribution significantly deviating from the one specified by the program specification.

We propose definitions of test and test assessment to reveal these types of failures. Moreover, the non-deterministic nature of quantum programs requires that a given input is executed multiple times. Therefore, we define a test input as follows.

Definition 4 (Test input). A *test input* is a pair $\langle i, n \rangle$, being i an assignment to qubits (i.e., $i \in D_I$), and n the number of times that program QP must be executed with i.

Definition 5 (Test execution and test result). Given a test input $\langle i, n \rangle$ for a quantum program QP, the *test execution* consists in running QP n times with input i. We identify with $res(\langle i, n \rangle, QP) = [QP(i), \ldots, QP(i)] = [o_1, \ldots, o_n]$ the *test result*, where o_j is the output value of the jth execution of the program.

Test Assessment. To check whether a test passes or fails, we need to check whether at least one of the two types of failures (i.e., *uof* or *wodf*) occurred.

To check *uof*, it is enough to check if some produced output is unexpected, i.e.,

$$\mathtt{fail}_{uof} := (\exists o_j \in res(\langle i, n \rangle, QP) : PS(i, o_j) = 0)$$

If a failure of type *uof* is detected (i.e., $\mathtt{fail}_{uof}$ is *true*), the assessment for *wodf* is not performed[2], because we can already assess that the test is not passing. Otherwise, it is performed as described in the following.

Checking *wodf* requires to check if the frequency distribution of the measured output values follows the expected distribution. We check this by doing a *goodness of fit* test with the Pearson's chi-square test [1]. The test checks whether the observed frequencies of the values of the categorical variable follow the expected distribution. In our setting, the categorical values are the possible output values of the quantum program QP for a given input i, i.e., those having their expected probabilities being non-zero, and the expected distribution is given by the program specification (i.e., $PS_{NZ}(i)$ in Definition 3). Concretely, given a test input $\langle i, n \rangle$ and its test result $res(\langle i, n \rangle, QP) = [o_1, \ldots, o_n]$, we apply the chi-square test as follows:

– from the program specification, we retrieve the expected probabilities of the outputs that can occur given the input i, i.e., $PS_{NZ}(i) = [p_{j_1}, \ldots, p_{j_k}]$, with $j_1, \ldots, j_k \in D_O$ (see Definition 3); $j_1, \ldots, j_k$ are the categorical values of the test;

---

[2] In this case, we directly set $\mathtt{fail}_{wodf}$ (see Eq. 1 later) to *false*.

- then, from the test result, we collect, in $[c_{j_1}, \ldots, c_{j_k}]$, the number of occurrences of each possible output $j_1, \ldots, j_k$, where $c_{j_h} = |\{o \in res(\langle i, n \rangle, \mathrm{QP}) \mid o = j_h\}|$.[3] This is the *one-dimensional contingency table* of the chi-square test; and
- finally, we apply the chi-square test, that takes in input the contingency table $[c_{j_1}, \ldots, c_{j_k}]$ and the expected occurrence probabilities $[p_{j_1}, \ldots, p_{j_k}]$, and checks whether the recorded occurrences follow the expected probability distribution.

The null hypothesis is that there is no statistical significant difference. If the p-value is less than a given significance level α ($\alpha = 0.01$ in our experiments), we can reject the null hypothesis and claim that there is a statistical significant difference. In our case, this means that a *wrong output distribution failure wodf* occurred, which can be detected with the following predicate:

$$\mathtt{fail}_{wodf} := (\text{p-value} < \alpha) \tag{1}$$

Note that the chi-square test requires to have at least two categories. Therefore, the assessment for *wodf* cannot be done when there is only one possible output for a given input (i.e., $|\mathrm{PS}_{NZ}(i)| = 1$).[4] However, in this case, checking *uof* is enough. Indeed, if the program QP is not faulty for *uof*, it means that it always produces the unique output expected from the program specification and, so, also *wodf* is satisfied.

To conclude, the test is considered *failed* if one of the two failures is observed. So, we introduce a predicate recording the result of the test assessment as follows:

$$\mathtt{fail} := \mathtt{fail}_{uof} \vee \mathtt{fail}_{wodf}$$

Remark 1. Note that the absence of a failure for an input i does not guarantee that the program behaves correctly for i. For *uof*, it could be that other additional executions would show a wrong output. For *wodf*, instead, the significance level of the test specifies the confidence on the absence of the fault. The argument is a little bit different for the case that the test fails. If $\mathtt{fail}_{uof} = true$, we are sure that the program is faulty, because an output that should be never returned has been returned. Instead, if $\mathtt{fail}_{wodf} = true$, it could still be that, with more executions, the observed frequencies of the output values would better align with the expected probability distribution specified in the program specification. In this case, the lower the p-value, the higher the confidence on the result.

Definition of the Number of Repetitions. Definitions 4 and 5 say that a test must specify the number of times n that the input i must be executed for

---

[3] Note that the assessment for *wodf* is done only if the assessment for *uof* did not reveal any failure. If this is the case, it is guaranteed that the program returned outputs only from $j_1, \ldots, j_k$, i.e., those having their expected probabilities being non-zero. Therefore, it is guaranteed that each returned output is considered in one of the counts $c_{j_1}, \ldots, c_{j_k}$.

[4] Note that a quantum program can still be deterministic for some given inputs.

its assessment. It is well recognized that selecting such a number is difficult [9], and most approaches do not specify it nor provide a rationale for the selection of a particular number (e.g., [8]). Intuitively, the higher the number of repetitions, the better, as this gives a higher confidence on the result of the test assessment. However, a too high number of repetitions makes the assessment of tests infeasible, in particular when multiple tests must be assessed (as, for example, in a test generation approach as the one proposed in this paper).

In QuSBT, we select a number of repetitions that is sufficient to have a reasonable confidence on the result of the test assessment, but also makes the test assessment feasible to compute. We start observing that not all the inputs need the same number of repetitions: inputs for which a program specification specifies few possible output values, require fewer repetitions than those having a lot of possible outputs. Consider the case in which input $i1$ has two possible outputs, while input $i2$ has four possible outputs. Then, more repetitions are needed for input $i2$ than for $i1$, as we need to provide comparable evidence for each of the possible outputs. On the basis of this intuition, we define a function that, given an input i, specifies the required number of repetitions:

$$\texttt{numRepetitions}(i) = |\mathsf{PS}_{NZ}(i)| \times 100$$

So, the number of repetitions n of the test input i is proportional to the number of possible output values that, according to the program specification, can be obtained by executing the program with i (see Definition 3).

5.2   Test Case Generation

For a given program QP, QuSBT generates a test suite of M tests, being M an approach's parameter. It uses a GA, where search variables $\overline{x} = [x_1, \ldots, x_M]$ are integer variables, each one representing an input for QP taken from D_I. QuSBT finds an assignment $\overline{v} = [v_1, \ldots, v_M]$ for the M tests, such that as many of them as possible fail the program. Fitness is computed as follows. For each test assignment v_j of the jth test:

- We identify the required number of repetitions n_j, as described in Sect. 5.1;
- We execute QP n_j times with the input v_j, obtaining the result $res(\langle v_j, n_j \rangle, \text{QP})$;
- The result is assessed (see Sect. 5.1). We identify with $\texttt{fail}_j$ the assessment result.

Let $ta = [\texttt{fail}_1, \ldots, \texttt{fail}_M]$ be the assessments of all the M tests. The fitness function that we want to maximize is given by the number of failed tests, i.e.,

$$f(\overline{v}) = |\{\texttt{fail}_j \in ta \mid \texttt{fail}_i = true\}| \tag{2}$$

Selection of the Number of Tests. QuSBT requires to select the number of tests M to be added in each searched test suite. Users can specify M, e.g., based on available budgets. However, selecting a value M without considering the program under test might not be a good practice. So, we propose to select M as the percentage β of the number of possible inputs D_I of the quantum program, i.e., $M = \lceil \beta \cdot |D_I| \rceil$. The user must then select the percentage β, rather than the absolute number M.

6   Experimental Design

We describe the experimental design to evaluate QuSBT in terms of research questions, benchmark programs, experimental settings, evaluation metrics, and statistical tests employed to answer the research questions. The used benchmarks and all the experimental results are available online[5].

Research Questions (RQs). We evaluate QuSBT using the following RQs:

- **RQ1:** Does QuSBT (which is GA-based) perform better than Random Search (RS)? RQ1 assesses whether GA can identify test inputs that contribute to failures, as compared to RS.
- **RQ2:** How does QuSBT perform on the benchmark programs? RQ2 assesses the variability on the final results, and how fast the GA converges to better solutions.

Benchmarks Programs. We selected six programs with different characteristics (see Table 1): (i) cryptography programs: Bernstein-Vazirani (BV) and Simon (SM) algorithms; (ii) QRAM (QR) implements an algorithm to access and manipulate quantum random access memory, and invQFT (IQ) implements inverse quantum Fourier transform; (iii) mathematical operations in superposition, i.e., Add Squared (AS); (iv) conditional execution in superposition, i.e., Conditional Execution (CE).

Considering that there are no common known metrics available in the literature for characterizing quantum programs, we here propose to use the number of input qubits, the number of gates, and the circuit depth as the characterization metrics. The number of input qubits (i.e., $|I|$) intuitively characterizes the dimension of the input space (as in classical programs). Since we want to evaluate our approach with relatively complex programs, we selected four programs having 10 input qubits. Moreover, we selected two programs with a lower number of input qubits (i.e., QR and SM) to check whether the proposed approach is also advantageous on less complex programs.

The other two metrics, i.e., the number of gates and circuit depth, instead, to a certain extent, characterize the complexity of the program logic. The *number of gates* is the number of individual operators (e.g., HAD, NOT), while the *circuit depth* is given by the length of the longest sequence of quantum gates (the output of a gate used as the input of another gate determines a unit of the length). As shown in Table 1, IQ has the largest *number of gates*, BV has the least *circuit depth*, and AS has the longest *circuit depth*. We are aware that these

---

[5] https://github.com/Simula-COMPLEX/qusbt/.

Table 1. Benchmark programs (Legend. AI: right after the inputs, MP: middle of the program, BR: right before reading the output)

Program	$|I|$	# gates	depth	Faulty versions (benchmarks)
AS	10	41	38	AS_1: AI, CNOT added; AS_2: AI, SWAP added; AS_3: BR, CNOT added; AS_4: BR, CSWAP added; AS_5: MP, CNOT added
BV	10	30	3	BV_1: AI, CNOT added; BV_2: AI, SWAP added; BV_3: AI, CCNOT added; BV_4: BR, CNOT added; BV_5: BR, CSWAP added
CE	10	25	20	CE_1: AI, CNOT added; CE_2: AI, SWAP added; CE_3: AI, CSWAP added; CE_4: BR, NOT added; CE_5: BR, HAD added
IQ	10	60	56	IQ_1: AI, CHAD added; IQ_2: MP, CHAD added; IQ_3: MP, replace H as CHAD; IQ_4: AI, CHAD added; IQ_5: MP, CHAD added
QR	9	15	12	QR_1: MP, CCPhase added; QR_2: MP, CHAD added; QR_3: MP, CNOT added; QR_4: AI, SWAP added; QR_5: BR, CSWAP added
SM	7	56	5	SM_1: AI, SWAP added; SM_2: AI, CCNOT added; SM_3: BR, CNOT added; SM_4: BR, CSWAP added; SM_5: BR, HAD added

metrics are coarse-grained, and in the future we plan to define and employ more fine-grained metrics.

For our selected programs, we derived the program specification (see Definitions 3) to assess the passing or failing of tests. For each correct program, we produced five faulty versions of it by introducing different types of faults at different locations of the circuit. These 30 faulty programs are the *benchmarks* that we test in our experiments, which are described in details in Table 1. The benchmark name (e.g., AS_1) recalls the original correct program acting as the program specification (e.g., AS). The table also reports the location where a fault has been injected (i.e., right after the inputs, middle of the program, or right before reading the output). A short description is also provided for each benchmark program to tell which kind of gates were added. For instance, a CNOT gate is added right after the input to the original program to produce AS_1.

Experimental Settings. We use Qiskit 0.23.2 [13] to write quantum programs in Python. It also provides a simulator for executing quantum programs, which we used for each evaluation of a given input i (i.e., $QP(i)$).

We adopted GA from the jMetalPy 1.5.5 framework [5], and used the default settings of jMetalPy: the binary tournament selection of parents, the integer SBX crossover (the crossover rate = 0.9), the polynomial mutation operation being equal to the reciprocal of the number of variables. The population size is set as 10, and the termination condition is the maximum number of generations which is set as 50. As the baseline comparison, we also implemented a Random Search (RS) version of the approach from jMetalPy. RS has been given the same number of fitness evaluations as GA, i.e., 500. Note that there is no existing baseline with which we can compare QuSBT.

Search variables $\overline{x} = [x_1, \ldots, x_M]$ (see Sect. 5.2) of QuSBT represent the input values of the tests (i.e., the values i of tests; see Definition 4) of the searched test suite. So, the search interval of each variable is given by the set of possible input values D_I of the program; since inputs of a quantum program are non-negative integers (see Sect. 4), the search space is defined as $x_k \in [0, |D_I| - 1]$ for $k = 1, \ldots, M$.

QuSBT requires to select, as parameter, the number of tests M of each generated test suite. This can be selected as percentage β of the size of the input domain of the program (see Sect. 5.2). We here use $\beta = 5\%$; this results in having $M=50$ for programs with 10 qubits (and so 1024 input values), $M = 26$ for the program with 9 qubits (and so 512 input values), and $M = 7$ for the program with 7 qubits (and so 128 input values).[6]

For the fitness evaluation, assessing whether a test passes or fails requires to perform the Pearson Chi-square test for checking failures of type *wodf* (see Sect. 5.1). To this aim, we adopt *rpy2 3.4.2*, a Python interface to the R framework. We use $\alpha = 0.01$ as the significance level in the Chi-square test (see Eq. 1). Notice that correct inputs may still provide distributions slightly different from the expected ones (due to the limited number of repetitions); therefore, to be more confident on the failure of an input, we use the value 0.01 for the Chi-square test, instead of 0.05 or a higher confidence level.

Experiments have been executed on the Amazon Elastic Compute Cloud, using instances with a 2.9 GHz Intel Xeon CPU and 3.75 GB of RAM. To consider the randomness in search algorithms, each experiment (i.e., the execution of QuSBT for a given benchmark using either GA or RS) has been executed 30 times, as suggested by guidelines to conduct experiments with randomized algorithms [3].

Evaluation Metrics and Statistical Tests. In order to evaluate the quality of the results of the search algorithms (GA and RS), we directly use the fitness function defined in Eq. 2 as the *evaluation metric*, which counts the number of failing tests in a test suite (i.e., an individual of the search). We call it the *Number of Failed Tests* metric (NFT). The NFT of GA is given by the best individual of the last generation, while the NFT of RS is given by the best of all the generated individuals.

To answer RQ1, we selected the Mann-Whitney U test as the statistical test and the Vargha and Delaney's $\hat{A}_{12}$ statistics as effect size measure based on the guidelines [3]. Namely, given a benchmark program, we run the generation approach 30 times with GA and 30 times with RS. The Mann-Whitney U test (with the significance level of 0.05) is used to compare the 30 NFT values obtained by GA and the 30 NFT values of RS. The null hypothesis is that there is no

---

[6] Note that we manually approximated the value of programs with 1024 inputs values. Indeed, the correct number of tests would be $\lceil 0.05 \cdot 1024 \rceil = 52$.

Table 2. Comparison between GA and RS ($\equiv$: there is no statistically significant difference between GA and RS. ✓: GA is statistically significantly better.)

AS$_1$	AS$_2$	AS$_3$	AS$_4$	AS$_5$	BV$_1$	BV$_2$	BV$_3$	BV$_4$	BV$_5$	CE$_1$	CE$_2$	CE$_3$	CE$_4$	CE$_5$	IQ$_1$	IQ$_2$	IQ$_3$	IQ$_4$	IQ$_5$	QR$_1$	QR$_2$	QR$_3$	QR$_4$	QR$_5$	SM$_1$	SM$_2$	SM$_3$	SM$_4$	SM$_5$
✓	✓	✓	$\equiv$	✓	✓	✓	✓	✓	✓	✓	✓	✓	✓	✓	✓	✓	$\equiv$	✓	✓	✓	✓	✓	✓	✓	✓	$\equiv$	$\equiv$	✓	✓

statistical difference between GA and RS. If the null hypothesis is not rejected, then we consider GA and RS equivalent. Otherwise, if the null hypothesis is rejected, we apply the $\hat{A}_{12}$ statistics. If $\hat{A}_{12}$ is 0.5, then it means that the results are obtained by chance. If $\hat{A}_{12}$ is greater than 0.5, then GA has a higher chance to achieve a better performance than RS, and vice versa if $\hat{A}_{12}$ is less than 0.5.

7   Results and Discussions

7.1   Results and Analyses

RQ1. To assess the usefulness of using a search algorithm, in our case GA, we compared it with RS. For each experiment (i.e., the test generation for a benchmark program), we executed 30 runs with GA and 30 runs with RS. We selected the *Number of Failing Tests* NFT as the evaluation metric (see Sect. 6). Then, we compared 30 values of GA and 30 values of RS, with the Mann-Whitney U test and the $\hat{A}_{12}$ statistics as described in Sect. 6. Comparison results are summarized in Table 2.

We observe that in 26 out of 30 cases, GA is significantly better than RS. This shows that GA is able to identify failing inputs in individuals. By considering the different types of the benchmarks, (see Table 1), we notice the differences in results. For some programs such as BV, CE, and QR, GA consistently performed significantly better than RS. In other programs such as AS and IQ, instead, in one out of the five cases, there are no differences between GA and RS. Note that, even for a simple program such as SM (for which we need to generate only 7 tests), GA is still better in three out of the five cases. This means that the task of selecting qubit values leading to failures is a difficult task also for programs with small numbers of input qubits such as those of SM (with 7 input qubits), and this further motivates the need for a search-based approach.

RQ2. Figure 3 reports, for all the benchmarks, the quality of the final results in all the 30 runs, in terms of the evaluation metric NFT, which counts the number of failing tests in the returned test suite (see Sect. 6). In almost all the cases of the four groups of the most complex benchmarks (i.e., Figs. 3a–3d) for which we built test suites of 50 tests, the variability of the final results across the runs is high. Moreover, in these four complex benchmarks, the search was almost always not able to find all 50 failing tests. Similar results can be found in QR (i.e., Fig. 3e), for which we built test suites of 26 tests, the search cannot always find 26 failing tests. This could be due to the fact that there are not so many failing tests, or the search was not given enough time.

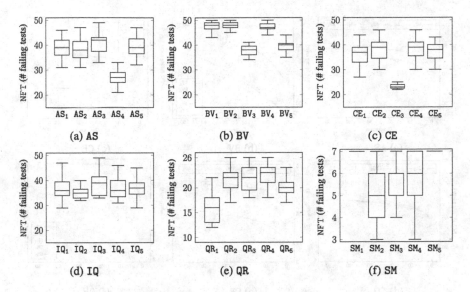

Fig. 3. Final results (# of failing tests in the final test suite) of GA across the 30 runs

These observations tell us that a dedicated and large-scale empirical study is needed to investigate whether such a large variability and inability to find, e.g., 50 or 26 failing tests, is due to the randomness of the search (which perhaps can be mitigated with a better fitness function), is specific to fault characteristics (such as their types and seeding locations (Table 1)) or characteristics of quantum programs under test such as their circuit depth and numbers of gates.

For the benchmark programs of SM (Fig. 3f), instead, the required test suite size is much smaller (i.e., 7). Among its five SM benchmarks, for two of them (i.e., SM_1 and SM_5), the search found, in all 30 runs, 7 failing inputs, showing that the task is relatively easy. On the other hand, for the other three SM benchmarks, the search found less than 7 failing inputs (as low as 3 failing inputs).

We now want to assess how fast the test generation approach optimizes its objective (i.e., the maximization of the number of failing tests in a test suite). Figures 4a–4f show, for each group of the benchmark programs, how the fitness (see Eq. 2) of the best individual in the population increases over generations. The reported plots are the averages across the 30 runs. First of all, we observe that, for all the benchmark programs, the first generation already finds some failing inputs. The number of discovered failing inputs in the first generation is positively correlated to the total number of failing inputs in the input space. Moreover, the number of identified failing inputs varies across the benchmark programs and depends on the types of faults and their locations in the benchmark programs (e.g., seeding a CSWAP gate right after the input or a HAD gate right before reading the output, see Table 1). Note that sometimes finding some failing inputs in a faulty circuit is not difficult, since RS can also do it. However, the maximization of the number of the failing tests is not trivial, as already evidenced

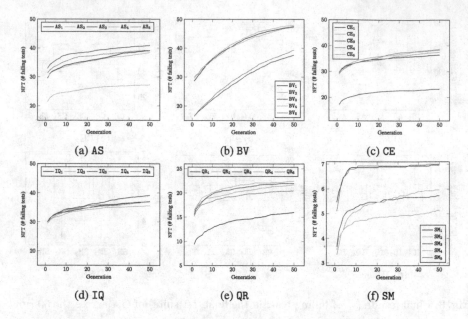

Fig. 4. Results – evolution of the fitness values over generations

by the observations reported for answering RQ1: GA is better than RS in finding more failing tests for most of the benchmark programs.

By observing the trends, we notice that they are increasing with different degrees of improvements. Three benchmarks of BV (i.e., BV_1, BV_2, and BV_4, Fig. 4b) reach the point of almost discovering all the 50 failing tests in the final generation. SM_1 and SM_5 even reach a plateau after around 10 generations. Instead, all the other 25 benchmarks do not achieve high scores on detecting failing tests, possibly implying that further improvements would be still possible with additional generations.

For benchmarks of BV (see Fig. 4b), the increment in the fitness function is faster than the other benchmarks (those that must generate 50 tests). This does not necessarily mean that the problem is easy; indeed, for all the BV benchmarks, GA is better than RS (see Table 2). Instead, we believe that each fault of the BV benchmarks can be captured by a single well-defined pattern of input qubit values. So, once a pattern is discovered by the search, it is successfully migrated in new failing tests. We believe that, in other benchmarks, there is no such a single pattern of failing qubit values and, so, the search has more problems in finding new failing tests. As future work, we plan to perform an extensive investigation of how different types of in failing inputs, and how these failing inputs relate to each other (i.e., if they share some failing qubit values or not).

7.2 Discussion

The faults seeded in the quantum programs used for the evaluation can have different complexity (see Table 1). For instance, introducing a CNOT gate as a fault requires that the CNOT gate is applied to two qubits, which is intuitively considered more complex than introducing a HAD gate (operating on one qubit). However, seeding a fault to a *critical* location might significantly change the logic of the circuit. For instance, seeding a NOT gate *right before reading the output* might completely reverse the output of a circuit, which may make the observation of failures easy and then generate a program for which it is easy to generate failing tests. In Table 1, we classify the fault seeding locations into three categories: right after the inputs, middle of the program, and right before reading the output. This classification is coarse-grained, and a better mechanism is required to characterize fault seeding locations. So, we need larger-scale experiments, designed based on well understanding of faults characteristics, their relations to test inputs, and characteristics of quantum programs under tests. Consequently, more comprehensive test strategies will be proposed in the future. Nevertheless, considering that quantum software testing is an emerging area, QuSBT contributes to building a body of knowledge in this area.

In this paper, we limit the scope of our study to identifying as many failing tests as possible. To assess passing and failing of a test, we defined two types of failures: *uof* and *wodf*, both of which do not consider the phase changes of qubits. Therefore, QuSBT currently can not reveal faults that only change the phases of output qubits, but not their occurrence probabilities.

The test input assessment requires to specify the number of repetitions (see Sect. 5.1). Note that, to the best of our knowledge, there is no existing criterion on how such a value should be set. So, our proposed mechanism provides a baseline for future research.

Even though our evaluation is performed on Qiskit in Python, QuSBT is general as it can be applied to other quantum platforms and quantum programming languages. In this paper, we performed all the experiments on the quantum computer simulator provided with Qiskit without simulating hardware faults. Thus, QuSBT needs to be extended in the future to deal with potential hardware faults in real quantum computers.

8 Threats to Validity

External Validity. We experimented only with six quantum programs and 30 (faulty) benchmark programs; thus, our results can be generalized to only quantum programs of similar characteristics. More experiments with varying characteristics of quantum programs are needed to generalize the results. Another threat is related to the selection of faults that were introduced in the quantum programs to create faulty benchmark programs. We chose a set of arbitrary faults, which could potentially affect our results. However, currently, there does not exist any bug repository for quantum programs that we could use to seed realistic faults in quantum programs.

Internal Validity. We choose GA's default parameter settings. Different GA settings may produce different results that could potentially affect our results.

However, the evidence has shown that even default settings of GA provide good results in search-based testing of classical software [4]. To assess the passing and failing of tests with *wodf*, we used the Pearson's Chi-square test. Other tests may be relevant; however, the Chi-square test has been used for this purpose in existing related literature [7,8].

Conclusion Validity. Since GA and RS have inherent randomness, we repeated experiments 30 times for each faulty program to ensure that the results weren't obtained by chance. Followed by this, we compared the results of GA with RS with statistical tests according to the well-established guides in search-based software engineering [3].

9   Conclusion and Future Work

We presented a search-based approach for testing quantum programs that uses a Genetic Algorithm (GA) and employs a fitness function to search for test suites of a given size, containing as many failing tests as possible. We assessed the effectiveness of our approach as compared with Random Search (RS) with 30 faulty benchmark quantum programs. The results showed that GA significantly outperformed RS for 87% of the faulty quantum programs, whereas for the rest, there were no significant differences.

Our future work includes experimenting with more algorithms and quantum programs and running them on quantum computers (e.g., by IBM). Moreover, we will perform analyses, e.g., studying the search space of solutions and the effect of search operators on the effectiveness of QuSBT. Finally, we will devise systematic methods to create realistic faulty quantum programs and publish a public repository.

References

1. Agresti, A.: An Introduction to Categorical Data Analysis, 3 edn. Wiley-Blackwell (2019)
2. Ali, S., Arcaini, P., Wang, X., Yue, T.: Assessing the effectiveness of input and output coverage criteria for testing quantum programs. In: 2021 14th IEEE Conference on Software Testing, Verification and Validation (ICST), pp. 13–23 (2021). https://doi.org/10.1109/ICST49551.2021.00014
3. Arcuri, A., Briand, L.: A practical guide for using statistical tests to assess randomized algorithms in software engineering. In: Proceedings of the 33rd International Conference on Software Engineering, ICSE 2011, pp. 1–10. ACM, New York (2011)
4. Arcuri, A., Fraser, G.: Parameter tuning or default values? An empirical investigation in search-based software engineering. Empir. Softw. Eng. **18**, 594–623 (2013)
5. Benítez-Hidalgo, A., Nebro, A.J., García-Nieto, J., Oregi, I., Del Ser, J.: jMetalPy: a Python framework for multi-objective optimization with metaheuristics. Swarm Evol. Comput. **51**, 100598 (2019)
6. Gimeno-Segovia, M., Harrigan, N., Johnston, E.: Programming Quantum Computers: Essential Algorithms and Code Samples. O'Reilly Media, Inc., Newton (2019)

7. Honarvar, S., Mousavi, M.R., Nagarajan, R.: Property-based testing of quantum programs in Q#. In: Proceedings of the IEEE/ACM 42nd International Conference on Software Engineering Workshops, ICSEW 2020, pp. 430–435. Association for Computing Machinery, New York (2020)
8. Huang, Y., Martonosi, M.: QDB: from quantum algorithms towards correct quantum programs. In: 9th Workshop on Evaluation and Usability of Programming Languages and Tools (PLATEAU 2018). OpenAccess Series in Informatics (OASIcs), vol. 67, pp. 4:1–4:14. Schloss Dagstuhl-Leibniz-Zentrum fuer Informatik, Dagstuhl (2019)
9. Li, G., Zhou, L., Yu, N., Ding, Y., Ying, M., Xie, Y.: Projection-based runtime assertions for testing and debugging quantum programs. Proc. ACM Program. Lang. 4(OOPSLA), 1–29 (2020)
10. Liu, J., Byrd, G.T., Zhou, H.: Quantum circuits for dynamic runtime assertions in quantum computation. In: Proceedings of the Twenty-Fifth International Conference on Architectural Support for Programming Languages and Operating Systems, pp. 1017–1030 (2020)
11. Miranskyy, A., Zhang, L.: On testing quantum programs. In: 2019 IEEE/ACM 41st International Conference on Software Engineering: New Ideas and Emerging Results (ICSE-NIER), pp. 57–60 (2019)
12. Wang, J., Ma, F., Jiang, Y.: Poster: fuzz testing of quantum program. In: 2021 14th IEEE Conference on Software Testing, Verification and Validation (ICST), pp. 466–469 (2021). https://doi.org/10.1109/ICST49551.2021.00061
13. Wille, R., Van Meter, R., Naveh, Y.: IBM's Qiskit tool chain: working with and developing for real quantum computers. In: 2019 Design, Automation Test in Europe Conference Exhibition (DATE), pp. 1234–1240 (2019)

Preliminary Evaluation of SWAY in Permutation Decision Space via a Novel Euclidean Embedding

Junghyun Lee, Chani Jung, Yoo Hwa Park, Dongmin Lee, Juyeon Yoon, and Shin Yoo[(✉)]

KAIST, Daejeon, South Korea
{jh_lee00,1016chani,16ypark,theresaldm,juyeon.yoon,shin.yoo}@kaist.ac.kr

Abstract. The cost of a fitness evaluation is often cited as one of the weaknesses of Search-Based Software Engineering: to obtain a single final solution, a meta-heuristic search algorithm has to evaluate the fitness of many interim solutions. Recently, a sampling-based approach called SWAY has been introduced as a new baseline that can compete with state-of-the-art search algorithms with significantly fewer fitness evaluations. However, SWAY has been introduced and evaluated only in numeric and Boolean decision spaces. This paper extends SWAY to permutation decision space. We start by presenting the theoretical formulation of the permutation decision space and the distance function required by SWAY, and subsequently present a proof-of-concept study of Test Case Prioritisation (TCP) problem using our permutative SWAY. The results show that our embedding works well for permutative decision spaces, producing results that are comparable to those generated by the additional greedy algorithm, one of the most widely used algorithms for TCP.

Keywords: SWAY · Permutations · TCP

1 Introduction

Search Based Software Engineering (SBSE) formulates software engineering problems as metaheuristic optimisations and applies various search techniques [10]. These search techniques typically navigate the decision (or solution) space guided by a fitness function that maps a solution in the decision space to one or more values in the fitness (or objective) space. The mapping is achieved by dynamically evaluating the decision against the actual problem instance and measuring the fitness. The dynamic and concrete nature of fitness evaluation allows us to search for properties that cannot be easily measured otherwise: for example, Search Based Software Testing has successfully applied to find test inputs that satisfy non-functional test requirements such as increased memory consumption [13] or worst case execution time [16].

J. Lee, C. Jung, Y. H. Park and D. Lee—Equal contribution.

© Springer Nature Switzerland AG 2021
U.-M. O'Reilly and X. Devroey (Eds.): SSBSE 2021, LNCS 12914, pp. 26–40, 2021.
https://doi.org/10.1007/978-3-030-88106-1_3

However, such dynamic and concrete nature of fitness evaluation is accompanied by the cost of the actual execution. Given the wide adoption of population based optimisation algorithms such as genetic algorithm, the cost of fitness evaluation poses a serious threat not only to practical applications of SBSE but also to research and experimental use of these techniques.

Recently, a new type of search algorithm based on random sampling, called SWAY, has been introduced [2]. Suppose we are optimising an objective variable by searching for a decision variable. The fitness evaluation can be formulated as:

$$o = fitness(d)$$

where $d \in \mathcal{D}$ is the decision variable and $o \in \mathcal{O}$ is the objective variable. Chen et al. empirically showed that, in many cases of SBSE formulations, there exists a close association between $\mathcal{D}$ and $\mathcal{O}$ [2]. SWAY exploits this by recursively clustering, and searching for, possible candidate solutions *in the decision space* rather than in the objective space. By doing so, it admits a logarithmic time complexity in terms of fitness evaluations. Such scalability, along with its simplicity, qualifies SWAY as a baseline optimizer [21]. However, the current form of SWAY is limited to decision spaces that are either numerical or Boolean. The aim of this paper is to extend SWAY to permutative decision space.

The technical contributions of this paper are as follows:

- We present a formulation of SWAY in permutative decision spaces. Instead of coarse-grained grouping followed by the use of binary SWAY (as suggested by authors of SWAY), we present a novel Euclidean embedding of permutations that can be used with continuous SWAY.[1]
- We conduct a proof-of-concept evaluation of SWAY in a permutative decision space with instances of Test Case Prioritisation problems. The results show the feasibility of our embedding.

The rest of the paper is organised as follows. Section 2 introduces the original SWAY, proposes our novel Euclidean embedding of permutative decision spaces, and introduces the adaptation of SWAY to the proposed embedding. Section 3 describes the settings of the case study of the application of SWAY to Test Case Prioritisation problem, whose results are presented in Sect. 4. Section 5 discusses the related work, and Sect. 6 concludes.

2 SWAY for Permutative Decision Spaces

This section first introduces the basic SWAY algorithm, and subsequently presents the design of our embedding scheme for permutation decision variables.

---

[1] Here, embedding for a permutative decision space simply refers to a mapping of each permutation to some Euclidean space that is structure-preserving (as in "node embedding" in machine learning). In the following sections, we shall describe which structure to preserve.

2.1   The Original SWAY

SWAY [2,3] is an effective random sampling algorithm that can be used as a baseline for more sophisticated search algorithms. Algorithm 1 shows the pseudocode of the original, continuous SWAY. At its core, SWAY simply seeks to choose a cluster of solutions that are superior to others. If the clustering is performed based on the solution phenotype, SWAY would have to spend a lot of fitness evaluations. Instead, SWAY exploits the fact that, in many SBSE problems, there exists a close association between the genotype (i.e., decision) and the phenotype (i.e., objective) spaces [3], and recursively clusters the solutions in the genotype space using FastMap heuristic [9] (implemented in SPLIT), only evaluating the representatives of each cluster.

Algorithm 1: Continuous SWAY with its subroutine Split

---

1 **Given:** inner product $\langle \cdot, \cdot, \rangle$ and its induced norm $\langle \|\cdot\| \rangle$, objective computing function $obj : \mathcal{D} \to \mathcal{O}$, ordering on $\mathcal{O} \preccurlyeq$

2 **Hyperparameters:** *enough*

3 **Function** contSWAY(*candidates*):

4   **if** $|candidates| < enough$ **then**

5   **return** *candidates*

6   **else**

7          $[west, westItems], [east, eastItems] \longleftarrow$ Split(*candidates*)

8          $\Delta_1, \Delta_2 \longleftarrow \emptyset, \emptyset$

9   **if** $obj(east) \preccurlyeq obj(west)$ **then**

10            $\Delta_1 \longleftarrow$ contSWAY(*westItems*)

11   **end**

12   **if** $obj(west) \preccurlyeq obj(east)$ **then**

13            $\Delta_2 \longleftarrow$ contSWAY(*eastItems*)

14   **end**

15   **return** $\Delta_1 \cup \Delta_2$

16   **end**

17 **End Function**

18 **Function** Split(*candidates*):

19     $rand \longleftarrow$ randomly selected candidate from *candidates*

20     $east \longleftarrow \text{argmax}_{x \in candidates} \|x - rand\|$

21     $west \longleftarrow \text{argmax}_{x \in candidates} \|x - east\|$

22   **for** $x \in candidates$ **do**

23         $x_d \longleftarrow \frac{\langle east-west, x-west \rangle}{\|east-west\|}$

24   **end**

25   Sort candidates by x_d

26     $eastItems \longleftarrow$ first half of *candidates*

27     $westItems \longleftarrow$ second half of *candidates*

28   **return** $[west, westItems], [east, eastItems]$

29 **End Function**

For problem with continuous numerical genotypes, the FastMap heuristic that is based on cosine rules and Euclidean distance works well (Line 22 of Algorithm 1); for binary decision spaces, SWAY adopts a radial coordinate system. Finally, for non-binary discrete decision spaces, Chen et al. propose coarse-grained binary groupings of such solutions fed into the binary version of SWAY [2,3]. However, even with sufficient domain knowledge, certain decision spaces may not allow an easy and intuitive coarse-grained grouping that would enable us to use binary SWAY. For example, it is not clear what coarse-grained groupings can be used in a permutative decision space without knowing which ordering is better than others.

We propose a formulation of SWAY for permutative decision spaces that uses the continuous SWAY. Our intuition is that we can use the continuous SWAY as long as we can *embed* permutations into an alternative vector form in such a way that the Euclidean distance between embedding vectors is closely correlated with Kendall τ distance, i.e., the combinatorial distance between permutations (i.e., the number of pairwise disagreement between two permutations). Note that the use of continuous SWAY, which depends on the cosine rule and Euclidean space, forces us to use Euclidean embedding.

The remainder of this section investigates such an embedding of the set of all possible permutations, denoted as S_n. To the best of our knowledge, S_n cannot be endowed with an easy-to-be-implemented inner product, or even a well-defined one. Thus, we need to embed S_n into a simple inner vector space.

2.2 Preliminaries

This section provides an overview of the necessary mathematical concepts. Let us start with a basic definition:

Definition 1. *A **permutation** of $[n] := \{1, 2, \ldots, n\}$ is a bijection from $[n]$ to itself. Denote S_n as the set of all possible permutations of $[n]$.[2] Especially, let $i = (1, \ldots, n) \in S_n$ be the identity permutation. Moreover, depending on the context, $\pi \in S_n$ may be regarded as a vector in $\mathbb{R}^n$.*

Unlike a p-dimensional space $\mathbb{R}^p$, which has a natural metric endowed from its Euclidean norm[3], defining the distance between two permutations in an analogous manner is not trivial. First, let us start with the "natural" definition of metric on S_n (much discussion has been taken from Deza and Deza [4]):

Definition 2. *Given a connected[4] graph $G = (V, F)$, its **path metric** is a metric on V, defined as the length of a shortest path connecting $x, y \in V$.*

Definition 3. *Given a finite set X and a finite set $\mathcal{O}$ of unary editing operations on X, the **editing metric** on X is the path metric of the graph $G(X, \mathcal{O})$ whose vertices are X and whose edge set is $\{\{x, y\} \mid \exists o \in \mathcal{O} : y = o(x)\}$. (If $X = S_n$, then it is also called **permutation metric**).*

---

[2] S_n with composition operation forms the symmetric group of order n.
[3] For $x = (x_i) \in \mathbb{R}^p$, its Euclidean norm is defined as $\|x\| := \left(\sum_{i=1}^{p} x_i^2\right)^{1/2}$.
[4] $G = (V, E)$ is connected if for every $x, y \in V$, there exists a path from x to y.

Since we are dealing with the decision space of permutations, it would be reasonable to assume that the objective value of candidate solutions is heavily dependent on the *relative orderings* in the permutations. Consider an example in TCP: a test case t_f has high fault detection capability and, consequently, contribute to higher APFD if executed early on. Swapping t_f with the next adjacent test case will delay the fault detection only a little, when compared to swapping t_f with the last test case in the ordering. The distance in relative ordering can be reflected by counting the number of *switches of two adjacent elements* required to move from one permutation to another, formalized as follows:

Definition 4. *The* **swap distance** *(also known as* **Kendall** τ *distance in statistical ranking theory) of* $\pi, \pi' \in S_n$, *denoted as* $d_K(\pi, \pi')$, *is the editing metric on* S_n *with* $\mathcal{O}$ *being the set of all possible swaps i.e. it is the minimum number of swaps required to go from* π *to* π'.

Proposition 1. $d_K : S_n \times S_n \to \mathbb{R}_{\geq 0}$ *is indeed a permutation metric.*

The following proposition provides a very intuitive way of computing the swap distance[5]:

Proposition 2. *Given* $\pi, \pi' \in S_n$, $d_K(\pi, \pi')$ *is precisely the number of relative inversions between them i.e. number of pairs* $(i, j), 1 \leq i < j \leq n$ *with* $(\pi_i - \pi_j)(\pi'_i - \pi'_j) < 0$.

All in all, we want an Euclidean embedding scheme with the following property: embeddings of two permutations are close together if the swap distance between them is small, and vice versa.

Remark 1. One may ask why not stop now and just use the swap distance in SWAY. However, continuous SWAY [2,3] is designed to be used for Euclidean space, only; specifically, the usage of Euclidean distance is crucial for splitting the candidates via cosine rule, which is not applicable for other metrics.

2.3   Consideration of Naive Embedding

The most trivial Euclidean embedding of permutations would be to take a permutation π of n items directly as a vector in $\mathbb{R}^n$, as mentioned in Definition 1. More formally, it can be defined as follows:

Definition 5. *For fixed* n, *the* **permutahedron**, *denoted as* Π_{n-1}, *is defined as the convex hull of the set* $V_n = \{(\pi(1), \ldots, \pi(n)) \mid \pi \in S_n\}$, *which can be thought of as the "direct" embedding of* S_n *onto* $\mathbb{R}^n$.

Based on the study of permutahedron in combinatorics [18], we can derive the following propositions about Π_{n-1}.[6]

---

[5] This proposition indicates a $\mathcal{O}(n \log n)$ algorithm based on sorting. Apart from our consideration, a more efficient algorithm has been proposed; see [1].

[6] Refer to [19,24] for the full proofs and more detailed discussions on related topics.

Proposition 3. Π_{n-1} *is a simple* $(n-1)$*-dimensional polytope with* V_n *as its set of vertices.*

Proposition 4. *Two vertices of* Π_{n-1} *are adjacent iff they differ by a swap, when considered as permutations.*

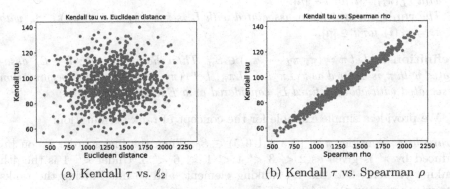

(a) Kendall τ vs. ℓ_2 (b) Kendall τ vs. Spearman ρ

Fig. 1. Scatter plots showing correlations between swap distance and different embedding distances

Simplicity and convexity of the underlying polytope, shown in Proposition 3, ensures that the SPLIT function in Algorithm 1 does not show any unexpected behaviour. What is more interesting is Proposition 4, which *seems* to suggest a positive correlation between the ℓ_2-distance[7] and the swap distance, d_K. However, empirical evidence shows that such correlation either does not exist, or is very weak if it does, rendering the naive and trivial embedding inapplicable. In Fig. 1a, the x-axis is the Euclidean distance between two random permutations, $\pi, \pi' \in S^n$, embedded naively using the permutahedron (i.e., $\|\pi - \pi'\|^2$), whereas the y-axis is the swap distance (i.e., $d_K(\pi, \pi')$). No strong positive correlation can be observed. Consequently, we are forced to consider another embedding scheme.

2.4 Motivations for Rank Based Embedding

We start with the following crucial observation: S_n is in bijection with the set of all possible linear orders on $[n]$, denoted as $\mathcal{L}_n$. By dealing with the linear orders instead of permutations, we can leverage several useful results from statistical ranking theory. To start, let us first define such bijection [15]:

---

[7] For simplicity, let us refer to the distance of the embedded permutations as the ℓ_2-distance of the permutations.

Definition 6. *Let $L \in \mathcal{L}_n$.*

1. *The **rank function** of L is the function $r_L : [n] \to [n]$, defined as*

$$r_L(x) = 1 + |\{y \in [n] : \; yLx\}|$$

2. *The **position permutation** associated with L is $\pi = (\pi_1 \; \pi_2 \; \cdots \; \pi_n) \in S_n$ with $r_L(\pi_i) = i$ for $i \in [n]$.*
3. *The **rank permutation** associated with L is $\pi = (\pi_1 \; \pi_2 \; \cdots \; \pi_n) \in S_n$ with $\pi_i = r_L(i)$ for $i \in [n]$.*

Definition 7. *Let $\pi = (\pi_1 \; \pi_2 \; \cdots \; \pi_n) \in S_n$. Then the linear order $L \in \mathcal{L}_n$ associated with π is defined as $\pi_1 L \pi_2 L \cdots L \pi_n$. Let $r(\pi)$ denote the rank permutation associated with above-defined L, considered as a Euclidean vector.*

We provide a simple example for the concept of rank permutation:

Example 1. Consider $\pi = (2 \; 3 \; 4 \; 1 \; 6 \; 5) \in S_6$. Then the linear order $<'$ on $[n]$ induced by π' is given as $2 <' 3 <' 4 <' 1 <' 6 <' 5$. Under $<'$, 1 is the 4th ranking element, 2 is the 1st ranking element, and so on. Putting the ranks altogether gives $r(\pi) = (4 \; 1 \; 2 \; 3 \; 6 \; 5)$.

Above definition motivates another "distance" between two permutations, which can be formally defined as follows:

Definition 8. *Spearman ρ **distance** of $\pi, \pi' \in S_n$, denoted as $d_S(\pi, \pi')$, is precisely the Euclidean distance between $r(\pi)$ and $r(\pi')$, considering them as vectors (vertices of Π_{n-1} in $\mathbb{R}^n$)*

Proposition 5. *$d_S : S_n \times S_n \to \mathbb{R}_{\geq 0}$ is indeed a permutation metric.*

Our embedding scheme is based on the following non-trivial results by Monjardet [15]. Here, $d_G(\cdot, \cdot)$ is a function from $S_n \times S_n$ to $\mathbb{R}_{\geq 0}$ that is combinatorially well-defined.

Theorem 1 (Monjardet, 1998 [15]).

$$d_S^2(\pi, \pi') = n d_K(\pi, \pi') - d_G(\pi, \pi') \quad \forall \pi, \pi' \in S_n \tag{1}$$

Equation 1 implies that *if the effect of d_G is insignificant with respect to d_S^2 and $n d_K$, then there is a positive correlation between d_S and d_k.* To see this, we perform similar experiment as the one with the naive embedding; we sample sufficient number of pairs of permutations, and for each sampled $(\pi, \pi') \in S_n \times S_n$ we plot a scatter plot of $d_S(\pi, \pi')^2$ vs. $d_K(\pi, \pi')$, shown in Fig. 1b. Observe how there is an almost linear relationship between the two quantities, which is precisely what we need.

Based on previous discussions, we propose the following Euclidean embedding scheme of S_n (note how r is a bijection from Π_{n-1} to itself):

$$\pi \in S_n \iff r(\pi) \in \Pi_{n-1} \subset \mathbb{R}^n$$

3 Preliminary Evaluation: Test Case Prioritisation (TCP)

We consider Test Case Prioritisation (TCP) problem [22] as the subject of our proof-of-concept, preliminary evaluation of our embedding scheme. Intuitively, the goal of TCP is to find the optimal ordering of the test cases such that "early fault detection" is maximized, which can be defined as follows [17]:

Definition 9 (Test Case Prioritisation (TCP)). *Given a test suite, T, the set of permutations of T, PT, and a function from PT to $\mathbb{R}$, $f : PT \to \mathbb{R}$, find $T' \in PT$ such that $(\forall T'')\, (T'' \in PT)\, (T'' \neq T')\, [f(T') \geq f(T'')]$.*

The ideal choice of f would be the function that measures the real fault detection rate of the given ordering. In reality, such measurement is not available before the entire test suite is executed, forcing us to use surrogates such as structural coverage [17,22]. We focus on the coverage-based approach.

3.1 Performance Metrics

We consider two metrics, Average Percentage of Statement Coverage (APSC) and Average Percentage of Fault Detection (APFD) [17], to evaluate the orderings produced by SWAY. Let T be an ordered test suite. APSC measures the rate of coverage achieved, and can be formally defined as follows:

$$APSC(T) = 1 - \frac{TS_1 + \cdots + TS_m}{nm} + \frac{1}{2n} \tag{2}$$

where TS_i is the index of the first test case that covers statement i, n is the number of test cases in the test suite, and m is the number of statements in the program. Note that it is possible to compute APSC using coverage of each test case measured from the previous version of the System Under Test (SUT). APFD, in comparison, measures the actual rate of fault detection *a posteriori*, because information about fault detection is only available after all test cases have been executed. It is defined as follows:

$$APFD(T) = 1 - \frac{TF_1 + \cdots + TF_m}{nm} + \frac{1}{2n} \tag{3}$$

where TF_i is the index of the first test case that covers fault i, n is the number of test cases in the test suite, and m is the number of faults in the program

3.2 Baseline Approaches

Currently there exists no alternative way of applying SWAY to permutative decision spaces: since ours is the first embedding for such decision spaces, we do not have a direct baseline approaches to compare against. Instead, we simply investigate the feasibility of our embedding by applying it to TCP.

As a basic sanity check of its results, we compare the results from permutative SWAY to those obtained by additional greedy algorithm, which has been widely used in the regression testing literature [8,14,23]. Our aim is not to evaluate SWAY itself for TCP problem: a proper evaluation of the efficiency of SWAY would require careful parameter tuning for the sampling size as well as sufficiently optimized implementation. As a proof-of-concept evaluation, we simply check whether our permutative SWAY can produce comparable results to the additional greedy algorithm, and leave the direct comparison between SWAY and other population based optimisation algorithms for future work.

3.3 SWAY for TCP

We make the following changes to the original SWAY to adapt it to the proposed embedding of permutations. Our implementation is available from our GitHub repository.[8]

Initial Sampling. For even a medium sized problem, using the entire S_n is infeasible due to the excessive memory required for storing and doing various operations on $n!$ permutations. To avoid this issue, we initialize the population (i.e., samples) by generating random permutations from S_n using Fisher-Yates shuffle[9], which outputs uniformly distributed permutations [6].

Given a set of all test cases, $T = \{t_1, \ldots, t_n\}$, it can be observed that *each permutation of $[n]$ corresponds to a unique ordering of T*, giving us a direct problem-specific interpretation: the decision space of TCP is precisely S_n. The objective score that we are optimizing for is APSC with respect to the already-known execution information of each test case. Typically, this is calculated using the previous version of the SUT.

Stopping Population. Stopping population is a user-defined threshold: SWAY stops once the size of the population falls below that threshold. For multi-objective problems, it is natural to set the stopping population to be high [2,3], since diversity is one of the important quality metrics for such problems [20]. However, if the fitness evaluation is sufficiently expensive for a single objective problem, it would be natural to use SWAY for single objective problems as well.

Suppose that we initially have N candidate solutions as input to SWAY, and set the stopping population as N_0. SWAY will compare all remaining N_0 candidates after stopping. Subsequently, the number of fitness evaluations would be $\mathcal{O}(\log N + N_0)$. Note that if $N_0 = \mathcal{O}(\log N)$, then the number of required fitness evaluations will simply be $\mathcal{O}(\log N)$. We set the stopping population for TCP to be five which is small enough to satisfy such a condition. Out of the five solutions, we choose the one with the highest APSC, and report its APFD.

---

[8] https://github.com/chanijung/sway-perm.
[9] This is implemented by `random.shuffle` function in Python.

Table 1. Linux utilities

Name	SLOC	$|T|$	Description
flex	3,453–4,008	21	Lexer generator
gzip	3,195–3,443	193	Data compression utility
grep	1.744–2,018	211	Pattern matching engine
sed	3,729	36	Stream text editor

3.4   Benchmarks

All four Unix utilities we use with our empirical evaluation were obtained from the SIR repository [5]: flex, gzip, grep, and sed. Table 1 contains the details of these subject programs and their test suites[10]. The test cases are built to exercise each parameter as well as to achieve coverage, and artificial faults have been injected for the evaluation of regression testing techniques. We consider four versions of flex, three versions of grep, two versions of gzip, and a single version of sed.

3.5   Research Questions

We structure our preliminary evaluation of SWAY for permutation decision space around the following research questions:

1. **RQ1. Effectiveness:** How well SWAY performs compared to the greedy prioritisation for TCP?
2. **RQ2. Sensitivity:** How sensitive is SWAY to the initial population?

As mentioned in Sect. 3.2, we only consider the additional greedy algorithm as our competitor since it is simple to implement, and it shows comparable performance with the other search-based algorithms. In addition, for sanity check, we also consider a random algorithm, which just outputs a random permutation. However, note that the objective of our study is to show the feasibility of our embedding of permutations, and not to present a novel TCP approach.

Each algorithm was executed with a fixed test suite for each program. SWAY and random algorithm were repeated 30 times in order to account for their randomness. For SWAY, the initial population of the candidate permutations was fixed as 2^{19} for all of the programs.[11]

---

[10] Test suites v0.cov.universe, v0.tsl.universe, v0.cov.universe.esc, and v0_2.universe.single have been used for flex, gzip, grep, and sed, respectively. Individual test cases that resulted in segmentation fault in our test environment have been filtered out, resulting in smaller test suites than those reported in SIR. Please note that this does not interfere with the feasibility evaluation of our embedding.

[11] This was the maximum feasible value allowed by our available resource.

4   Results

This section presents the results of our preliminary evaluation.

4.1   RQ1: How Well Does Our Approach Perform?

Figures 2a and 2b show the resulting error bar plots of APSC and APFD for the
studied subjects. The observable trend is that greedy and SWAY achieve similar
APSC values, but SWAY can sometimes outperform greedy, especially for some
of the Linux utility runs.

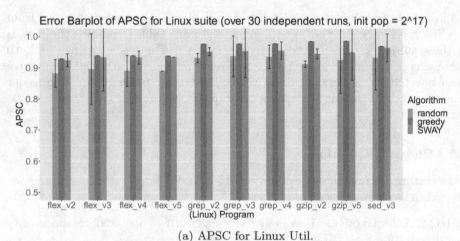

(a) APSC for Linux Util.

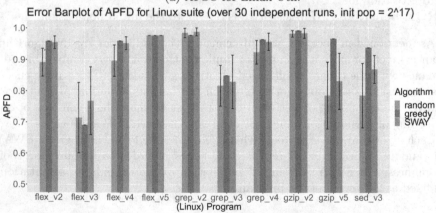

(b) APFD for Linux Util.

Fig. 2. Error bar plots for Linux Utils (RQ1)

To compare the results of greedy and SWAY more precisely, we apply Mann-
Whitney U test [11], a non-parametric test for comparing two statistically independent groups. The null hypothesis, H_0, is that, for X and Y randomly selected

from each group, $\Pr[X \geq Y] = \Pr[X \leq Y]$. For each APSC and APFD, we set the alternative hypothesis H_1 as that SWAY performs better than greedy. Table 2 contains the results: statistically significant results are typeset in **bold**.

Table 2. Mann-Whitney U test of APSC and APFD between SWAY and Greedy

Name	p_{APSC}	p_{APFD}	Name	p_{APSC}	p_{APFD}
flex-v2	1.00	0.89	grep-v3	1.00	0.97
flex-v3	1.00	**0.00**	grep-v4	1.00	0.32
flex-v4	1.00	**0.02**	gzip-v2	1.00	0.97
flex-v5	1.00	1.00	gzip-v5	1.00	1.00
grep-v2	1.00	**0.00**	sed-v3	1.00	1.00

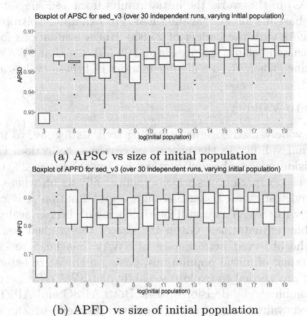

(a) APSC vs size of initial population

(b) APFD vs size of initial population

Fig. 3. Boxplots for **RQ2**. Here, log is treated as binary log i.e, $\log_2$.

The results show that greedy outperforms SWAY on APSC in general, which is to be expected since greedy directly (and deterministically) maximizes APSC. However SWAY and greedy algorithm are more at par in terms of APFD: for some programs, SWAY outperforms greedy with statistically significant p-values. Note that, given that the aim of SWAY is to provide an efficient baseline based on random sampling, our aim here is not to consistently outperform greedy. Based on these results, we answer RQ1 that SWAY can produce comparable results to those of the additional greedy algorithm when applied to the TCP problem using the proposed embedding.

4.2 RQ2: Sensitivity of SWAY to Initial Sample Size

We perform the sensitivity analysis only using sed, due to the large number of candidate samples required for the sensitivity analysis. We vary the size of the initial population from 2^3 up to 2^{19}, doubling the size at each step. For each size, we run SWAY 30 times to cater for the randomness in sampling.

Figures 3a and 3b show the resulting bar plots of APSC and APFD, respectively. Both APSC and APFD show monotonically increasing trends as the size of the initial population increases: the correlation is stronger with APSC. We posit that this trend is to be expected since, intuitively, greater initial population implies that the search space being covered by SWAY is greater. However, also note that after certain threshold population, increasing it does not seem to have a significant effect on APFD. Consequently, we answer RQ2 that, above certain size, SWAY is not overtly sensitive to the size of the initial population.

While we do not compare SWAY with other population based Evolutionary Algorithms (EAs) in this work, the initial results from sed suggest that SWAY can be a viable baseline for TCP against EAs. For example, Epitropakis et al. [8] configures MOEAs with the budget of 25,000 fitness evaluations for SIR Linux utilities, of which sed belongs. Figures 3a and 3b indicate that SWAY can achieve stable performance when given a similar number of fitness evaluations.

4.3 Threats to Validity

We depend on widely used coverage profiling tool, GNU gcov, to minimise any threat to internal validity in the process of coverage collection. Compared to a Boolean decision space whose size grows exponentially as 2^n, the size of a permutation decision space grows super-exponentially as $n!$, where n is the size of the considered test suite. Using Stirling's approximation[12], it can be easily seen that even with SWAY, we still need $\mathcal{O}(n \log n)$ fitness evaluations when using all possible permutations. Given the size of the studied test suites, it is possible that the observed performance of SWAY has been severely affected by our chosen range of initial populations, posing a threat to external validity. Further studies are needed to explore scalability of SWAY for permutation, as well as other combinatorial decision spaces. Both APSC and APFD are widely studied and used evaluation metrics for the TCP problem, which minimises the threat to construct validity of our study.

5 Related Work

A baseline optimiser is an optimiser that is simple, widely and publicly available, fast, offer comparable performance to the SOTA methods, and computationally inexpensive [21]. It is beneficial to have a baseline optimizer for an optimisation problem because it provides a floor performance values to it. This helps the

---

[12] $n! \sim \sqrt{2\pi n} \left(\frac{n}{e}\right)^n$.

developers to rule out the optimizers with lower performance. SWAY satisfies all such criteria [2,3], which motivates us to extend it to additional decision spaces.

We compare SWAY to coverage based greedy prioritisation due to the availability of coverage data as well as the ease of implementing the additional greedy algorithm. However, there are numerous TCP techniques that are not focused on early increase of coverage only. For example, history based prioritisation [7,12] aims to execute the least recently executed test cases first. As a preliminary evaluation, we also focus on single objective TCP for the sake of simplicity. However, Multi Objective Evolutionary Algorithms (MOEAs) have been successfully applied to TCP with multiple objectives [8]. We leave the evaluation of multi-objective formulation of SWAY for TCP for future work.

While the primary intended use of SWAY is a baseline and not an efficient search algorithm in itself, the efficiency of SWAY can be improved by adopting optimised fitness evaluation. For example, SWAY can benefit from the coverage compaction [8] like any other TCP technique, as the compaction can make each fitness evaluation faster.

6 Conclusions and Future Work

This paper presents a novel embedding of the permutations into the Euclidean space, allowing us to directly use (continuous) SWAY without any additional modifications. We base our embedding on well-established fields of combinatorics and statistical ranking theory, and show that our embedding scheme is suitable for the framework of SWAY. A proof of concept evaluation of our embedding, applied to TCP using continuous SWAY, shows that it can successfully measure the distance between solutions in permutative decision spaces, enabling SWAY to be applied to such spaces. For future work, we will focus on improving the scalability of SWAY in permutation decision space by applying (non)linear dimensionality reduction techniques after our embedding.

References

1. Chan, T.M., Pătraşcu, M.: Counting inversions, offline orthogonal range counting, and related problems. In: Proceedings of the Twenty-First Annual ACM-SIAM Symposium on Discrete Algorithms, SODA 2010, pp. 161–173. Society for Industrial and Applied Mathematics, USA (2010)
2. Chen, J., Nair, V., Krishna, R., Menzies, T.: "Sampling" as a baseline optimizer for search-based software engineering. IEEE Trans. Softw. Eng. 45(6), 597–614 (2019)
3. Chen, J., Nair, V., Menzies, T.: Beyond evolutionary algorithms for search-based software engineering. Inf. Softw. Technol. 95, 281–294 (2018)
4. Deza, M.M., Deza, E.: Encyclopedia of Distances, 4th edn. Springer, Heidelberg (2018)
5. Do, H., Elbaum, S., Rothermel, G.: Supporting controlled experimentation with testing techniques: an infrastructure and its potential impact. Empir. Softw. Eng. 10(4), 405–435 (2005)

6. Durstenfeld, R.: Algorithm 235: random permutation. Commun. ACM **7**(7), 420 (1964)
7. Engström, E., Runeson, P., Ljung, A.: Improving regression testing transparency and efficiency with history-based prioritization - an industrial case study. In: 2011 Fourth IEEE International Conference on Software Testing, Verification and Validation, pp. 367–376 (2011)
8. Epitropakis, M.G., Yoo, S., Harman, M., Burke, E.K.: Empirical evaluation of pareto efficient multi-objective regression test case prioritisation. In: Proceedings of the 2015 International Symposium on Software Testing and Analysis, ISSTA 2015, pp. 234–245. ACM, New York (2015)
9. Faloutsos, C., Lin, K.I.: FastMap: a fast algorithm for indexing, data-mining and visualization of traditional and multimedia datasets. SIGMOD Rec. **24**(2), 163–174 (1995)
10. Harman, M., Mansouri, S.A., Zhang, Y.: Search-based software engineering: trends, techniques and applications. ACM Comput. Surv. **45**(1), 11:1–11:61 (2012)
11. Hollander, M., Wolfe, D.A., Chicken, E.: Nonparametric Statistical Methods. Wiley Series in Probability and Statistics, 3rd edn. Wiley, Hoboken (2014)
12. Kim, J.M., Porter, A.: A history-based test prioritization technique for regression testing in resource constrained environments. In: Proceedings of the 24th International Conference on Software Engineering, pp. 119–129. ACM Press (2002)
13. Lakhotia, K., Harman, M., McMinn, P.: A multi-objective approach to search-based test data generation. In: Proceedings of the 9th Conference on Genetic and Evolutionary Computation, pp. 1098–1105, July 2007
14. Li, Z., Harman, M., Hierons, R.M.: Search algorithms for regression test case prioritization. IEEE Trans. Softw. Eng. **33**(4), 225–237 (2007)
15. Monjardet, B.: On the comparison of the Spearman and Kendall metrics between linear orders. Discret. Math. **192**(1), 281–292 (1998)
16. Puschner, P., Nossal, R.: Testing the results of static worst-case execution-time analysis. In: 19th IEEE Real-Time Systems Symposium (RTSS 1998), Los Alamitos, California, USA, pp. 134–143 (1998)
17. Rothermel, G., Untch, R., Chu, C., Harrold, M.: Prioritizing test cases for regression testing. IEEE Trans. Softw. Eng. **27**(10), 929–948 (2001)
18. Schoute, P.H.: Analytic treatment of the polytopes regularly derived from the regular polytopes. Verhandelingen Koninklijke Akademie Wetenschappen Amsterdam **11**(3), 370–381 (1911)
19. Stanley, R.P.: Enumerative Combinatorics: Volume 1, Cambridge Studies in Advanced Mathematics, vol. 49, 2nd edn. Cambridge University Press, Cambridge (2012)
20. Wang, S., Ali, S., Yue, T., Li, Y., Liaaen, M.: A practical guide to select quality indicators for assessing pareto-based search algorithms in search-based software engineering. In: 2016 IEEE/ACM 38th International Conference on Software Engineering (ICSE), pp. 631–642 (2016)
21. Whigham, P.A., Owen, C.A., Macdonell, S.G.: A baseline model for software effort estimation. ACM Trans. Softw. Eng. Methodol. **24**(3), 1–11 (2015)
22. Yoo, S., Harman, M.: Regression testing minimization, selection and prioritization: a survey. Softw. Test. Verif. Reliabil. **22**(2), 67–120 (2012)
23. Yoo, S., Harman, M.: Pareto efficient multi-objective test case selection. In: Proceedings of International Symposium on Software Testing and Analysis, ISSTA 2007, pp. 140–150. ACM Press, July 2007
24. Ziegler, G.M.: Lectures on Polytopes, Graduate Texts in Mathematics, vol. 152. Springer, New York (2007)

Search-Based Selection and Prioritization of Test Scenarios for Autonomous Driving Systems

Chengjie Lu[1]([✉])[iD], Huihui Zhang[2][iD], Tao Yue[1,3][iD], and Shaukat Ali[3][iD]

[1] Nanjing University of Aeronautics and Astronautics, Nanjing, China
chengjielu@nuaa.edu.cn, taoyue@ieee.org
[2] Weifang University, Weifang, China
huihui@wfu.edu.cn
[3] Simula Research Laboratory, Oslo, Norway
shaukat@simula.no

Abstract. Violating the safety of autonomous driving systems (ADSs) could lead to fatal accidents. ADSs are complex, constantly-evolving and software-intensive systems. Testing an individual ADS is challenging and expensive on its own, and consequently testing its multiple versions (due to evolution) becomes much more costly. Thus, it is needed to develop approaches for selecting and prioritizing tests for newer versions of ADSs based on historical test execution data of their previous versions. To this end, we propose a multi-objective search-based approach for Selection and Prioritization of tEst sCenarios for auTonomous dRiving systEms (SPECTRE) to test newer versions of an ADS based on four optimization objectives, e.g., demand of a test scenario put on an ADS. We experimented with five commonly used multi-objective evolutionary algorithms and used a repository of 60,000 test scenarios. Among all the algorithms, IBEA achieved the best performance for solving all the optimization problems of varying complexity.

Keywords: Test optimization · Multi-objective search · Autonomous driving

1 Introduction

Autonomous Driving Systems (ADSs) are safety-critical systems, thus requiring a high degree of dependability. Testing ADSs provides confidence that such systems are dependable; however, due to their complex implementation and the mandate to deal with complex environment, testing ADSs is challenging [3]. Moreover, in practice, ADSs evolve, e.g., because of introducing a new functionality and updating an existing one. Thus, testing ADSs, in general, is costly, especially considering that their new versions need to be tested continuously. Thus, it is important to optimize tests for ADSs. Motivated by this, we propose a search-based approach for Selection and Prioritization of tEst sCenarios for

© Springer Nature Switzerland AG 2021
U.-M. O'Reilly and X. Devroey (Eds.): SSBSE 2021, LNCS 12914, pp. 41–55, 2021.
https://doi.org/10.1007/978-3-030-88106-1_4

auTonomous dRiving systEms (SPECTRE) to test a new version of an ADS from existing test scenarios designed for its previous versions.

Figure 1 shows SPECTRE's overview. SPECTRE relies on test scenario execution results from a previous version of an ADS to prioritize test scenarios to be executed on its newer version. In contrast, the existing works on Search-based Testing (SBT) of ADSs (e.g. [4,5,10]) focus on generating test scenarios for testing ADSs.

In SPECTRE, each scenario is characterized with a set of properties of the ego vehicle with the ADS under test deployed (e.g., acceleration, speed) and its environment (e.g., weather, number of obstacles). The simulation of each test scenario leads to output four key values (*Execution Results* in Fig. 1): (1) whether a collision occurred with the scenario, (2) collision probability associated with the scenario, (3) the extent of demand on the ADS put by the scenario, and (4) diversity of the scenario as compared to the others. Based on these attributes, we define four optimization objectives.

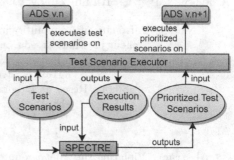

Fig. 1. SPECTRE – overview

To solve our optimization problem, we implemented SPECTRE with five Multi-Objective Evolutionary Algorithms (MOEAs): NSGA-II, NSGA-III, IBEA, SPEA2 and MOCell. Random Search (RS) was used for sanity check. To evaluate SPECTRE, we employed a repository with 60,000 test scenarios and their execution results, Baidu Apollo[1] as the software under test, together with the LGSVL simulator[2]. Results showed that IBEA performed the best in terms of producing quality solutions for all the optimization problems of varying complexity.

The paper is organized as follows: Sect. 2 formulates the search problem and Sect. 3 presents the evaluation, followed by experiment results in Sect. 4. Section 5 is the related work and Sect. 6 concludes the paper.

2   Problem Representation and Objective Function

2.1   Problem Representation

Given a set of test scenarios $SS = \{S_1, S_2...S_{ns}\}$, with ns being the total size of SS, SPECTRE selects a subset of test scenarios from SS and prioritize them to construct a new test suite to test a new version of the ADS. A scenario $S \in SS$ is characterized with a list of properties (e.g., speed of the ego vehicle, weather of the environment): $\{p_1, p_2, p_3...p_{np}\}$, where np is the total number of properties.

[1] https://apollo.auto/.
[2] https://www.svlsimulator.com/.

Basic Concepts. Based on historical execution results of test scenarios, in our context, each scenario S is attached with values of the attributes below. Notice that values of these attributes are extracted from execution results of test scenarios, which are different from properties characterizing test scenarios.

Attribute-1 (Collision (COL)) is a Boolean attribute telling if a scenario S led the ADS collide with obstacles. With COL, we classify all scenarios into either *Collision Scenarios* (S_{COL}) or *Non-Collision Scenarios* (S_{NCOL}).

Attribute-2 (Collision Probability (CPT) measures how close the ADS is to collide with obstacles in a scenario S. We use current distance (CD) and safety distance (SD) [7] to measure CPT as:

$$CPT = \begin{cases} \dfrac{SD - CD}{SD}, & CD < SD \\ 0.0, & else \end{cases} \tag{1}$$

where, SD is a function of accelerations and velocities of the ego vehicle and an obstacle: $F_{SD}(a_{ego}, a_{obstacle}, v_{ego}, v_{obstacle})$; CD is a function of positions of the ego vehicle and an obstacle: $F_{CD}(Pos_{ego}, Pos_{obstacle})$. Notice that, based on Equation (1), the greater the degree of the current distance violation, the higher the collision probability. Based on CPT, a scenario S is defined as *Potential Collision Scenario* (S_{PCOL}) if $CPT \in (0,1)$, implying that when driving in S with $CPT \in (0,1)$, the ego vehicle has a chance to collide with obstacles.

Attribute-3 (Demand (DEM)). Inspired by [8], we use the concept of *demand* to measure how much difficulty the generated scenarios put the ego vehicle in, based on their np properties. Concretely, each scenario property (e.g., the speed) has a corresponding *demand* value. For example, considering that when facing the same or a similar environment, a higher speed of the ego vehicle would possibly result in a higher *demand*. For instance, the speed ranges from 0 to 80 km per hour when driving on an urban road, and its demand can be classified into four categories (based on the level of risk that the vehicle will drive from SFMTA[3]): 0, 1, 3, and 4 for the *Zero*, *Slow*, *Moderate*, and *Fast* speed, respectively. Similarly, demand values for property *rain* can be: 0, 1, 2, and 3, representing no rain, light, moderate or heavy rain, respectively.

Furthermore, we consider test scenarios with demand values of one of its properties equal or greater than the medium value, i.e., $(Max_D - Min_D)/2$ as high demand values, where, Max_D and Min_D denote the maximum and minimum demands of one property. For instance, for property *rain* (i.e., medium $= (3 - 0)/2$), *Moderate* (2) or *Heavy* (3) rain can be considered as high demand. When combining the np properties of a scenario together, its DEM is defined as the number of high *demand* properties, taking an integer values in $[0, np]$. Based on DEM, a scenario is defined as *High Demand Scenario* (S_{HighD}) if more than half of its properties are high demand properties.

Attribute-4 (Diversity (DIV)). Considering that values of different properties (e.g., speed and throttle) of a scenario S are not comparable, we first apply the normalization function [11] below to ensure all the values fall into $[0, 1]$.

---

[3] https://www.sfmta.com.

$$nor(F(x)) = \frac{F(x) - F_{min}}{F_{max} - F_{min}} \tag{2}$$

Based on the definition of scenarios, first, we define the diversity of the k_{th} property in two scenarios S_i, S_j as below:

$$PDIV_k = nor(|p_{ik} - p_{jk}|), \tag{3}$$

where, p_{ik} and p_{jk} are the k_{th} property values of S_i and S_j, respectively. Then we compute the scenario diversity $SDIV$ of two scenarios S_i, S_j as below:

$$SDIV_{i,j} = \frac{\sum_{k=0}^{np} PDIV_k}{np}. \tag{4}$$

where np is the number of property used to define scenarios. DIV of a scenario S_i is then calculated as:

$$DIV = \sum_{j=0}^{ns} SDIV_{i,j}, j \neq i. \tag{5}$$

where ns is the total number of scenarios in the test scenario set SS. Let test suite TS be a set of prioritized test scenarios $TS = \{S_1, S_2, S_3...S_{nts}\}$ selected from SS, where nts is the size TS, a search budget given by users. $PS = \{TS_1, TS_2, TS_3...TS_{nps}\}$ (with nps being its size) is the entire search space of all possible solutions, i.e., the set of permutations of the ordering of all the scenarios from SS. So, if we want to select and prioritize nts scenarios, the size of the search space nps is: $nps = A_{ns}^{nts} = ns*(ns-1)*(ns-2)*...*(ns-nts+1)$. The search space nps will exponentially increase with the growth of ns and exhaustively exploring the entire search space is practically infeasible. Thus, search algorithms can be applied to find optimal solutions within a given budget.

Given $TS = \{S_1, S_2, S_3...S_{nts}\}$, a prioritization solution $X = \{x_1, x_2, ..., x_{nts}\}$ is a particular permutation of TS, where x_i $(0 \leq x_i \leq nts - 1)$ denotes the unique position of test scenario S_i. Note that the value of x_i is unique and ranges from 0 to $nts - 1$. If $x_i = $ j, S_i is the $(j+1)_{th}$ scenario in the sequence. A smaller value of x_i means a preceding position in the sequence X, that is, 0 means the first position while $nts - 1$ indicates the last position of a test scenario.

Optimization Problem. Given a set of test scenarios $SS = \{S_1, S_2...S_{ns}\}$ and a desired budget nts ($nts \leq ns$), find solution $TS_k \in PS$ with a particular permutation $X_{kp} = \{x_1^{kp}, x_2^{kp}, x_3^{kp}...x_{nts}^{kp}\}$, where TS_k includes nts scenarios selected and prioritized from SS that satisfy:

(1) $\forall TS_i \in PS : \#S_{COL}^{TS_i} \leq \#S_{COL}^{TS_k}$, telling that TS_k has the maximum number of collision scenarios.
(2) $\forall TS_i \in PS : \#S_{PCOL}^{TS_i} \leq \#S_{PCOL}^{TS_k}$, implying that TS_k has the maximum number of potential collision scenarios.
(3) $\forall TS_i \in PS : \#S_{HighD}^{TS_i} \leq \#S_{HighD}^{TS_k}$, which denotes that TS_k has the maximum number of highly demand scenarios.

(4) $\forall TS_i \in PS : DIV(TS_k) \geq DIV(TS_j)$, which indicates that TS_k has the most diverse scenarios.

(5) $\forall (x_i < x_j (x_i, x_j \in X_{kp} \wedge i \neq j)) :$
$$\begin{cases} COL^{X_{kp}}(x_j) \leq COL^{X_k}(x_i) \wedge \\ CPT^{X_{kp}}(x_j) \leq CPT^{X_k}(x_i) \wedge \\ DEM^{X_{kp}}(x_j) \leq DEM^{X_k}(x_i) \wedge \\ DIV^{X_{kp}}(x_j) \leq DIV^{X_k}(x_i) \end{cases} \text{ which}$$

means values of the four attributes of the scenarios in TS_k will descend.

2.2 Objective Functions

Based on the definitions in Sects. 2.1, we formally define the objectives.

Objectives 1 to 4 are for selecting NTS test scenarios that maximize these objectives, whereas objective 5 is devised to prioritize the selected test scenarios.

Objective 1. *Number of Collision Scenarios* (NS_{COL}) is the number of *Collision Scenarios* S_{COL} in TS_k which led the ego vehicle to collide.

$$NS_{COL}^{TS_k} = Count(S_{COL}), \tag{6}$$

Objective 2. *Number of Potential Collision Scenarios* (NS_{PCOL}) counts the number of *Potential Collision Scenarios* (S_{PCOL}) (Sect. 2.1):

$$NS_{PCOL}^{TS_k} = Count(S_{PCOL}) \tag{7}$$

Objective 3. *Number of High Demand Scenarios* (NS_{HighD}) is the number of *High Demand Scenarios* S_{HighD} defined in Sect. 2.1:

$$NS_{HighD}^{TS_k} = Count(S_{HighD}) \tag{8}$$

Objective 4. *Test Solution Diversity* ($TSDIV$) measures the differences of each pair of scenarios (calculated with Eq. 4) in TS_k as:

$$TSDIV_{TS_k} = \frac{\sum_{i=0}^{nts-1} \sum_{j=i+1}^{nts} SDIV_{i,j}}{nts} \tag{9}$$

Objective 5. Attribute Prioritization ($APrio$) differentiates scenarios based on positions of attribute values. In Eq. 11, $\frac{nts-x_i}{nts}$ indicates that a value of an attribute (e.g., COL) in a preceding position has a higher contribution to $APrio$. When putting equal weights to each attribute, we can obtain one value: $APrio_{TS_k}$ (Eq. 10), telling that the objective function tries to permute scenarios with higher collision, collision probability, demand and diversity in the front positions of the permutation sequence as early as possible.

$$APrio_{TS_k} = \omega 1 * APrio_{col} + \omega 2 * APrio_{cpt} + \omega 3 * APrio_{dem} + \omega 4 * APrio_{div};$$
$$(\omega 1 = \omega 2 = \omega 3 = \omega 4 = 0.25) \tag{10}$$

$$APrio_{col} = \frac{\sum_{i=1}^{nts} * \frac{nts-x_i}{nts} * COL_i}{nts}; APrio_{cpt} = \frac{\sum_{i=1}^{nts} * \frac{nts-x_i}{nts} * CPT_i}{nts};$$
$$APrio_{dem} = \frac{\sum_{i=1}^{nts} * \frac{nts-x_i}{nts} * DEM_i}{nts}; APrio_{div} = \frac{\sum_{i=1}^{nts} * \frac{nts-x_i}{nts} * DIV_i}{nts}$$
(11)

3   Empirical Evaluation

3.1   DataSet

Test Scenarios. A test scenario for ADSs, in our experiment, is defined with 19 properties; 5 of them are about the ego vehicle (e.g., acceleration and speed) and the other 14 properties describe the environment (e.g., pedestrians, weather). To produce the dataset, we employed the Baidu Apollo Open Platform 5.0 as the ADS under test and integrated it with the LGSVL simulator. We chose the San Francisco map for scenarios collecting because it has a large number of different types of roads such as one-way roads, two-way roads and cross walks.

Collecting Data. The test scenarios in the dataset were automatically collected when we were testing Apollo 5.0 with a machine learning based environment configuration generation strategy. We executed the strategy, together with LGSVL for nearly 1000 times on four different roads of the San Francisco map loaded in LGSVL. In the end, we managed to collect the dataset of 90K test scenarios, each of which is characterized with the 19 properties.

Processing Data. First, we removed duplicated test scenarios from the original dataset, to reduce unnecessary effort for prioritization In the end, we obtained a dataset containing 60K scenarios. To save time on calculating diversity during the execution of the MOEAs, we further calculated all the pair-wise comparison diversity values of the test scenarios in advance, i.e., *SDIV*.

Labelling Test Scenarios with Their Attributes. After data collecting and pre-processing, for each test scenario, we calculated four values for each of the four attributes (Sect. 2.1). The labeled dataset was then fed to SPECTRE for selection and prioritization. The replication package is available at Github[4].

3.2   Research Questions (RQs)

RQ1: How do the selected MOEAs compare to each other in terms of solving our optimization problem?

RQ2: How the selected MOEAs compare to each other when solving optimization problems of various search budgets?

RQ3: How does the search budget affect the effectiveness of the selected MOEAs?

RQ4: How is the time performance of the selected MOEAs?

---

[4] https://github.com/ssbse2021/SPECTRE.

3.3   Experiment Design and Evaluation Metrics

To answer RQs, we integrated SPECTRE with five commonly used MOEAs: NSGA-II, NSGA-III, IBEA, SPEA2 and MOCell for solving different Search-Based Software Engineering (SBSE) problems (e.g., test selection [19], test minimization [21], requirements prioritization [20]). Among them, NSGA-II and SPEA2 were chosen because a large number of works studied them and have proven to be effective for solving SBSE problems [16]; MOCell is an effective Pareto-based MOEA used in [16]; NSGA-III aims to handle many-objective (i.e., 3 to 15) optimization problems; and IBEA represents Indicator-based evolutionary algorithms. For IBEA, we employed the $I_{\epsilon+}$-indicator [22]. As recommended in [2], RS was used for sanity check. We used the default parameter settings of MOEAs from jMetal [9], except for NSGA-III's population size, which was changed to 100 from the default size of 92 to be consistent with the other MOEAs. All parameter settings are presented in SPECTRE's online repository.

SPECTRE is configured to select test scenarios with eight NTS settings, where NTS is the number of test scenarios to be selected from the dataset, ranging from 1,000 to 8,000 with an increment of 1,000. We executed SPECTRE for 30 times for each MOEA and with each NTS.

Based on the published guide [1], we used the Inverted Generational Distance (IGD) quality indicator. IGD computes the distance of the solutions of the Pareto front from those of the reference Pareto front to assess the performance of the MOEAs. Thus, a smaller IGD value indicates a better performance. For each NTS, a reference Pareto front is computed by merging all the Pareto fronts from all the 30 runs of all the MOEAs and RS.

3.4   Statistical Tests

Based on the guidelines in [2], we selected statistical tests with the significance level of 0.05. First, we applied the Kolmogorov-Smirnov test to test if the samples are normally distributed. Results tell that they are not normally distributed. Then, we used the non-parametric Kruskal-Wallis rank test to compare the samples. Results reveal a significant difference among them. Thus, we performed the Mann-Whitney U test for pairwise comparisons, and used the Vargha and Delaney effect size to calculate $\hat{A}_{12}$. Given metric χ, $\hat{A}_{12}$ was used to compare the probability of yielding higher values of χ for algorithms AlgA and AlgB. If $\hat{A}_{12}$ is 0.5, then the results were obtained by chance. If $\hat{A}_{12}$ is greater than 0.5, then AlgA has a higher chance to achieve a better performance than AlgB in terms of χ, and vice versa. The Mann-Whitney U test returns p-values to check if the difference between AlgA and AlgB is significant. We also adjusted all p-values with the Bonferroni Correction to avoid type I errors.

To study the correlation between IGD and NTS, we performed the Spearman's rank correlation (ρ) test. The ρ value ranges from -1.0 to 1.0, i.e., there is a positive correlation if ρ is close to 1.0 and a negative correlation when ρ closes to -1.0. If ρ closes to 0 then there is no correlation between IGD and NTS. We also reported the significance of the correlation using p-value, i.e., a p-value less than 0.05 tells that the correlation is statistically significant.

4   Results and Analyses

To check if the problem is complex, we compared the selected MOEAs with RS. Results show that all the MOEAs performed significantly better than RS in terms of IGD for all the NTSs. Thus, for answering our RQs, we didn't include RS. Detailed results can be found in SPECTRE's online repository.

4.1   Results of RQ1

Results for RQ1, comparing each MOEA with the others in terms of p-values and $\hat{A}_{12}$, are reported in Table 1. For IBEA, when comparing with the other MOEAs, all the p-values are less than 0.05 and $\hat{A}_{12} < 0.5$, thus suggesting that IBEA is significantly better than the other MOEAs. NSGA-II is significantly better than MOCell, but significantly worst than NSGA-III, SPEA2, and IBEA. NSGA-III is significantly better than MOCell and NSGA-II, whereas significantly worst than IBEA. MOCell was significantly worst than the rest. We

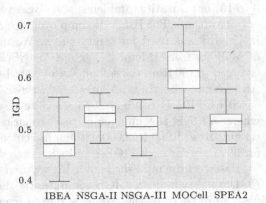

Fig. 2. Descriptive statistics of IGD when combining all NTS results – RQ1

can then rank the MOEAs as: IBEA, NSGA-III/SPEA2, NSGA-II, and MOCell.

Figure 2 better illustrates the results, especially the variance of 30 IGD values produced by each MOEA in its 30 runs. From the figure, we see that MOCell performed the worst and also produced results with the largest variance. The variances of IGD values of the other four MOEAs are smaller and comparable.

We therefore recommend using IBEA for solving our search problem.

Table 1. Results for comparing MOEAs when combining all NTS results – RQ1

Metric	IBEA vs.				NSGA-II vs.			NSGA-III vs.		MOCell vs.
	NSGA-II	NSGA-III	MOCell	SPEA2	NSGA-III	MOCell	SPEA2	MOCell	SPEA2	SPEA2
$\hat{A}_{12}$	**0.121**	**0.287**	**0.008**	**0.207**	0.754	**0.044**	0.678	**0.009**	0.399	0.973
p-value	<0.05	<0.05	<0.05	<0.05	<0.05	<0.05	<0.05	<0.05	0.183	<0.05

*A bold $\hat{A}_{12} < 0.5$ with a $p-value < 0.05$ implies that the upper algorithm is significantly better than the bottom one, whereas $\hat{A}_{12} > 0.5$ with $p-value < 0.05$ means vice versa. A $p-value > 0.5$ means no significant differences.

4.2   Results of RQ2

Table 2 reports pair-wise comparisons of MOEAs with respect to IGD. Among all the MOEAs, MOCell achieved the worst performance for all NTSs. For $NTS \in \{1000, 3000\}$: IBEA achieved the best performance, followed by NSGA-III; NSGA-III significantly outperformed SPEA2 and SPEA2 was significantly better than NSGA-II. For $NTS \in \{2000, 4000, 6000, 7000\}$, IBEA significantly outperformed the others and NSGA-III achieved the second best. No significant difference was observed between SPEA2 and NSGA-II. For $NTS = 5000$, IBEA performed the best. Both NSGA-III and SPEA2 were significantly better than NSGA-II and there was no significant difference between NSGA-III and SPEA2. For $NTS = 8000$, both IBEA and NSGA-III achieved the best, and there was no significant difference between them, and no significance difference was observed between SPEA2 and NSGA-II. Table 3 better organizes the results of the pair-wise comparisons of the MOEAs for each NTS.

Table 2. Results of comparing MOEAs for each NTS – RQ2

NTS	IBEA *vs.*				NSGA-II *vs.*			NSGA-III *vs.*		MOCell *vs.*
	NSGA-II	NSGA-III	MOCell	SPEA2	NSGA-III	MOCell	SPEA2	MOCell	SPEA2	SPEA2
1000	**.027**/<.05	**.249**/<.05	**.009**/<.05	**.098**/<.05	.834/<.05	**.032**/<.05	.653/<.05	**.018**/<.05	**.289**/<.05	.972/<.05
2000	**.040**/<.05	**.239**/<.05	**.013**/<.05	**.052**/<.05	.826/<.05	**.121**/<.05	.629/.08	**.039**/<.05	**.227**/<.05	.922/<.05
3000	**.044**/<.05	**.258**/<.05	**.007**/<.05	**.062**/<.05	.904/<.05	**.128**/<.05	.707/<.05	**.016**/<.05	**.182**/<.05	.943/<.05
4000	**.061**/<.05	**.271**/<.05	**.029**/<.05	**.096**/<.05	.851/<.05	**.177**/<.05	.578/.304	**.071**/<.05	**.210**/<.05	.858/<.05
5000	**.068**/<.05	**.206**/<.05	**.002**/<.05	**.146**/<.05	.770/<.05	**.036**/<.05	.707/<.05	**.009**/<.05	.410/.234	.984/<.05
6000	**.038**/<.05	**.258**/<.05	**.014**/<.05	**.088**/<.05	.826/<.05	**.116**/<.05	.599/.191	**.046**/<.05	**.267**/<.05	.898/<.05
7000	**.100**/<.05	**.257**/<.05	**.004**/<.05	**.116**/<.05	.769/<.05	**.044**/<.05	.559/.438	**.023**/<.05	**.264**/<.05	.963/<.05
8000	**.144**/<.05	.359/.061	**.001**/<.05	**.204**/<.05	.808/<.05	**.060**/<.05	.636/.072	**.003**/<.05	**.289**/<.05	.976/<.05

*The value before/is $\hat{A}_{12}$ and after is p-value. A bold $\hat{A}_{12} < 0.5$ with a $p-value < 0.05$ implies that the upper algorithm is significantly better than the bottom one, whereas $\hat{A}_{12} > 0.5$ with $p-value < 0.05$ means vice versa. A $p-value > 0.5$ means no significant differences.

Table 3. Ranking of MOEAs for each NTS value – RQ2

NTS	Ranking	NTS	Ranking	NTS	Ranking	NTS	Ranking
1000	I, N-III, S, N-II, M	2000	I, N-III, S/N-II, M	3000	I, N-III, S, N-II, M	4000	I, N-III, S/N-II, M
5000	I, N-III/S, N-II, M	6000	I, N-III, S/N-II, M	7000	I, N-III, S/N-II, M	8000	I/N-III, S/N-II, M

*I: IBEA, N: NSGA; S: SPEA2. M: MOCell; a/means two MOEAs have the same ranking.

The variance of 30 IGD values for each MOEA corresponding to its 30 runs for each NTS value are reported in Fig. 3. For almost all the NTSs, MOCell is the worst with the large variances. For the other MOEAs, we can observe smaller variances and they are comparable for most of NTS values. This observation is consistent with the results we obtained for RQ1.

4.3   Results of RQ3

RQ3 aims to study how the increasing number of NTSs affects the performance of each MOEA. To this end, we plot the average of 30 IGD values for NTS in Fig. 4. From the figure, we can observe that along with the increase of the NTS, the IDG values of all the

Table 4. Results of the Spearman's rank correlation test – RQ3

Metric	MOSA				
	IBEA	NSGA-II	NSGA-III	MOCell	SPEA2
ρ	0.936	0.933	0.930	0.713	0.930
p-value	<0.05	<0.05	<0.05	<0.05	<0.05

MOEAs increase as well. Recall that a lower value of IGD means a better quality of solutions. This suggests that when the NTS is increasing, it affects the quality

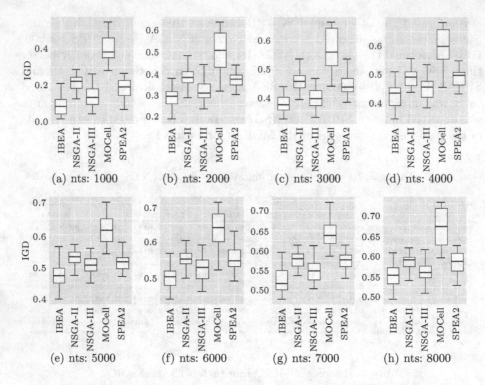

Fig. 3. Descriptive statistics of IGD in terms of various NTS – RQ2

of solutions produced by each MOEA. This is because an optimization problem with a larger NTS has a larger search space (Sect. 2); therefore, the problem is more challenging to solve.

We further studied the statistical significance of this pattern with the Spearman's rank correlation (ρ) test. Results are shown in Table 4, from which we can see that all the ρ values are near 1.0, except for MOCell. This tells that there is a near perfect positive correlation between IGD and NTS. For MOCell, the ρ value is 0.713, indicating a strong positive correlation. In addition, all p-values are less than 0.05, suggesting that this positive correlation is statistically significant.

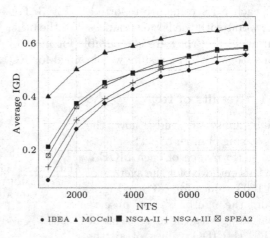

Fig. 4. Results of IGD of various MOEAs when increasing NST – RQ3

These results suggest that the ability of the MOEAs producing high-quality solutions significantly decreases with the increase of NTS. One reason could be that with while increasing NTS, the optimization problem is getting more complex, and hence MOEAs need more generations to find good quality solutions. This aspect needs to be assessed with additional experiments in the future.

4.4 Results of RQ4

Table 5 shows that a MOEA needs nearly 17 to 137 min to solve the optimization problems of different complexity (i.e., NTS). When looking at each NTS value, we can see that there aren't much time differences among the studied MOEAs that practically matter. For example, the best performed algorithm, i.e., IBEA, for the NTS of 8000, took 126 min, which is only approximately 8 min more than RS (with the best time performance). Practically, such minor time difference doesn't matter. Moreover, since SPECTRE is executed offline, it is not critical to select a MOEA in terms of its time performance and we care more about the quality of produced solutions. In summary, the time performance of SPECTRE is acceptable in practice, as, e.g., IBEA spending 17.6 min on selecting and prioritizing 1,000 out of 60,000 test scenarios.

Table 5. Average running time of each MOEA (Time Unit: Minute) – RQ4

MOSA	NTS							
	1000	2000	3000	4000	5000	6000	7000	8000
IBEA	17.58	32.09	47.05	62.42	77.03	98.61	110.15	126.01
NSGA-II	16.19	30.89	46.14	61.87	76.82	97.35	108.92	122.09
NSGA-III	16.21	31.04	46.34	61.41	77.12	97.39	109.19	125.16
MOCell	17.36	33.01	49.77	66.52	82.22	106.89	118.56	136.68
SPEA2	16.81	31.10	46.23	61.81	77.73	97.93	111.35	126.14
Random	14.82	28.56	42.98	56.27	72.14	91.51	102.79	117.68

4.5 Overall Discussion

Research Implications. Based on the evaluation results, we recommend IBEA for SPECTRE as IBEA achieves the best performance among all the selected MOEAs (RQ1 and RQ2). When looking into the performance of the selected MOEAs along with the increase in NTS, IGD values of all the MOEAs increase. This tells that when increasing NTS, the search space increases as well, hence possibly requiring more generations or evaluations to explore good solutions. Moreover, we observed that running time (RQ4) increases with the increase of NTS because of the increased search space and the cost of calculating all the five objectives. For example, as shown in Table 5, for IBEA, selecting 8000 scenarios (126.01 mins) takes about 7 times the running time of selecting 1000 scenarios (17.58 mins). Thus, improving SPECTRE's scalability is one of our future works.

SPECTRE can also be extended to address other optimization problems in testing ADSs, for instance, considering the uncertainty aspect of the attributes of test scenarios. The current implementation of SPECTRE has four attributes, among which CPT (Sect. 2.1) is naturally an uncertain factor. In the future, we can develop solutions by taking into account the uncertain nature of these attributes. Moreover, SPECTRE can be easily extended by introducing new optimization objectives of newly introduced attributes.

Practical Implications. In practice, testing a new version of an ADS with all existing test scenarios is costly due to limited time-wise and monetary-wise resources. Hence, it is important to have an approach like SPECTRE for cost-effectively construct a new test suite by benefiting from prior knowledge on the cost-effectiveness of already executed test scenarios. SPECTRE requires an organization to construct and maintain a test scenario repository for test optimization (like the one described in Sect. 2.1). This requirement is reasonable as a lot of organizations always have their test management tools (e.g., Bugzilla).

SPECTRE selects and prioritizes a subset of test scenarios out of all available ones based on their attributes (Sect. 2.1) to avoid arbitrary decisions of intuition and experience. Without SPECTRE, the selection and prioritization process may mainly rely on managers' experience and domain expertise.

4.6   Threats to Validity

We employed quality indicator *IGD* to assess the performance of the MOEAs, which is comparable among the selected MOEAs. The total number of evaluations (i.e., 30,000) was used as the stopping criterion for all the MOEAs. We used the same cost measure, i.e., NTS, and repeated the experiments with a given NTS. Regarding parameter settings of the MOEAs, we however mostly used the default parameter settings of the MOEAs from [9], which have shown good results for various SBSE problems [3].

We followed a rigorous statistical procedure to analyze the collected data. Thirty independent runs of each MOEA were performed based on existing guidelines to deal with MOEA's randomness [2]. We chose appropriate tests, i.e., the Mann-Whitney U test with the Bonferroni Correction and $\hat{A}_{12}$ to assess effect based on the established guideline from [2]. We choose an appropriate quality indicator (i.e., IGD) based on the guideline from [1]. Generalization of the results is a key issue with all experiments. Our experiments were conducted with one dataset of 60,000 test scenarios, which is sufficiently large. Nonetheless, additional datasets are needed for future investigation.

5   Related Work

Search-Based Testing (SBT) of ADSs. Ben Abdessalem et al. [4] used NSGA-II and surrogate models to identify most critical behaviors of Advanced Driver Assistance Systems (ADASs) used in ADSs within limited computation resources. They experimented with an industrial ADAS and results show that their approach can automatically identify test cases indicating critical ADAS behaviors with higher quality compared to random search, especially under resource sensitive situations. Another related work combines multi-objective search and decision tree classification models, i.e., NSGAII-DT [5]. This approach tests vision-based control systems of ADSs to find critical scenarios quickly and accurately. NSGAII-DT was compared with NSGA-II on an industrial ADS, and the results shows that NSGAII-DT significantly outperforms NSGA-II in terms of generating more distinct and critical test scenarios.

FITEST [6] is an SBT approach for detecting feature interaction failures in autonomous driving. FITEST has a combination of traditional coverage based heuristics and novel heuristics specifically proposed for revealing feature interaction failures. They evaluated FITEST using two versions of an industrial ADS. Results show that FITEST is effective in terms of identifying more feature interaction failures than approaches with coverage-based and failure-based test objectives. Gambi et al. [10] addressed challenges of simulation-based testing by combining procedural road generation and genetic algorithms to generate virtual roads, by utilizing *procedural content generation*, for testing ADSs. Their evaluation on two different ADSs shows that the proposed method can generate effective virtual road networks, which can lead car departures from lanes. Li et al. [12] proposed AV-FUZZER which combines genetic algorithms with a local fuzzer to increase the ability of generating AV safety violation scenarios. The approach was evaluated on Baidu Apollo and was proven to be able to find safety violations in a short time.

All the above-mentioned related research focus on generating test scenarios for an ADS, but none of them study the reuse of test scenarios obtained from previous versions of the ADS and used for testing its new version. We, instead, focus on reusing existing test scenarios by selecting and prioritizing them from a repository of test scenarios that have been executed for testing old versions of an ADS, with multi-objective search.

Search-Based Test Case Prioritization (TCP). TCP approaches consider various prioritization criteria such as fault detection rate, time cost estimates, and code coverage. Search-based techniques have been widely used in addressing TCP problems. For instance, in [13], Li et al. described five algorithms for the sequencing problem in test case prioritization for regression testing, defined a fitness function with three objectives, and prioritized test cases with hill climbing and GAs. To study TCP problems with limited budget, many works have been proposed. For instance, Singh et al. [17] used ant colony optimization to prioritize test cases under limited time and cost constrains, with the goal to maximum the number of faults to cover and minimum time cost. Wang et al. [18] proposed a multi-objective search-based prioritization approach, aiming at prioritizing test cases with limited test resources and time budget, with one cost measure on test execution time and three effectiveness measures on prioritization density, test resources usage and fault detection capability. TCP approaches focusing on the fault detection capability also attracted much attention. For instance, Pradhan et al. [15] proposed a multi-objective approach to prioritize test cases with the high coverage of configurations, test APIs, statuses, and high fault detection capability as quickly as possible. Moreover, Luo et al. [14] conducted an empirical study to evaluate the performance of a TCP approach in terms of its fault detection efficiency.

Though, our aim is similar to these works, i.e., test prioritization for regression testing, we focus on prioritization on test scenario prioritization for ADSs, which is not much studied in the literature.

6   Conclusion and Future Work

This paper presented a multi-objective search approach for test scenario selection and prioritization for autonomous driving systems (ADSs) with the ultimate aim of decreasing the testing cost of newer versions of ADSs based on historical test data collected for testing their previous versions. The approach integrated five multi-objective evolutionary algorithms (MOEAs), i.e., NSGA-II, NSGA-III, IBEA, SPEA2, and MOCell. To evaluate our approach with the selected MOEAs, we experimented with one large-scale dataset collected from testing an open-source ADS. The dataset is of 60,000 test scenarios. Our evaluation results showed that IBEA performed the best in terms of producing high quality solutions, and therefore is recommended for addressing our optimization problem.

In the future, we will test other ADSs to assess SPECTRE's performance and scalability. Moreover, attribute values associated with each scenario are required to be continuously updated due to continuous testing of newer versions of ADSs. Thus, we will provide a framework for automatically updating these values together with an online repository. We will also perform parameter tuning for MOEAs and study their effect on the performance of our approach.

Acknowledgements. The work is supported by the National Natural Science Foundation of China under Grant No. 61872182. The work is also partially supported by the Co-evolver project (No. 286898/F20) funded by the Research Council of Norway. Huihui Zhang is supported by the Science and Technology Program of Public Wellbeing (No. 2020KJHM01).

References

1. Ali, S., Arcaini, P., Pradhan, D., Safdar, S.A., Yue, T.: Quality indicators in search-based software engineering: an empirical evaluation. ACM Trans. Softw. Eng. Methodol. (TOSEM) **29**(2), 1–29 (2020)
2. Arcuri, A., Briand, L.: A practical guide for using statistical tests to assess randomized algorithms in software engineering. In: Proceedings of the 33rd International Conference on Software Engineering (ICSE 2011), pp. 1–10 (2011)
3. Arcuri, A., Fraser, G.: On parameter tuning in search based software engineering. In: Cohen, M.B., Ó Cinnéide, M. (eds.) SSBSE 2011. LNCS, vol. 6956, pp. 33–47. Springer, Heidelberg (2011). https://doi.org/10.1007/978-3-642-23716-4_6
4. Ben Abdessalem, R., Nejati, S., Briand, L.C., Stifter, T.: Testing advanced driver assistance systems using multi-objective search and neural networks. In: Proceedings of the Conference on Automated Software Engineering, pp. 63–74. ACM (2016)
5. Ben Abdessalem, R., Nejati, S., Briand, L.C., Stifter, T.: Testing vision-based control systems using learnable evolutionary algorithms. In: Proceedings of the Conference on Software Engineering, pp. 1016–1026. ACM (2018)

6. Ben Abdessalem, R., Panichella, A., Nejati, S., Briand, L.C., Stifter, T.: Testing autonomous cars for feature interaction failures using many-objective search. In: Proceedings of the Conference on Automated Software Engineering, pp. 143–154. ACM (2018)
7. Corso, A., Du, P., Driggs-Campbell, K., Kochenderfer, M.J.: Adaptive stress testing with reward augmentation for autonomous vehicle validatio. In: 2019 IEEE Intelligent Transportation Systems Conference (ITSC), pp. 163–168. IEEE (2019)
8. Czarnecki, K.: Operational design domain for automated driving systems: Taxonomy of basic terms. Waterloo Intelligent Systems Engineering (WISE) Lab, University of Waterloo, Canada (2018)
9. Durillo, J.J., Nebro, A.J.: jMetal: a Java framework for multi-objective optimization. Adv. Eng. Softw. **42**(10), 760–771 (2011)
10. Gambi, A., Mueller, M., Fraser, G.: Automatically testing self-driving cars with search-based procedural content generation. In: Proceedings of International Symposium on Software Testing and Analysis, pp. 318–328. ACM (2019)
11. Greer, D., Ruhe, G.: Software release planning: an evolutionary and iterative approach. Inf. Softw. Technol. **46**(4), 243–253 (2004)
12. Li, G., et al.: AV-FUZZER: finding safety violations in autonomous driving systems. In: International Symposium on Software Reliability Engineering, pp. 25–36. IEEE (2020)
13. Li, Z., Harman, M., Hierons, R.M.: Search algorithms for regression test case prioritization. IEEE Trans. Softw. Eng. **33**(4), 225–237 (2007)
14. Luo, Q., Moran, K., Poshyvanyk, D., Di Penta, M.: Assessing test case prioritization on real faults and mutants. In: 2018 IEEE International Conference on Software Maintenance and Evolution (ICSME), pp. 240–251. IEEE (2018)
15. Pradhan, D., Wang, S., Ali, S., Yue, T., Liaaen, M.: STIPI: using search to prioritize test cases based on multi-objectives derived from industrial practice. In: Wotawa, F., Nica, M., Kushik, N. (eds.) ICTSS 2016. LNCS, vol. 9976, pp. 172–190. Springer, Cham (2016). https://doi.org/10.1007/978-3-319-47443-4_11
16. Ramirez, A., Romero, J.R., Ventura, S.: A survey of many-objective optimisation in search based software engineering. Syst. Softw. Eng. **149**, 382–395 (2019)
17. Singh, Y., Kaur, A., Suri, B.: Test case prioritization using ant colony optimization. ACM SIGSOFT Softw. Eng. Notes **35**(4), 1–7 (2010)
18. Wang, S., Ali, S., Yue, T., Bakkeli, Ø., Liaaen, M.: Enhancing test case prioritization in an industrial setting with resource awareness and multi-objective search. In: Proceedings of the 38th International Conference on Software Engineering Companion, pp. 182–191 (2016)
19. Yoo, S., Harman, M.: Pareto efficient multi-objective test case selection. In: Proceedings of the International Symposium on Software Testing and Analysis, pp. 140–150 (2007)
20. Zhang, H., Zhang, M., Yue, T., Ali, S., Li, Y.: Uncertainty-wise requirements prioritization with search. ACM Trans. Softw. Eng. Methodol. (TOSEM) **30**(1), 1–54 (2020)
21. Zhang, M., Ali, S., Yue, T.: Uncertainty-wise test case generation and minimization for cyber-physical systems. J. Syst. Softw. **153**, 1–21 (2019)
22. Zitzler, E., Künzli, S.: Indicator-based selection in multiobjective search. In: Yao, X., et al. (eds.) PPSN 2004. LNCS, vol. 3242, pp. 832–842. Springer, Heidelberg (2004). https://doi.org/10.1007/978-3-540-30217-9_84

Search-Based Automated Play Testing of Computer Games: A Model-Based Approach

Raihana Ferdous[1], Fitsum Kifetew[1(✉)] (iD), Davide Prandi[1] (iD),
I. S. W. B. Prasetya[2] (iD), Samira Shirzadehhajimahmood[2] (iD), and Angelo Susi[1] (iD)

[1] Fondazione Bruno Kessler, Trento, Italy
{rferdous,kifetew,prandi,susi}@fbk.eu
[2] Utrecht University, Utrecht, The Netherlands
{s.w.b.prasetya,s.shirzadehhajimahmood}@uu.nl

Abstract. Computer game technology is increasingly more complex and applied in a wide variety of domains, beyond entertainment, such as training and educational scenarios. Testing games is a difficult task requiring a lot of manual effort since the interaction space in the game is very fine grained and requires a certain level of intelligence that cannot be easily automated. This makes testing a costly activity in the overall development of games.

This paper presents a model-based formulation of game play testing in such a way that search-based testing can be applied for test generation. An abstraction of the desired game behaviour is captured in an extended finite state machine (EFSM) and search-based algorithms are used to derive abstract tests from the model, which are then concretised into action sequences that are executed on the game under test.

The approach is implemented in a prototype tool EvoMBT. We carried out experiments on a 3D game to assess the suitability of the approach in general, and search-based test generation in particular. We applied 5 search algorithms for test generation on three different models of the game. Results show that search algorithms are able to achieve reasonable coverage on models: between 75% and 100% for the small and medium sized models, and between 29% and 56% for the bigger model. Mutation analysis shows that on the actual game application tests kill up to 99% of mutants. Tests have also revealed previously unknown faults.

Keywords: Game play testing · Search-based testing · Model-based testing

1 Introduction

A common approach to test a computer game is by *play testing* it, where human users are deployed to play the game in order to find flaws, usability issues,

This work is a result of iv4XR project, funded by the EU Horizon 2020 research and innovation programme under grant agreement No. 856716.

U.-M. O'Reilly and X. Devroey (Eds.): SSBSE 2021, LNCS 12914, pp. 56–71, 2021.
https://doi.org/10.1007/978-3-030-88106-1_5

and to give feedback on the game user experience. This process is expensive, so introducing automation could greatly reduce the cost. Unfortunately, so far there is not much automated testing technology available for computer games. A handful that exist are tailored for specific games (and not publicly available).

Computer games also come in a great variety of genres such as action, adventure, puzzle, strategy, building, etc. [1]. The difference between genres (or even within the same genre) is large, e.g. an action game is usually a fast moving event driven system but the story is linear, while an adventure game is much less event driven, but the story is often complex. While such variety is good to keep users entertained, it certainly does not help in developing an automated testing approach that would work for all, or at least most, game genres.

This paper presents model-based approach for automated play testing of computer games, relying on search-based testing for generating tests. Outside the Game domain, model-based testing (MBT) [12] has long been known as a versatile testing approach. Similarly, search-based testing (SBT) [9] has proven effective for generating tests, in particular when the search space is large and exact methods are not applicable. This paper aims to formulate game play testing in such a way that SBT can be applied for automated test generation.

We present an approach for modelling game behaviour using extended finite state machines (EFSMs) in such a way that the tester can model the desired aspect of the game behaviour. Once the model is defined, SBT is applied for test generation from the model, following a typical MBT cycle.

The approach is implemented in a prototype tool EvoMBT which allows the generation of abstract tests from EFSM models by applying search-based algorithms. Empirical evaluation is carried out by applying EvoMBT on a 3D game called Lab Recruits. The concretisation and execution of abstract tests on Lab Recruits is implemented by means of an agent-based API of Lab Recruits. Results show that the proposed application of SBT and MBT are effective in achieving reasonable levels of coverage on the model and exposing faults.

The main contributions of this work are:

1. an approach combining SBT and MBT for automated game play testing
2. a tool EvoMBT for generation of tests from an EFSM model, allowing experimentation with existing search algorithms
3. publicly available artifacts (tool, models, data) that enable reproducibility of results and facilitate further research.

The rest of the paper is organised as follows: Sect. 2 presents the running example used throughout the paper. Section 3 discusses issues in modelling games and presents definitions used in the rest of the paper. Section 4 introduces the testing problem and Sect. 5 presents our proposed search-based test generation approach. Experimental results are presented in Sect. 6 and related work is discussed in Sect. 7. Section 8 concludes, and outlines future work.

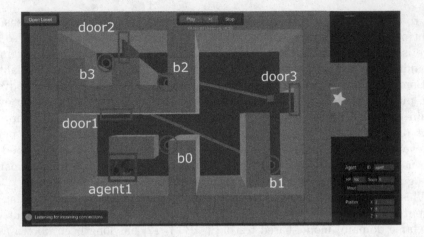

Fig. 1. Level `buttonDoors1` in `Lab Recruits`.

2   Running Example

This section introduces `Lab Recruits`[1], a 3D game developed for experimenting with intelligent agents. The application allows the definition of mazes, a set of rooms connected by doors. Each door is opened by one or more buttons, and each button activates one or more doors. The goal is to find the path to reach a certain room by opening doors in the right order. The game can be played by both humans and artificial agents [10]. `Lab Recruits` levels are defined as csv (comma-separated value) human-readable files allowing researchers to specify their tests of variable complexity.

As a running example, Fig. 1 shows a level of the `Lab Recruits` game named `buttonDoors1`. The level features three doors, `door1`, `door2`, and `door3`, and four buttons, `b0`, `b1`, `b2`, and `b3`. Door `door1` is activated by buttons `b1`, `b2`, and `b3`, while `door2` and `door3` are connected only to `b2`. Note that `b0` is not connected, therefore pressing it has not effect in the game. Agent `agent1` aims to reach the room marked with a star, and therefore to open `door3`. A possible path requires `agent1` to press `b1` to open `door1` and then `b2` to open `door3`. Since `b2` also acts on `door1`, at this point `agent1` cannot reach `door3`, but need to traverse `door2` and press `b3` to open `door1`. Now, `agent1` walks through `door1` and `door3`, finally reaching the star room. Even if the layout of the level is simple, the path to reach the final room is not trivial and it is not trivial for automated play testing.

3   Modelling Games

Computer games are stateful systems, and hence using state-based models to model them is natural. They are also very complex systems, so abstraction will

---

[1] https://github.com/iv4xr-project/labrecruits.

have to be applied, but not to the degree that we lose control and observability of the system. Plain finite state machines (FSM) or labelled transition systems are in most cases either cumbersome or insufficient, and we will need to use, for instance, EFSM that allow variables and assignments to be superimposed over a finite state model. The running example presented in Sect. 2 with buttons and doors whose states change dynamically can be modelled with a plain FSM, but its size would be quite large; whereas an EFSM model would be much more succinct and easy to understand.

Unlike other types of systems, modelling a computer game has an additional challenge due to the presence of the 'world' where the game is played on. E.g. the Lab Recruits game in Sect. 2 is played in a virtual lab building as its 'world'. A world imposes certain constraints. Triggering a state might require a certain interactable to be interacted with, but a test agent can only do that if the interactable is physically reachable from its current position. If there is a wall between them, this is obviously problematic. So in terms of modelling, such physical constraints need to be taken into account as well. That is, a transition in the model should be translatable to a concrete sequence of actions by the agent, that are also physically possible. The same goes with observation. When the model requires that a certain condition should be checked, e.g. as an invariant to check, or as the guarding condition of a transition, it implies that the agent should be able to observe the condition. In the game setup this is not always given. A wall might be blocking the agent's sight, and hence the agent might first need to move itself to a spot where it can observe the said condition. In terms of modelling, this means that introducing guards and invariants in the model implies that there should exist a feasible way for the agent to actually observe them.

In the next subsection, we present the EFSM notation we adopt in the rest of the paper, and introduce the modelling of Lab Recruits (see Sect. 2) which takes into consideration the issues mentioned above regarding the modelling of games for testing purposes.

3.1 EFSM Notation

An FSM models the behaviour of a system as a finite set of states connected by transitions, where a transition could be fired by an input and returns an output. EFSMs [4] introduce data information into FSM behavioral representation. An EFSM has an internal memory, a set of variables, to store data and extends FSM transitions with guards and update transformations. Guards specify whether a transition can be performed according to the values of the variables stored in the memory. Updates allow changing variable values as a result of a transition. In this paper we adopt the following definition of EFSM.

Definition 1 (EFSM). An EFSM E is a 7-tuple (S, I, O, D, F, U, T), where

- S is a set of states
- I is s set of input symbols and O is a set of output symbols
- $\bar{D} : D_1 \times \ldots \times D_n$ is an n-dimensional space.
- F is a set of enabling functions $f_i : \bar{D} \to \{0, 1\}$
- U is a set of update transformations $u_i : \bar{D} \to \bar{D}$
- $T : S \times F \times I \to S \times U \times O$ is a transition relation.

Symbol $\bar{x} = (x_1, \ldots, x_n)$ indicates an element of $D_1 \times \ldots \times D_n$. Given states s_1, s_2, input i, output o, $f \in F$, and $u \in U$, $(s_1, f, i) \to (s_2, u, o)$ denotes $T(s_1, f, i) = (s_2, u, o)$. Given a vector variables $\bar{x} \in \bar{D}$ at s_1, the notation specifies a transition from s_1 to s_2, triggered by the input i, and *provided* $f(\bar{x}) = 1$. The transition produces the output o, and updates $\bar{x}$ to $u(\bar{x})$.

A finite *path* P over an EFSM $E = (S, I, O, D, F, U, T)$ is a finite sequence of transitions $t_0 \ldots t_n \in T$. A configuration of E is a pair state $s \in S$ and vector variables $\bar{x} \in D$. A feasible path over E from a configuration $(s_0, \bar{x})$ is a path $t_0 \ldots t_n$ such that the enabling function of t_0 is 1 for $\bar{x}$ and for each $i \in [1, n]$, $f_i(u_{i-1}(\bar{x}_{i-1})) = 1$ with f_i enabling function of t_i, u_{i-1} update function on t_{i-1}, and x_{i-1} vector variables at $i - 1$.

EFSM Model for Lab Recruits. A model for `Lab Recruits` captures the essential features of the game while abstracting away from details that are not of interest to the tester. For instance, to check the consistency of the button-door connections in the game, a candidate model could consider only buttons and doors and the actions the player can perform: move from a door to a button or to another door, walk trough a door, and toggle a button. Such a model for `buttonDoors1` in Fig. 1 could be EFSM $LR1 = (S, I, O, D, F, U, T)$ in Fig. 2. The set of states S are buttons and doors. For each door `door_`, `d_p` and `d_m` model the two sides of `door_`. The n-dimensional space D records door status with $D = \{0, 1\} \times \{0, 1\} \times \{0, 1\}$, where x_i control `door_i`. The EFSM in Fig. 2 has three types of transitions: solid edges for free travel, when the agent can move from one entity to the other without traversing a door; this type of transition has empty enabling and update functions. Dotted transitions model guarded movements that happen when the agent walks through a door; the enabling function check the status of the corresponding variable, while update function is empty. Dashed self loop transitions are for toggle actions, i.e., the agent presses the button; the update function changes the status of the doors connected to the pressed button. Note that the concept of 'transitions' here also incorporates 'world travel'. That is, a transition in the model is guaranteed to be physically possible in the `Lab Recruits` world, and furthermore the guards guarding the transitions can be physically checked as well (through some concretisation that guides the agent to observe them, achieved via automated navigation in the underlying testing framework [11]). Input set $I = \{\texttt{travel}, \texttt{toggle}\}$ defines the actions an agent can perform, i.e., move (`travel`) or press a button (`toggle`). Output set O is empty.

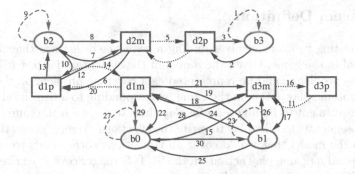

Fig. 2. EFSM model of `buttonDoors1` in Fig. 1

The game starts with the agent near b0 and with all the doors closed, therefore $\bar{x} = (0,0,0)$. A feasible path to reach star room in Fig. 1 has to include transition 16 (t16, for short), and therefore opening door3. The agent1 starts going to b1 (t30) and pressing it (t23). Update transformation changes $\bar{x}$ to $(1,0,0)$, i.e., door1 is open. Then, agent1 goes to d1m (t24) and walks through door1 reaching d1p (t20). Enabling function of t20 is 1, as $x_1 = 1$. After that, agent1 goes to b2 (t13) and presses it (t9), changing $\bar{x}$ to $(0,1,1)$, so door1 is closed, while door2 and door3 are open. At this point, the agent goes to door2 (t8), crosses it (t5), reaches b3 (t3), and toggles it (t1). Button b3 opens door1 so that $\bar{x} = (1,1,1)$, i.e., all the doors are open. Now, agent1 can reach star room following, for instance, t1, t4, t6, t14, t21, and t16. This gives an example of a feasible path from the initial position of the agent to the star room mimicking the steps an agent has to perform.

We also implemented a random level generator for Lab Recruits for experimental purposes. The generator builds on the observation that the EFSM of a Lab Recruits level has a specific structure. First, a room is represented by the set of buttons it contains. Given the total number of buttons $n\_buttons$ in a level and the mean $mean\_buttons$ number of buttons in a room, the algorithm extracts random integers from a Poisson distribution with mean $mean\_buttons$, until all buttons are used. For instance, given $n\_buttons = 10$ and $mean\_buttons = 2$, the generated sequence $2, 3, 2, 1, 2$ corresponds to the number of buttons in a level with 5 rooms. Then, given the number of doors n_doors, we randomly connect two rooms until all doors are used. The algorithm guarantees that there are not unconnected rooms. Given a room, the corresponding EFSM model has a state for each button and door side, and all the states are connected by a free travel Each button has a self loop with update function that represents button-door connections. Finally, the models corresponding to linked rooms are connected by guarded travel transition, where the enabling function checks the status of the door. The generated EFSM can be transformed into the corresponding csv file level and opened on Lab Recruits.

4   Problem Definition

The play testing problem involves finding a sequence of actions that achieve a desired goal in the game. Given the model of the system under test (SUT), the play testing problem could be represented as a coverage problem on the model. Testing a specific play action in the game (corresponding to a transition T in the model) is equivalent to finding a *prefix play* that would reach the source state of T, and subsequently a suffix play to verify the effect of T. Hence, generating a test suite from the model that would cover all transitions corresponds to exercising the corresponding game play actions in the SUT. Stronger coverage criteria, such as k-transition coverage and path coverage, represent more rigorous interactions of game play actions.

5   Test Generation

Our proposed approach follows the generic model-based test generation approach where the *SUT* is abstracted into a *model* which is then used to generate *abstract tests*. The abstract tests are then concretised into *concrete tests* that can be executed on the SUT.

The goal of the work presented in this paper is to investigate the feasibility of applying the model-based approach by incorporating search-based test generation for the *test generation* phase.

The *abstraction* phase, where the model of the SUT is built, typically involves human involvement as it requires a good understanding of the behaviour of the SUT. In our experiments, we have used models which were crafted manually as well as randomly generated ones. However, the test generation approach presented here is independent of how the model is generated, as long as it is as described in Sect. 3.1. The *concretisation* and *execution* phases are specific to the SUT and could be implemented in different ways, depending on the nature of the SUT. For our experiments we have built automated transformers from abstract tests to concrete tests, and adopted an agent-based API provided by the SUT for executing the tests. For a different SUT, different concretisation (and execution) mechanisms are needed, however the generation of abstract tests remains the same, as long as the model of the SUT is provided.

In the remainder of this section, we present the search-based test generation approach for deriving abstract tests from the model of the SUT.

5.1   Search-Based Test Generation

Test generation from models could be driven by different goals. In this paper we outline a search-based approach that can be applied to find test suits that satisfy a desired model coverage criterion, e.g., transition coverage. We present the various ingredients needed for applying a search algorithm for test generation, including individual representation, search operators, and fitness function.

Individual Representation. Given an EFSM, we represent an individual as a path (sequence of transitions), starting from the initial state of the model (see Sect. 3.1). Individuals can be of different length, up to a pre-defined maximum. For our running example (see Fig. 2), $I_1 = \langle t_{27}, t_{28}, t_{18}, t_{21} \rangle$ represents an example of an individual. Note that paths in the model may or may not be feasible, hence an individual, as generated initially, is not guaranteed to be feasible.

Search Operators. With individuals represented as paths in the model, different operators could be implemented. Here we describe crossover and mutation operators that we used in our experiments. Clearly, other operators could be implemented and experimented with.

Crossover: one possible way of implementing crossover is to adopt a straightforward application of *single point relative crossover*. Given two individuals, a common state is chosen at random and the tails of the two individuals are swapped. For our running example, if $I_1 = \langle t_{30}, t_{26}, t_{16}, t_{11} \rangle$ and $I_2 = \langle t_{29}, t_{21}, t_{17}, t_{25} \rangle$, crossover at state $d3m$ results in offspring $O_1 = \langle t_{30}, t_{26}, t_{17}, t_{25} \rangle$ and $O_2 = \langle t_{29}, t_{21}, t_{16}, t_{11} \rangle$.

Mutation: we propose three mutation operators, applied with equal probability:

1) insert self transition: insert a self transition on a randomly chosen state of the model, if such a transition is allowed
2) delete self transition: remove a self transition at random
3) delete a transition: remove a transition at random.

Fitness Function. Given an EFSM model and a given coverage criterion, the fitness function should guide the search towards covering all coverage targets. However, since the individual may not be feasible, the fitness function should also guide the search towards turning the individual into a feasible one. As a result, the fitness function has two components: 1) related to path feasibility, and 2) related to the search target. A high level algorithm of the fitness function we adopted is shown in Algorithm 1. To calculate the fitness of an individual with respect to a coverage target, first the individual is executed on the model and the execution trace as well as the outcome of the execution are returned (line 6 in Algorithm 1). If the individual is a feasible path, then the algorithm checks to see if the current target is present in the individual. If present (line 9) then target is covered, otherwise, the fitness value should estimate the distance from satisfying the target. In this case, we opt for a simple heuristic, i.e., penalising the individual by a predefined constant value ($PENALTY1$). Other heuristics could be applied here as well. If however the individual happens to be infeasible (line 14 in Algorithm 1, this means that a transition guard in the path represented by the individual has failed. In this case, we compute the approach level and branch distance for the path (lines 15 and 16). Approach level is computed as the number of transitions in the path yet to be traversed. Branch distance is

Algorithm 1. Fitness function

```
1: Input
2:    I     individual
3:    T     target
4: Output
5:    f     fitness value
6: trace, feasible ⟵ executeOnModel(I)
7: if feasible then                          ▷ individual I represents a feasible path in the model
8:    al_feasiblity, bd_feasiblity ⟵ 0
9:    if T ∈ I then
10:        al_target, bd_target ⟵ 0
11:    else
12:        al_target, bd_target ⟵ PENALTY1    ▷ even if I eventually turns feasible, T remains
   uncovered, but at least I is feasible
13:    end if
14: else if not feasible then                ▷ individual I represents an infeasible path
15:    al_feasiblity ⟵ length(I) − passdTransitions
16:    bd_feasiblity ⟵ computeBranchDistance(trace)
17:    if T ∈ I then
18:        al_target, bd_target ⟵ 0           ▷ fitness takes the value of feasiblity_fitness
19:    else
20:        al_target, bd_target ⟵ PENALTY2    ▷ even if I turns feasible, T remains uncovered
21:    end if
22: end if
23: f_feasiblity = al_feasibility + normalise(bd_feasibility)
24: f_target = al_target + normalize(bd_target)
25: f = f_feasibility + f_target
```

computed based on the guard expression of the failing transition, as typically done in code-based testing [9]. We then check whether the individual contains the current target (line 17). If yes, no penalty is applied, otherwise, a penalty is applied ($PENALTY2 \gg PENALTY1$). Finally, the algorithm computes the *feasibility fitness* and *target fitness* values, and sums them up to find the fitness value of the individual (lines 23–25).

Search Algorithms. Once the individual encoding, search operators, and fitness function are defined, existing search algorithms could be applied to generate tests. In practice though, the corresponding machinery for implementing the test generation is needed. We have implemented a prototype tool EvoMBT that uses EvoSuite [5] as a library. EvoMBT implements all the model related parts, including the operators discussed above. It implements EvoSuite's interfaces in such a way that search algorithms already implemented in EvoSuite can be used out-of-the-box. Details are discussed in Sect. 6.

6   Evaluation

In this section we present the experiment we carried out in order to get insight into the feasibility of the proposed test generation approach combining search based algorithms with model based testing.

6.1   Prototype: EvoMBT

EvoMBT provides an implementation of the EFSM used in this paper and the necessary machinery for generating/executing tests from/on the model, compute fitness values, and collect coverage. EvoMBT uses search algorithms implemented in EvoSuite [5] (i.e., EvoSuite is used as a library). EvoMBT currently implements state and transition coverage criteria, relative point crossover, and a number of mutation operators. At the moment, several search algorithm found in EvoSuite can be used with EvoMBT without any modification. For the purpose of experimentation, EvoMBT also implements mutation operations on the Lab Recruits application, and enables concretisation and execution of generated tests on Lab Recruits (both mutated and original). It generates different reports that enable analysis of results as well as debugging of eventual faults. EvoMBT is publicly available in Github: https://github.com/iv4xr-project/iv4xr-mbt. We also provide an executable jar with all the necessary resources, and additional plots that could not fit in the paper, here: https://doi.org/10.5281/zenodo.4768470.

6.2   Models of the System Under Test

We use three different models of Lab Recruits: i) buttonDoors1: the running example (see Sect. 2) with 10 states and 30 transitions, ii) randomMedium: randomly generated model as described in Sect. 3.1 with $n\_doors = 8$ and $n\_buttons = 10$ having 26 states and 116 transitions, and iii) randomLarge: randomly generated with $n\_doors = 15$ and $n\_buttons = 20$ having 50 states and 194 transitions.

6.3   Experiment Setup

Experiments are aimed at assessing: *feasibility of search-based algorithms for generating abstract test sequences from the model, practicality of abstract tests for execution on the actual system under test*, and *fault finding potential of the generated tests*. Consequently we formulate the following research questions to guide our experimental evaluation:

> **RQ1 - Suitability of SBT** how suitable are search based algorithms for test generation from the models?
>> **RQ1.1 - Model coverage** how much of the models are covered by the test generation algorithms?
> **RQ2 - Test execution** are the model-based tests feasible in terms of execution on the actual application?
> **RQ3 - Fault finding** what is the fault finding potential of the tests generated from the models?

For **RQ1**, we report on the search algorithms we used for test generation and the coverage they achieved on the models (**RQ1.1**). For this purpose we use

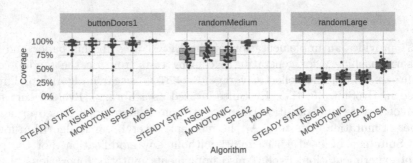

Fig. 3. Coverage achieved by the search algorithms for the three models

transition coverage criterion, computed as the ratio of covered transitions to the total number of transitions in the model. For **RQ2**, we measure the test execution time on the Lab Recruits application. For **RQ3**, we measure the mutation score of the tests on mutants injected into the Lab Recruits application. Mutation score is computed as the ratio of killed mutants to the total number of mutants generated.

Experimental Settings. For the search algorithms, we kept the default values in EvoSuite. For search budget, we use 300 s, collecting statistical data every 10 s. Experiments were run on computers with Intel Core i7 processors with 8 cores @2.80 GHz and 8 GB memory, running Ubuntu Linux.

Experiment Procedure. For **RQ1.1** we run each algorithm on a given model 20 times, to account for the random nature of the algorithms. Hence, we performed 5 algorithms × 3 (models) × 20 (repetitions) = 300 runs for a total of 300 × 300 (seconds) = 90000 s (25 h). For **RQ2**, we report test execution times on the Lab Recruits application for all test suites generated. For **RQ3**, we report the mutation scores for all algorithms generated on buttonDoors1, randomMedium, and randomLarge.

6.4 Results

Suitability of SBT (RQ1). The first set of results are related to the suitability of search based testing for the generation of tests from models. We have applied 5 different search algorithms: *MONOTONIC GA, MOSA, NSGAII, SPEA2, STEADY STATE GA* for the generation of tests from the models. Figure 3 shows the coverage achieved by each algorithm on the three models of Lab Recruits.

As can be seen from Fig. 3, the algorithms achieve different levels of coverage on the three models. On the running example (buttonDoors1), which is the least complex of the three with 30 transitions in total, all algorithms achieve high levels of coverage with MOSA achieving 100%. On the randomMedium model which has 116 transitions, MOSA still achieves full coverage, while the other algorithms achieve less than for the smaller model. On the largest of the three,

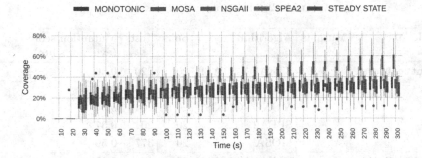

Fig. 4. Coverage achieved on `randomLarge` by the search algorithms over time

Table 1. Test execution time on `Lab Recruits` (in minutes), the tests are organized into 20 test suites for each algorithm

Model	Algorithm	Tests	Passed	Failed	Time (avg per test)
`buttonDoors1`	STEADY STATE	237	220	17	36 (0.15)
	NSGAII	222	195	27	34.2 (0.15)
	MONOTONIC	239	205	34	29.5 (0.12)
	SPEA2	227	204	23	28.4 (0.13)
	MOSA	400	380	20	36.1 (0.09)
`randomMedium`	STEADY STATE	436	391	45	661.3 (1.52)
	NSGAII	614	502	112	1176 (1.92)
	MONOTONIC	564	495	69	1324.5 (2.35)
	SPEA2	594	527	67	1104.8 (1.86)
	MOSA	919	833	86	1362.2 (1.48)
`randomLarge`	STEADY STATE	249	31	218	243.2 (0.98)
	NSGAII	401	22	379	412.8 (1.03)
	MONOTONIC	466	25	441	613.8 (1.32)
	SPEA2	307	31	276	267.4 (0.87)
	MOSA	546	28	518	430.1 (0.79)

which has 194 transitions, the coverage achieved by the algorithms decreases with MOSA achieving 59% median coverage while the others achieve below 37%. Given the size of the model, the results could potentially improve if search budget is increased. As can be seen in Fig. 4, the trend shows that the coverage is likely to increase with increased search budget.

*We answer **RQ1** positively: different search algorithms could be applied for test generation from models, achieving reasonable levels of transition coverage.*

Test Execution (RQ2). We measured the time it takes to execute the generated tests on the actual `Lab Recruits` application. The abstract tests are

Table 2. Mutation analysis results

Model	Mutants	Algorithm	Suits	Tests	Mutantion score (avg. per suite)
buttonDoors1	5	STEADY STATE	20	220	0.46
		NSGAII	20	196	0.41
		MONOTONIC	20	204	0.34
		SPEA2	20	204	0.37
		MOSA	20	377	0.59
randomMedium	8	STEADY STATE	20	386	0.83
		NSGAII	20	506	0.80
		MONOTONIC	20	487	0.79
		SPEA2	20	508	0.92
		MOSA	20	850	0.98
randomLarge	24	STEADY STATE	20	32	0.08
		NSGAII	20	20	0.03
		MONOTONIC	20	25	0.11
		SPEA2	20	31	0.08
		MOSA	20	29	0.12

concretised for automated execution on Lab Recruits via its agent based API. The execution of tests on Lab Recruits involves the player (driven by the test agent) actually interacting with the game environment (e.g., going from one room to another, pressing buttons, etc.). Hence, the execution of tests is time taking.

As can be seen from Table 1, test execution on Lab Recruits is rather time taking. Hence, if the test generation were to be done directly on Lab Recruits, it would have taken an extremely long period of time. To give an idea, on buttonDoors1, MOSA performed, on average, 54848 fitness evaluations (i.e., executed abstract tests on the model). Executing that many tests directly on Lab Recruits would take several days.

*For **RQ2**, overall the model based approach for test generation combined with search algorithms gives an efficient means for generating tests for such systems as Lab Recruits where test execution is slow.*

Fault Finding (RQ3). With **RQ3**, we assess the fault finding potential of the generated tests. We created mutants in the Lab Recruits application in which the association between buttons and doors is changed, i.e., a link between a button and a door is removed. We created a number of mutants and executed the generated test suites on each mutant. Given that the tests may not all run successfully on the original application (see Table 1, 'Failed' column), we executed only the passing tests on the mutants, and calculated the mutation score. The results, presented in Table 2, show that the generated tests are effective in detecting the injected faults. It is worth noting that the mutation scores for buttonDoors1 and randomLarge are low because several tests failed when executed on the original Lab Recruits application (see Sect. 6.4), reducing the coverage of the tests. These test failures are due to bugs in Lab Recruits and the agent based API. In particular, in Lab Recruits, under certain circumstances, pressing a button fails to open a door controlled by it. On the agent API, we found instances where the agent gets stuck while navigating the game world, which is not supposed to happen. All faults have been reported to the developers of Lab Recruits.

Concerning RQ3, experimental results show that generated tests are effective in detecting injected faults and revealing actual bugs in the application under test.

7   Related Work

Although SBT has been successful for various types of software, its application in computer games has not been much studied. Directly using a search algorithm to search for test sequences without any model has not been attempted, as far we as know. The search space is far too large for such an approach to work. Instead, existing works tend to employ search algorithms for optimizing learning-based automated agents. For example Holmgård et al. [6] uses Monte Carlo Search Tree (MCTS) based agents to replace human play testers. A genetic algorithm is used to evolve MCTS' selection policy towards a desired play style. The case study is small; a game played in a 10×20 grid. It is unclear if the approach would scale to bigger games.

There were very few studies, as far as we could find, on the use of MBT for testing computer games, e.g. [2,7,13]. Ariyurek et al. [2] use a scenario graph for generating abstract test sequences. Such a graph is essentially an FSM whose states are decorated with a set of predicates that abstractly describe the state of a game under test. MCTS is used to search for the concrete sequence of actions that implement the steps in an abstract test sequence. The case studies are however small scale games, played in a grid not larger than 10×11; it is not clear if MCTS would scale to a larger search space. To deal with larger game worlds Prasetya et al. investigate the use of navigation mesh as a model [11] of the game world under test, subjected to their agent-based automated testing framework iv4XR/aplib [10]. The idea is taken from pathplanning, where the walkable areas of a physical or virtual world is divided into a finite set of connected shapes (e.g. triangles). This reduces the initially infinite search space into a finite graph which is then used as a model to guide agents' navigation, e.g. using A*.

Iftikhar et al. [7] use UML state machine, which is an EFSM, to model an open source variant of the Super Mario game. The study does not however fully explore the implication of using *extended* FSMs. For generating tests, an N+ strategy is used [3], that is aimed at covering all transitions and round trips. This strategy is not strong enough to handle an EFSM with complex constellations of conditions. It essentially unrolls the FSM into a tree where along any full path in the tree no node is repeating, except if it is the last node.

Outside the game domain, search-based algorithms are used for generating tests from EFSMs. Many of the works are focused on finding valid paths from the models and eventually covering predefined goals (e.g., [8]). Our work is aimed at exploring the feasibility of SBT for automated play testing via modelling. In this regard, existing works on SBT from EFSMs are complementary with ours, and could eventually be experimented with in EvoMBT so as to increase the effectiveness and efficiency of test generation. For instance, the fitness function of Kalaji et al. [8] could be implemented in EvoMBT in order to assess its feasibility for the play testing use case.

8   Conclusion and Future Work

We have presented an approach for automated game play testing by employing the combined application of search-based and model-based testing. The main objective of the work presented is exploratory in nature where we tried to assess the suitability of search-based testing for automated game play testing. Game play behavior is abstracted into an EFSM model and search-based algorithms are used to generate abstract tests, which are then converted into concrete tests that can be executed on the game. Experimental results are promising where a number of search algorithms were experimented with and achieved reasonable model coverage, mutation score, and exposed real bugs in the game under test.

The current work makes a number of choices with respect to heuristics used for test generation, such as fitness function and search operators. There are different alternatives that could be implemented and experimented with as part of future work.

References

1. Apperley, T.H.: Genre and game studies: toward critical approach to video game genres. Simul. Gaming **37**(1), 6–23 (2006)
2. Ariyurek, S., Betin-Can, A., Surer, E.: Automated video game testing using synthetic and humanlike agents. IEEE Trans. Games **13**(1), 50–67 (2021). https://doi.org/10.1109/TG.2019.2947597
3. Binder, R.: Testing Object-Oriented Systems: Models, Patterns, and Tools. Addison-Wesley Professional (2000)
4. Cheng, K.T., Krishnakumar, A.S.: Automatic functional test generation using the extended finite state machine model. In: 30th ACM/IEEE Design Automation Conference, pp. 86–91. IEEE (1993)
5. Fraser, G., Arcuri, A.: EvoSuite: automatic test suite generation for object-oriented software. In: Proceedings of the 19th ACM SIGSOFT Symposium and the 13th European Conference on Foundations of Software Engineering, pp. 416–419 (2011)
6. Holmgård, C., Green, M.C., Liapis, A., Togelius, J.: Automated playtesting with procedural personas through MCTS with evolved heuristics. IEEE Trans. Games **11**(4), 352–362 (2018)

7. Iftikhar, S., Iqbal, M.Z., Khan, M.U., Mahmood, W.: An automated model based testing approach for platform games. In: 2015 ACM/IEEE 18th International Conference on Model Driven Engineering Languages and Systems (MODELS), pp. 426–435. IEEE (2015)
8. Kalaji, A.S., Hierons, R.M., Swift, S.: An integrated search-based approach for automatic testing from extended finite state machine (EFSM) models. Inf. Softw. Technol. **53**(12), 1297–1318 (2011). https://doi.org/10.1016/j.infsof.2011.06.004
9. McMinn, P.: Search-based software test data generation: a survey. Softw. Test. Verif. Reliab. **14**(2), 105–156 (2004). https://doi.org/10.1002/stvr.294
10. Prasetya, I.S.W.B., Dastani, M., Prada, R., Vos, T.E.J., Dignum, F., Kifetew, F.: Aplib: tactical agents for testing computer games. In: Baroglio, C., Hubner, J.F., Winikoff, M. (eds.) EMAS 2020. LNCS (LNAI), vol. 12589, pp. 21–41. Springer, Cham (2020). https://doi.org/10.1007/978-3-030-66534-0_2
11. Prasetya, I., et al.: Navigation and exploration in 3D-game automated play testing. In: Proceedings of the 11th ACM SIGSOFT International Workshop on Automating TEST Case Design, Selection, and Evaluation (ATEST), pp. 3–9 (2020)
12. Utting, M., Pretschner, A., Legeard, B.: A taxonomy of model-based testing approaches. Softw. Test. Verif. Reliab. **22**(5), 297–312 (2012). https://doi.org/10.1002/stvr.456
13. Zhao, H., Sun, J., Hu, G.: Study of methodology of testing mobile games based on TTCN-3. In: 2009 10th ACIS International Conference on Software Engineering, Artificial Intelligences, Networking and Parallel/Distributed Computing, pp. 579–584. IEEE (2009)

Hybrid Multi-level Crossover for Unit Test Case Generation

Mitchell Olsthoorn$^{(\boxtimes)}$ (iD), Pouria Derakhshanfar (iD), and Annibale Panichella (iD)

Delft University of Technology, Delft, The Netherlands
{M.J.G.Olsthoorn,P.Derakhshanfar,A.Panichella}@tudelft.nl

Abstract. State-of-the-art search-based approaches for test case generation work at test case level, where tests are represented as sequences of statements. These approaches make use of genetic operators (*i.e.,* mutation and crossover) that create test variants by adding, altering, and removing statements from existing tests. While this encoding schema has been shown to be very effective for many-objective test case generation, the standard crossover operator (single-point) only alters the structure of the test cases but not the input data. In this paper, we argue that changing both the test case structure and the input data is necessary to increase the genetic variation and improve the search process. Hence, we propose a hybrid multi-level crossover (*HMX*) operator that combines the traditional test-level crossover with data-level recombination. The former evolves and alters the test case structures, while the latter evolves the input data using numeric and string-based recombinational operators. We evaluate our new crossover operator by performing an empirical study on more than 100 classes selected from open-source Java libraries for numerical operations and string manipulation. We compare *HMX* with the single-point crossover that is used in EVOSUITE *w.r.t.* structural coverage and fault detection capability. Our results show that *HMX* achieves a statistically significant increase in 30% of the classes up to 19% in structural coverage compared to the single-point crossover. Moreover, the fault detection capability improved up to 12% measured using strong mutation score.

Keywords: Search-based software testing · Test case generation · Crossover operator · Empirical software engineering

1 Introduction

Genetic operators are a fundamental component of evolutionary search-based test case generation algorithms. These operators create variation in the test cases to help the search process explore new possible paths. The main genetic operators are mutation, which makes changes to a single test case, and crossover, which exchanges information between two test cases.

Over the years, related work has used three types of encoding schemata to represent test cases for search algorithms, namely data-level, test case-level,

© Springer Nature Switzerland AG 2021
U.-M. O'Reilly and X. Devroey (Eds.): SSBSE 2021, LNCS 12914, pp. 72–86, 2021.
https://doi.org/10.1007/978-3-030-88106-1_6

and test suite-level. These schemata typically implement genetic operators at the same level as the encoding. For example, the crossover operator at the data-level exchanges data between two input vectors [12]. The test case-level crossover exchanges statements between two parent test cases [19]. Lastly, the test suite-level crossover swaps test cases within two test suites [10]. Recent studies have shown that the test case-level schema combined with many-objective (MO) search is the most effective at generating test cases with high coverage [6, 15].

The current many-objective approaches use the single-point crossover to recombine groups of statements within test cases. Test cases consist of both test structures (method sequences) and test data [19]. Hence, the crossover operator only changes the test structure and simply copies over the corresponding input data. Therefore, input data has to be altered by the mutation operator, usually with a small probability.

In this paper, we argue that better genetic variation can be obtained by designing a crossover operator that alters the structure of the test cases and also the input data by creating new data that is in the neighborhood of the parents' data. To validate this hypothesis, we propose a new operator, called Hybrid Multi-level Crossover (HMX), that combines different crossover operators on multiple levels. We implement HMX within EvoSuite [10], the state-of-the-art unit-test generation tool for Java.

To evaluate the effectiveness of our operator, we performed an empirical study where we compare HMX with the single-point crossover used in EvoSuite, a state-of-the-art test case generation tool for Java, w.r.t. structural coverage and fault detection capability. To this aim, we build a benchmark with 116 classes from the Apache Commons and Lucene Stemmer projects, which include classes for numerical operations and string manipulation.

Our results show that HMX achieves higher structural coverage for ~30% of the classes in the benchmark. On average, HMX, covered 6.4% and 7.2% more branches and lines than our baseline, respectively (with a max improvement of 19.1% and 19.4%). Additionally, the proposed operator improved the fault detection capability in ~25% of the classes with an average improvement of 3.9% (max. 14%) and 2.1% (max. 12.1%) for weak and strong mutation, respectively.

In summary, we make the following contributions:

1. A novel crossover that works at both test case and input data-level to increase genetic variation in the search process. The data-level recombination combines multiple different techniques depending on the data type.
2. An open-source implementation of our operator in EvoSuite.
3. A full replication package containing the results and the analysis scripts [13].

The outline for the remainder of this paper is as follows. Section 2 explains the fundamental concepts used in the paper. Section 3 introduces our new crossover operator, called HMX, and breaks down how it works. Section 4 sets out our research questions and describes the setup of our empirical study. Section 5 details our results and highlights our findings. Section 6 discusses the threats to validity and Sect. 7 draws conclusions and identifies possible directions for future work.

2   Background and Related Work

Search-Based Unit Test Generation. Prior studies introduced search-based software test generation (SBST) approaches utilizing meta-heuristics (*e.g.,* genetic algorithm) to automate test generation for different testing levels [12], such as unit [10], integration [9], and system-level testing [3]. Search-based unit-test generation is one of the widely studied topics in this field, where a search process generates tests fulfilling various criteria (*e.g.,* structural coverage, mutation score) for a given class under test (CUT). Studies have shown that these techniques are effective at achieving high code coverage [6,16] and fault detection [1].

Single-Objective Unit Test Generation. Single-objective techniques specify one or more fitness functions to guide the search process towards covering the search targets according to the desired criteria. Rojas *et al.* [18] proposed an approach that aggregates all of the fitness functions for each criterion using a weighted sum scalarization and performs a single-objective optimization to generate tests. Additionally, Gay [11] empirically showed that combining different criteria in a single-objective leads to detect more faults compared to using each criterion separately.

Dynamic Many-Objective Sorting Algorithm (*DynaMOSA*). In contrast with single-objective unit test generation, Panichella *et al.* have proposed a many-objective evolutionary-based approach, called *DynaMOSA* [15]. This approach considers each coverage targets from multiple criteria as an independent search objective. *DynaMOSA* utilizes the hierarchy of dependencies between different coverage targets (*e.g.,* line, branch, mutants) to select the search objectives during the search dynamically. Moreover, recent work [17] introduced a multi-criteria variant of *DynaMOSA* that extends the idea of dynamic selection of the targets, based on an enhanced hierarchical dependency analysis. This recent study showed that this multi-criteria variant outperforms single-objective search-based unit test generation *w.r.t.* structural and mutation coverage and, therefore, can achieve a higher fault detection rate. These results have also been confirmed independently by Campos *et al.* [6]. Consequently, *DynaMOSA* is currently used as the default algorithm in EVOSUITE.

Crossover Operator. Like any other evolutionary-based algorithms, all variations of *DynaMOSA* need crossover and mutation operators for evolving the individuals in the current population to generate the next population. Since *DynaMOSA* encodes tests at a test case-level, the mutation operator alters statements in a selected test case according to a given *mutation probability*. This search algorithm uses the single-point crossover to recombine two selected individuals (parents) into new tests (offspring) for the next generation. This crossover operator randomly selects two positions in the selected parents and split them into two parts. Then, it remerges each part with the opposing part from the other parent. A more detailed explanation of this operator is available in Sect. 3.

Algorithm 1: HMX: hybrid multi-level crossover

Input: Two parent test cases P_1 and P_2
Output: Two offspring test cases O_1 and O_2

```
 1  begin
 2      O₁, O₂ ← SINGLE-POINT-CROSSOVER(P₁, P₂)
        // Constructor data store
 3      C₁ ← Map<signature, constructor[ ]> // For P₁
 4      C₂ ← Map<signature, constructor[ ]> // For P₂
        // Method data store
 5      M₁ ← Map<signature, method[ ]> // For P₁
 6      M₂ ← Map<signature, method[ ]> // For P₂
 7      forall the (S₁, S₂), in S₁ ∈ O₁ and S₂ ∈ O₂ do
 8          if SIGNATURE(S₁) == SIGNATURE(S₂) then
 9              if S₁ is constructor then
10                  C₁[SIGNATURE(S₁)].add(S₁)
11                  C₂[SIGNATURE(S₂)].add(S₂)
12              else if S₁ is method then
13                  M₁[SIGNATURE(S₁)].add(S₁)
14                  M₂[SIGNATURE(S₂)].add(S₂)
15      foreach SIG ∈ C₁.keys ∪ C₂.keys do
            // choose random constructor with same signature
16          S₁ ← random.choice(C1[SIG])
17          S₂ ← random.choice(C2[SIG])
18          O₁, O₂ ← DATA-CROSSOVER(O₁, O₂, PARAMS(S₁), PARAMS(S₂))
19      foreach SIG ∈ M₁.keys ∪ M₂.keys do
            // choose random method with same signature
20          S₁ ← random.choice(M1[SIG])
21          S₂ ← random.choice(M2[SIG])
22          O₁, O₂ ← DATA-CROSSOVER(O₁, O₂, PARAMS(S₁), PARAMS(S₂))
23      return O₁, O₂
```

While the single-point crossover brings diversity to the structure of the generated test cases, it does not work at the data-level (*i.e.*, crossover between the test inputs). Hence, this study introduces a hybrid multi-level crossover, called HMX, for the state-of-the-art in search-based unit test generation.

3 Approach

This section details our new crossover operator, called Hybrid Multi-level Crossover (HMX). This operator combines the traditional *single-point* test case-level crossover with multiple data-level crossovers.

Algorithm 1 outlines the pseudo-code of our crossover operator. HMX first performs the traditional *single-point* crossover at line 2. The *single-point* crossover is chosen for the test case-level operator as previous studies have shown that it is effective in producing a variation in the population over time [19]. It is also the default crossover operator used in the state-of-the-art test case generation tool EvoSuite [19]. This operator takes two parent test cases as input and selects a random point among the statements within the parents test cases. The parents are then split at this point, and their resulting parts are then recombined with its opposing part of the other parent to produce two new offspring test cases. Since these offspring test cases use a random crossover point, they might contain incomplete sequences of statements (*e.g.*, missing variable definition) and, therefore, will not compile. To make the crossover more effective, these broken references are fixed by introducing new random variable definitions that match the type of the broken reference [10]. Lines 3–22 contain the selection logic of the data-level crossover. Unlike the test case-level crossover, the data-level crossover can not be applied to every combination of input data. Performing the crossover on input data with different types (*e.g.*, strings and numbers) would not produce any meaningful output as there is no logical way to combine these dissimilar types. Furthermore, we should not perform a crossover on two identical data types from different methods. If the data-level crossover would be applied to parameters of the same type that belong to different methods, it could produce offspring that are farther from the desired objective than the original. Hence, the algorithm has to select which combinations of input data are compatible. *HMX* achieves this by selecting compatible functions (*i.e.*, constructors and methods calls) and applying the crossover pairwise to the function's parameters.

In lines 3–6, two pairs of maps are created that store the compatible functions for each parent for both constructors and methods. Each map stores a list of functions that share the same signature; The signature is the key of the map, and the functions are the values. The signature of the function is a string derived from the class name, function name, parameters types, and return type using the following format:

```
CLASS_NAME|FUNCTION_NAME(PARAM1_TYPE, PARAM2_TYPE, ...)RETURN_TYPE
```

In lines 7–14, *HMX* loops over all combinations of statements S_1 and S_2 in the offspring produced by the single-point crossover. For each combination, it checks if the signatures of the two functions match (line 8). If both statements are either constructors or methods, they are stored in their corresponding map with the signature as a key in lines 10–11 and 13–14, respectively. Note that if the test case contains constructor or method calls for other classes than the CUT, these are also considered by the selection of compatible functions. For example, additional objects (*e.g.*, strings, lists) might be needed as an input argument to one of the CUT's functions.

When all possible matching functions have been found, the operator loops through the signatures of the two function types separately in lines 15–18 and 19–22. For each signature, *HMX* selects a random function instance matching the signature from each parent. The operator then performs the data-level crossover on the parameters of these two randomly selected functions in lines 18 and 22.

For each signature in the map, *HMX* only selects one function instance per parent to proceed with the genetic recombination.

The data-level recombination pairwise traverses the parameters of the two compatible functions selected in lines 16–17 (for constructors) and 20–21 (for methods). For each pair of parameters, Algorithm 1 checks their types and determines if they are numbers or strings, the two supported types of *HMX*. If the two parameters are numbers (*i.e.*, byte, short, int, long, float, double, boolean, and char), the operator applies the *Simulated Binary Crossover* (SBX), which is described in Sect. 3.1. If the parameters are strings, it applies the string crossover described in Sect. 3.2. Lastly, in line 23, *HMX* returns the produced offspring.

Listing 1.1. Parent 1

```
1  @Test
2  public void test1() {
3      Fraction f0 = new Fraction(2, 3);
4      Fraction f1 = new Fraction(2, -1);
5      f0.divideBy(f1);
6      f0.add(Fraction.ZERO);
7  }
```

Listing 1.2. Parent 2

```
1  @Test
2  public void test2() {
3      Fraction f0 = new Fraction(3, 1);
4      Fraction f1 = new Fraction(1, 3);
5      f0.add(f1);
6      f0.pow(2.0);
7  }
```

To provide a practical example, let us consider the two parent test cases in Listings 1.1 and 1.2. Both parent 1 and parent 2 contain two invocations of the `Fraction` constructor. Since these constructors share the same signature: `Fraction|<init>(int, int)Fraction`; they are compatible. Similarly, the method `add` of the `Fraction` class is present in both parents, with the same signature: `Fraction|add(Fraction)V`; and are compatible, as well. In contrast, for example, method `divideBy`, in parent 1, and method `add`, in parent 2, are not compatible since their signatures are different.

3.1 Simulated Binary Crossover

The *Simulated Binary Crossover* (SBX) is a recombination operator commonly used in numerical problems with numerical decision variables and fixed-length chromosomes. It has been shown that Evolutionary Algorithms (EAs) that use this crossover operator produce better results compared to traditional numerical crossover operators [8]. The equation below outlines the algorithm of *SBX*:

$$u = rand_u \tag{1}$$

$$\beta = \begin{cases} 2 \cdot u^{1/(\eta_c+1)} & \text{if } u < 0.5 \\ 1 & \text{if } u = 0.5 \\ \frac{0.5}{1.0-u}^{1/(\eta_c+1)} & \text{if } u > 0.5 \end{cases} \tag{2}$$

$$b = rand_b \tag{3}$$

$$v = \begin{cases} ((v_1 - v_2) \cdot 0.5) - (\beta \cdot 0.5 \cdot |v_1 - v_2|) & \text{if } b = true \\ ((v_1 - v_2) \cdot 0.5) + (\beta \cdot 0.5 \cdot |v_1 - v_2|) & \text{if } b = false \end{cases} \tag{4}$$

where v (Eq. (4)) is the new value of parameter v_1, v_1 is the original value of the parameter, and v_2 is the value of the opposing parameter (the corresponding parameter from the matched function). η_c is the *distribution index* and it measures how close the new values should be to original values (proximity). For *HMX*, this variable is set to 2.5 as this is within the recommended range [2;5] [8]. *SBX* first creates a random *uniform* variable u (Eq. (1)), which is used to select one of three strategies for β. This scaling variable β (Eq. (2)), is used to scale an offset. This offset is either subtracted or added depending on the random *boolean* variable b. In general, *SBX* generates new values centered around the original parents, either in between the parents' values (contracting) or outside this range (expending) depending on the value of u. The algorithm is performed on both matching parameters, and the resulting new values are used as a replacement of the original values.

As an example, consider the two compatible constructors `Fraction(2,3)` (line 3 in Listing 1.1) and `Fraction(1,3)` (line 4 in Listing 1.2). The *SBX* recombination operator is applied for the following pairwise combinations: (2, 1) and (3, 3). To calculate the new value of the first element of the first pair, $v_1 = 2$ and $v_2 = 1$. Similarly, the second element can be calculated by switching the values of v_1 and v_2. The same procedure can be applied to calculate the new values of the second pair.

3.2   String Crossover

The single-point string crossover is used to exchange information between two string parameters of matching functions [12]. By recombining parts of each string, it makes it possible for promising substrings to collect together. The operator achieves this by picking two random numbers, $0 \leq x_i < \text{length}(x)$ and $0 \leq y_i < \text{length}(y)$ for both strings, respectively. It then recombines the two strings by concatenating the substrings in the following way: $x = x[: x_i] \,||\, y[y_i :]$ and $y = y[: y_i] \,||\, x[x_i :]$.

For example, given the following string $x = $ "*lorem*" and $y = $ "*ipsum*" and the random variables $x_i = 1$ and $y_i = 3$, the new values will be: $x = $ "*lom*" and $y = $ "*ipsurem*".

Table 1. Projects in our empirical study. # indicates the number of CUTs. cc indicates the cyclomatic complexity of CUTs. cc indicates the standard deviation. min and max indicate the minimum and maximum value of the metric, respectively. Also, str-par and nr-par are the average number of string and number input parameters for the selected CUTs.

Project	#	CCN				String parameter				Number parameter			
		$\overline{cc}$	σ	min	max	str-par	σ	min	max	$\overline{nr\text{-}par}$	σ	min	max
CLI	4	1.7	0.9	3.0	1.1	14.5	14.2	34.0	4.0	8.5	13.7	29.0	1.0
Geometry	13	1.8	0.4	2.5	1.2	3.4	5.5	21.0	1.0	10.2	6.7	21.0	1.0
Lang	34	3.0	1.6	7.4	1.1	17.4	36.7	209.0	1.0	26.6	48.3	249.0	1.0
Logging	1	3.0	-	3.0	3.0	6.0	-	6.0	6.0	3.0	-	3.0	3.0
Math	27	2.9	1.6	7.7	1.1	2.5	1.8	9.0	1.0	10.0	10.5	45.0	1.0
Numbers	5	2.8	1.1	4.5	1.6	1.4	0.9	3.0	1.0	31.6	33.5	89.0	4.0
RNG	4	3.3	1.4	5.0	1.7	2.2	2.5	6.0	1.0	2.0	1.4	4.0	1.0
Stemmer	16	1.0	0.0	1.0	1.0	0.0	0.0	0.0	0.0	0.0	0.0	0.0	0.0

4 Empirical Study

To assess the impact of *HMX* on search-based unit test generation, we perform an empirical evaluation to answer the following research questions:

RQ1 *To what extent does HMX improve structural coverage compared to the single-point crossover?*

RQ2 *How does HMX impact the fault-detection capability of the generated tests?*

Benchmark. For this study, we selected the CUTs from the APACHE COMMONS and SNOWBALL STEMMER libraries. The former is a commonly-used project containing reusable Java components for several applications[1]. The latter is a well-known library for stemming strings, which is part of the APACHE LUCENE[2]. As described in Sect. 3, *HMX* brings more advantages for search-based test generation in projects that utilize strings and numbers. Hence, to show the effect of this new crossover operator, we selected 100 classes from 9 components in APACHE COMMONS that have numeric and string input data: (i) MATH a library of lightweight, self-contained mathematics and statistics components; (ii) NUM-BERS includes utilities for working with complex numbers; (iii) GEOMETRY provides utilities for geometric processing; (iv) RNG a library of Java implementations of pseudo-random generators; (v) STATISTICS a project containing tools for statistics; (vi) CLI an API processing and validating a command line interface; (vii) TEXT a library focused on algorithms working on strings; (viii) LANG contains extra functionality for classes in java.lang; and (ix) LOGGING an adapter allowing configurable bridging to other logging systems.

---

[1] https://commons.apache.org.
[2] https://github.com/weavejester/snowball-stemmer.

In addition, we added the main 16 classes in SNOWBALL STEMMER to the benchmark, as these focus on string manipulation and were previously used in former search-based unit test generation studies [14].

Due to the large number of classes in the selected APACHE COMMONS components, we used CK [2], a tool that calculates the method-level and class-level code metrics in Java projects using static analysis. We collect the Cyclomatic Complexity (CC) and type of input parameters for each method in the selected 9 components. Using the collected information, we filter out the classes that do not have methods accepting strings or numbers (integer, double, long, or float) as input parameters. Then, we sort the remaining classes according to their average CC and pick the top 100 cases for our benchmark. Table 1 reports CC, number of string, and number arguments for each project used in this study. By doing a preliminary run of EvoSuite on the 116 selected classes, we noticed that this tool fails to start the search process in 9 of the CUTs. These failures stem from an issue in the underlying test generation tool EvoSuite. The tool fails to gather a critical statistic (*i.e.,* TOTAL_GOALS) for these runs in both the baseline and *HMX*. We also encountered 4 classes that did not produce any coverage for both the baseline and our approach. Consequently, we filtered out these classes from the experiment and performed the final evaluation on 103 remaining classes.

Implementation. We implemented *HMX* in EvoSuite [10], which is the state-of-the-art tool for search-based unit test generation in Java. By default, this tool uses the single-point crossover for test generation. We have defined a new parameter `multi_level_crossover` to enable *HMX*. Our Implementation is openly available as an artifact [13].

Preliminary Study. We performed a preliminary study to see how the probability of applying our data-level crossover influences the result. The single-point test case-level crossover is applied with a predefined probability. We experimented with how often the data-level crossover should be applied whenever the test case-level crossover was applied. From the probabilities we tried (*i.e.,* 0.25, 0.50, 0.75, 1.00), we found out that always applying the data-level crossover when the test case-level crossover produced the best results according to statistical analysis.

Parameter Settings. We run each search process with EvoSuite's default parameter values. As confirmed by prior studies [5], despite the impact of parameter tuning on the search performance, the default parameters provide acceptable results. Hence, we run each search process with a two-minute search budget and set the population size to 50 individuals. Moreover, we use mutation with a probability of $1/n$ (n = length of the generated test). For both crossover operators that we used in this study (single-point crossover for the baseline and our novel *HMX*), the crossover probability is 0.75. For the Simulated Binary Crossover (SBX), we used the *distribution index* $\eta_c = 2.5$ [8]. The search algorithm is the multi-criteria DynaMOSA [17], which is the default one in EvoSuite v1.1.0.

Experimental Protocol. We apply both default EvoSuite with single-point crossover and EvoSuite + *HMX* to each of the selected CUTs in the benchmark.

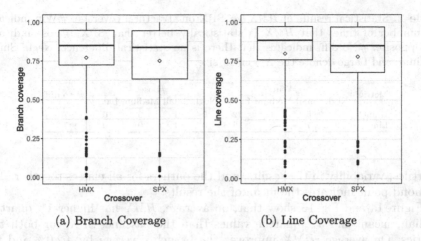

(a) Branch Coverage   (b) Line Coverage

Fig. 1. Boxplot of structural coverage comparing *HMX* to the baseline SPX. The diamond point indicates the mean coverage of the benchmark.

To address the random nature of search-based test generation tools, we repeat each execution 100 times, with a different random seed, for a total number of 23 200 independent executions. We run our evaluation on a system with an AMD EPYC™ 7H12 using 240 cores running at 2.6 GHz. With each execution taking 5 min on average (*i.e.*, search, minimalization, and assertion generation), the total running time is 80.6 days of sequential execution.

For our analysis, we report the average (median) results across the 100 repeated runs. To determine if the results (*i.e.*, structural code coverage and fault detection capability) of the two crossover operator are statistically significant, we use the unpaired Wilcoxon rank-sum test [7] with a threshold of 0.05. The Wilcoxon test is a non-parametric statistical test that determines if two data distributions are significantly different. Additionally, we use the Vargha-Delaney statistic [20] to measure the magnitude of the result, which determines how large the difference between the two operators is.

5   Results

This section discusses the results of our study with the aim of answering the research questions formulated in Sect. 4. All differences in results in this section are presented in absolute differences (percentage points).

5.1   Result for RQ1: Structural Coverage

Figure 1 shows the structural coverage achieved by our approach, *HMX*, compared to the baseline, SPX, on the benchmark. In particular, Fig. 1a shows branch coverage and Fig. 1b shows line coverage. The boxplots show the median,

Table 2. Statistical results of *HMX* vs. SPX on structural coverage. #Win indicates the number of times that *HMX* is statistically better than SPX. #Lose indicates the opposite. #No diff. indicates that there is no statistical difference. Negl., Small, Medium, and Large denote the $\hat{A}_{12}$ effect size.

Metric	#Win				#Lose				#No diff.
	Negl.	Small	Medium	Large	Negl.	Small	Medium	Large	
Branch	2	5	3	22	0	1	0	0	70
Line	3	1	3	19	0	1	0	0	76

quartiles, variability in the results, and the outliers for all classes together. The diamond point indicates the mean of the results.

Figure 1a and Fig. 1b show that, on average, *HMX* has higher 1st quartile, median, mean, and 3rd quartile values than the baseline, SPX, for both test metrics. On average, *HMX* improves the branch coverage by +2.0% and the line coverage by +1.9%. The largest differences are visible for the lower whisker and for the first quartile (25th percentile). In particular, the differences for the lower whisker are around +20% branch and line coverage when using *HMX*; the improvements in the first quartile are around +10% and +8% for branch and line coverage, respectively. These results indicate that *HMX* improves both line and branch coverage for some of the CUTs in our benchmark. Finally, as we can see in both of the plots in Fig. 1, the variation in the results for *HMX*, measured by the Interquartile Range (IQR), is smaller than for SPX. This observation shows that *HMX* helps EvoSuite to generate tests with a more stable structural coverage.

Table 2 shows the results of the statistical comparison between *HMX* and the baseline, SPX, based on a p-value ≤ 0.05. *#Win* indicates the number of times that *HMX* has a statistically significant improvement over SPX. *#Equal* indicates the number of times that there is no statistical difference in the results between the two operators; *#Lose* indicates the number of times that *HMX* has statistically worse results than SPX. The *#Win* and *#Lose* columns also include the magnitude of the difference through the $\hat{A}_{12}$ effect size, classified in *Small*, *Medium*, *Large*, and *Negligible*.

From Table 2, we can see that *HMX* has a statistically significant non-negligible improvement in 30 and 23 classes for branch and line coverage, respectively. For the branch coverage metric, *HMX* improves with a large magnitude for 22 classes, medium for 3 classes, and small for 5 classes. For line coverage, *HMX* improves with a large magnitude for 19 classes, medium for 3 classes, and small for 1 class. *HMX* only loses in one case in comparison to the baseline for both branch and line coverage: StrSubstitutor from the Lang project. However, in this case, the effect size is small (magnitude).

For branch coverage, we observe a maximum increase in coverage of +19.1% for the *finnishStemmer* class from the Stemmer project. For line coverage, the class with the maximum increase in coverage is hungarianStemmer (also from Stemmer) with an average improvement of +19.4%. Compared to the baseline,

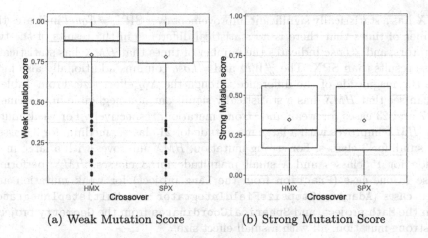

(a) Weak Mutation Score   (b) Strong Mutation Score

Fig. 2. Boxplot of structural coverage comparing *HMX* to the baseline SPX.

Table 3. Statistical results of *HMX* vs. SPX for fault-detection capability.

Metric	#Win				#Lose				#No diff.
	Negl.	Small	Medium	Large	Negl.	Small	Medium	Large	
Weak mutation	3	3	3	21	0	1	0	0	72
Strong mutation	0	8	0	15	0	3	0	0	77

all classes in the SNOWBALL STEMMER string manipulation library improve based on branch and line coverage with an average improvement of +11.4% and +11.0%, respectively. For the APACHE COMMONS library, *HMX* significantly improves the branch and line coverage in 16 (9 string-related and 7 number-related) and 10 (6 string-related and 4 number-related) classes, respectively.

> In summary, the proposed *HMX* crossover operator achieves significantly higher (~30% of the cases) or equal structural code coverage for unit test case generation compared to the baseline SPX.

5.2   Result for RQ2: Fault Detection Capability

Figure 2 shows the fault detection capability of *HMX* compared to SPX measured through the mutation score. Figure 2a shows the weak mutation score and Fig. 2b shows the strong mutation score. The boxplots show the median, quartiles, variability in the results, and the outliers for all classes in the benchmark together. The diamond point indicates the mean of the results. From Fig. 2a, we can see that, on average, *HMX* improves the weak mutation score by +1.2% compared to SPX. However, from Fig. 2b we can see that overall, the strong mutation scores only show marginal improvements (+0.5%).

Table 3 shows the statistical comparison between *HMX* and SPX, based on a *p*-value ≤ 0.05. Similarly to Table 2, #*Win* indicates the number of times that

HMX has a statistically significant improvement over SPX, *#Equal* indicates the number of times that there is no statistical difference in the results of the two operators, and *#Lose* indicates the number of times that *HMX* has statistically worse results than SPX. The *#Win* and *#Lose* columns additionally also indicate the magnitude of the difference through the $\hat{A}_{12}$ effect size. From Table 3, we can see that *HMX* has a statistically significant non-negligible improvement in 27 and 23 cases for weak and strong mutation, respectively. For weak mutation, *HMX* improves with a large magnitude for 21 classes, medium for 3 classes, and small for 3 classes. For strong mutation, *HMX* improves with a large magnitude for 15 classes and a small magnitude for 8 classes. *HMX* performes worse in one case (`Fraction` from the `Lang` project) for weak mutation and three cases (`AdaptiveStepsizeFieldIntegrator` and `MultistepIntegrator` from the `Math` project, and `SphericalCoordinates` from the `Geometry` project) for strong mutation, all with a small effect size.

We observe a maximum increase in weak mutation score of +14.0% for the `hungarianStemmer` class (`Stemmer`) and +12.2% for the `ExtendedMessage Format` class (`Text`) on strong mutation score. Among the classes that improve on weak and strong mutation score, 27 and 20, respectively, also improve *w.r.t.* branch coverage. Interestingly, four classes among both mutation scores improve *w.r.t.* mutation score without improving the structural coverage.

In summary, *HMX* achieves significantly higher (~25% of the cases) or equal fault detection capability compared to SPX and is outperformed in one and three classes for weak and strong mutation, respectively.

---

6   Threats to Validity

This section discusses the potential threats to the validity of our study.

Construct Validity: Threats to *construct validity* stem from how well the chosen evaluation metrics measure the intended purpose of the study. Our study relies on well-established evaluation metrics in software testing to compare the proposed hybrid multi-level crossover with the current state-of-the-art, namely structural coverage (*i.e.,* branch and line) and fault detection capability (*i.e.,* weak and strong mutation). As the stopping condition of the search process, we used a time-based budget rather than a budget based on the number of test evaluations or generations. A time-based budget provides a fairer measure since the two crossover operators have a different overhead and execution time and might otherwise provide an unfair advantage to our operator.

Internal Validity: Threats to *internal validity* stem from the influence of other factors onto our results. The only difference between the two approaches in our study is the crossover operator. Therefore, any improvement or diminishment in the results must be attributed to the difference in the two crossover operators.

External Validity: Threats to *external validity* stem from the generalizability of our study. We selected 116 classes from popular open-source projects based on their cyclomatic complexity and type of input parameters to create a representative benchmark. These classes have previously been used in the related literature on test case generation [14,15].

Conclusion Validity: Threats to *conclusion validity* stem from the deduction of the conclusion from the results. To minimize the risk of the randomized nature of EAs, we performed 100 iterations of the experiment in our study with different random seeds. We have followed the recommended guidelines for running empirical experiments with randomized algorithms using sound statistical analysis as recommend in the literature [4]. We used the unpaired Wilcoxon rank-sum test and the Vargha-Delaney $\hat{A}_{12}$ effect size to determine the significance and magnitude of our results.

7 Conclusions and Future Work

In this paper, we have proposed a novel crossover operator, called *HMX*, that combines different crossover operators on both a test case-level and a data-level for generating unit-level test cases. By implementing such a hybrid multi-level crossover operator, we can create genetic variation in not only the test statements but also the test data. We implemented *HMX* in EVOSUITE, a state-of-the-art Java unit test case generation tool. Our approach was evaluated on a benchmark of 116 classes from two popular open-source projects. The results show that *HMX* significantly improves the structural coverage and fault detection capability of the generated test cases compared to the standard crossover operator used in EVOSUITE (*i.e.*, single-point). Based on these promising results, there are multiple potential directions for future work to explore. In this paper, we detailed the crossover operator for two types of primitive test data inputs (*i.e.*, numbers and strings). In future work, we are planning to extend this with additional operators for arrays, lists, and maps. Additionally, we want to experiment with alternative crossover operators for numbers (*e.g.*, parent-centric crossover, arithmetic crossover) and strings (*e.g.*, multi-point crossover).

Acknowledgements. We gratefully acknowledges the Horizon 2020 (EU Commission) support for the project *COSMOS*, Project No. 957254-COSMOS.

References

1. Almasi, M.M., Hemmati, H., Fraser, G., Arcuri, A., Benefelds, J.: An industrial evaluation of unit test generation: finding real faults in a financial application. In: 2017 IEEE/ACM 39th International Conference on Software Engineering: Software Engineering in Practice Track (ICSE-SEIP), pp. 263–272. IEEE (2017)
2. Aniche, M.: CK calculator v0.0.6. https://doi.org/10.5281/zenodo.35668
3. Arcuri, A.: RESTful API automated test case generation with evomaster. ACM Trans. Softw. Eng. Methodol. **28**(1), 1–37 (2019)

4. Arcuri, A., Briand, L.: A Hitchhiker's guide to statistical tests for assessing randomized algorithms in software engineering. Softw. Test. Verification Reliab. **24**(3), 219–250 (2014)
5. Arcuri, A., Fraser, G.: Parameter tuning or default values? An empirical investigation in search-based software engineering. Empir. Softw. Eng. **18**(3), 594–623 (2013)
6. Campos, J., Ge, Y., Albunian, N., Fraser, G., Eler, M., Arcuri, A.: An empirical evaluation of evolutionary algorithms for unit test suite generation. Inf. Softw. Technol. **104**(August), 207–235 (2018). https://doi.org/10.1016/j.infsof.2018.08.010
7. Conover, W.J.: Practical Nonparametric Statistics, vol. 350. Wiley, Hoboken (1998)
8. Deb, K., Sindhya, K., Okabe, T.: Self-adaptive simulated binary crossover for real-parameter optimization. In: Proceedings of the 9th Annual Conference on Genetic and Evolutionary Computation, pp. 1187–1194 (2007)
9. Derakhshanfar, P., Devroey, X., Panichella, A., Zaidman, A., van Deursen, A.: Towards integration-level test case generation using call site information. arXiv preprint arXiv:2001.04221 (2020)
10. Fraser, G., Arcuri, A.: Evosuite: automatic test suite generation for object-oriented software. In: Proceedings of the 19th ACM SIGSOFT Symposium and the 13th European Conference on Foundations of Software Engineering, ESEC/FSE 2011, pp. 416–419. ACM, New York (2011)
11. Gay, G.: Generating effective test suites by combining coverage criteria. In: Menzies, T., Petke, J. (eds.) SSBSE 2017. LNCS, vol. 10452, pp. 65–82. Springer, Cham (2017). https://doi.org/10.1007/978-3-319-66299-2_5
12. McMinn, P.: Search-based software test data generation: a survey. Softw. Test. Verification and Reliab. **14**(2), 105–156 (2004)
13. Olsthoorn, M., Derakhshanfar, P., Panichella, A.: Replication package of "Hybrid Multi-level Crossover for Unit Test Case Generation", July 2021. https://doi.org/10.5281/zenodo.5102597
14. Panichella, A., Kifetew, F.M., Tonella, P.: Reformulating branch coverage as a many-objective optimization problem. In: 2015 IEEE 8th International Conference on Software Testing, Verification and Validation (ICST), pp. 1–10. IEEE (2015)
15. Panichella, A., Kifetew, F.M., Tonella, P.: Automated test case generation as a many-objective optimisation problem with dynamic selection of the targets. IEEE Trans. Softw. Eng. **44**(2), 122–158 (2017)
16. Panichella, A., Kifetew, F.M., Tonella, P.: A large scale empirical comparison of state-of-the-art search-based test case generators. Inf. Softw. Technol. **104**(June), 236–256 (2018). https://doi.org/10.1016/j.infsof.2018.08.009
17. Panichella, A., Kifetew, F.M., Tonella, P.: Incremental control dependency frontier exploration for many-criteria test case generation. In: Colanzi, T.E., McMinn, P. (eds.) SSBSE 2018. LNCS, vol. 11036, pp. 309–324. Springer, Cham (2018). https://doi.org/10.1007/978-3-319-99241-9_17
18. Rojas, J.M., Campos, J., Vivanti, M., Fraser, G., Arcuri, A.: Combining multiple coverage criteria in search-based unit test generation. In: Barros, M., Labiche, Y. (eds.) SSBSE 2015. LNCS, vol. 9275, pp. 93–108. Springer, Cham (2015). https://doi.org/10.1007/978-3-319-22183-0_7
19. Tonella, P.: Evolutionary testing of classes. ACM SIGSOFT Softw. Eng. Notes **29**(4), 119–128 (2004)
20. Vargha, A., Delaney, H.D.: A critique and improvement of the CL common language effect size statistics of McGraw and Wong. J. Educ. Behav. Stat. **25**(2), 101–132 (2000)

Multi-objective Test Case Selection Through Linkage Learning-Based Crossover

Mitchell Olsthoorn[(✉)][iD] and Annibale Panichella[iD]

Delft University of Technology, Delft, The Netherlands
{M.J.G.Olsthoorn,A.Panichella}@tudelft.nl

Abstract. Test Case Selection (TCS) aims to select a subset of the test suite to run for regression testing. The selection is typically based on past coverage and execution cost data. Researchers have successfully used multi-objective evolutionary algorithms (MOEAs), such as NSGA-II and its variants, to solve this problem. These MOEAs use traditional crossover operators to create new candidate solutions through genetic recombination. Recent studies in numerical optimization have shown that better recombinations can be made using machine learning, in particular linkage learning. Inspired by these recent advances in this field, we propose a new variant of NSGA-II, called L2-NSGA, that uses linkage learning to optimize test case selection. In particular, we use an unsupervised clustering algorithm to infer promising patterns among the solutions (subset of test suites). Then, these patterns are used in the next iterations of L2-NSGA to create solutions that preserve these inferred patterns. Our results show that our customizations make NSGA-II more effective for test case selection. The test suite sub-sets generated by L2-NSGA are less expensive and detect more faults than those generated by MOEAs used in the literature for regression testing.

Keywords: Regression testing · Test case selection · Multi-objective optimization · Search-based software engineering

1 Introduction

Software testing is one of the main phases in the software development life cycle. Developers write test cases for newly developed functionalities and maintain and update the existing test base. Regression testing aims to assess that changes to the production code do not affect the behavior of unchanged parts [27]. Ideally, regression testing can be tackled by running the entire test suite within a DevOps pipeline [24]. However, this strategy becomes unfeasible for very large systems in terms of resources (*e.g.,* build servers) and time. For this reason, researchers in the software engineering community proposed various techniques to reduce the cost of regression testing by removing redundant tests (*test suite minimization* [20]); or sorting the test cases with the goal of detecting regression

© Springer Nature Switzerland AG 2021
U.-M. O'Reilly and X. Devroey (Eds.): SSBSE 2021, LNCS 12914, pp. 87–102, 2021.
https://doi.org/10.1007/978-3-030-88106-1_7

faults earlier (*test case prioritization* [19]); or selecting fewer tests to run (*test case selection* [2]).

Multi-objective Evolutionary Algorithms (MOEAs) (and NSGA-II in particular) have been successfully used in the literature to produce Pareto efficient subsets of the test suites *w.r.t.* different testing criteria [27–29]. MOEAs that rely on Pareto ranking and problem decompositions have been shown to achieve good performance also compared to greedy algorithms and local solvers [29]. Further studies tailored the individual elements of MOEAs for test case selection, such as the initialization phase (*e.g.,* [14,21,30]) and selection operators [17].

One limitation for classic MOEAs (including NSGA-II) is that new solutions are generated using fully randomized recombination (crossover) operators [22,26]. For example, the single-point and the multi-point crossovers randomly cut the chromosomes and exchange the genetic materials between two parent solutions, potentially breaking "promising" patterns. The latest advances in the evolutionary computation literature showed that a more effective search could be performed by identifying and preserving *linkage structures, i.e.,* groups of genes (problem variables) that should be replicated altogether into the offspring. *Linkage learning* [26] is a broad umbrella of methods to infer linkage structures and exploit this knowledge within more "competent" variation operators [16].

While *linkage learning* has been shown to be effective for single-objective numerical problems [16,22,26], we argue that it can also have huge potential for multi-objective test case selection. In this context, a solution is a binary vector where each bit i indicates whether the i-th test case is selected or not for regression testing. MOEAs can generate partial solutions that contain promising patterns, *i.e.,* groups of test cases (bits) that together allow achieving high coverage with minimal execution cost. Hence, detecting and preserving these patterns (group of bits) using linkage learning can improve overall the search process.

This paper introduces L2-NSGA, a variant of NSGA-II that integrates key elements of *linkage learning* for the test case selection problem. In particular, L2-NSGA uses Agglomerative Hierarchical Clustering (AHC) to identify linkage structures in the non-dominated solutions produced by NSGA-II in every other generation. These structures (patterns) are groups of bits (subsets of test suites) that are found to be statistically frequent within the non-dominated solutions according to the AHC algorithm. Then, L2-NSGA uses a novel crossover operator that stochastically selects and replicates some of the inferred structures into new individuals. Given the multi-objective nature of regression testing, L2-NSGA optimizes all testing criteria simultaneously by using the *fast non-dominated sorting* algorithm and the *crowding distance* defined by Deb *et al.* for NSGA-II [3].

We conduct an empirical study on four software systems with multiple versions and regression faults. We analyze the quality and fault detection capability of the solutions produced by L2-NSGA. We compare its performance against NSGA-II, which is the most widely-employed MOEA in the regression testing literature (*e.g.,* [14,21,28,30]). Our results suggest that the sub-test suites produced by L2-NSGA achieve higher coverage while incurring lower execution costs than the baseline (RQ1). Furthermore, the solutions created by L2-NSGA detect more regression faults than the solutions produced by NSGA-II (RQ2).

2   Background and Related Work

Three main approaches have been proposed in the literature to reduce the cost of regression testing [27]: *test suite minimization* [20], *test case prioritization* [19], and *test case selection* (TCS) [2]. Test case minimization aims to reduce the size of the test suite (number of test cases) by removing test cases that are redundant according to the chosen test criteria. Test case prioritization prioritizes (sorts) the test cases with the goal of running the fault-detecting tests earlier. Finally, TCS aims to select a subset of the original test suite taking into account test software changes and balancing cost (*e.g.*, execution time and resource usage) and test quality (*e.g.*, branch coverage). Given the conflicting nature of test quality and test resources, TCS is inherently a *multi-objective* problem [29] and, therefore, addressed using multi-objective evolutionary algorithms (MOEAs).

A common practice to decide which tests to select consists of using *test quality* metrics (or adequacy criteria) as surrogates for fault detection capability. These quality metrics reflect different aspects that software testers might be interested in maximizing, such as running test cases that exercise most of the production code as possible (code coverage [27,29,30]) or test cases that cover certain requirements first (requirement coverage [30]).

Yoo and Harman [29] introduced the first explicit formulation of TCS using a multi-objective paradigm. Given a program P, its new version P', and a test suite T, the goal is to find Pareto efficient subset of test suites $T' \subseteq T$ that correspond to optimal trade-offs among the different testing criteria to optimize.

Let $\mathcal{Q} = \{Q_1, \ldots, Q_m\}$ be the set of quality metrics to maximize; and let C be the cost metric to minimize, the multi-objective TCS problem can be formulated using the following formula:

$$min \; \Omega(T') = [C(T'), -Q_1(T'), \ldots, -Q_1(T')] \qquad (1)$$

where $T' \subseteq T$; $Q_i(T)$ denotes the quality value of T' based on the metric Q_i; and $C(T')$ is the cost of the sub-set T'.

Solutions to the TCS are encoded as *binary chromosomes*, where the i-th binary element (or *gene*) is set to 1 if the test case $t_i \in T$ is selected; 0 otherwise. A solution $T_x \subseteq T$ is said to *dominate* another solution $T_y \subseteq T$ (denoted by $T_x \succ T_y$), if T_x is better than or equal to T_y for all test objectives, and there is at least one objective (*e.g.*, test cost) in which $T_x \subseteq T$ is strictly better than T_y. A solution T^* is *Pareto optimal* if there exists no other solution $T_x \subseteq T$ such that $T_x \succ T^*$. The set of all Pareto optimal solutions (subsets of T) is called *Pareto optimal set*, and the corresponding objective vectors form the *Pareto front*. The goal of multi-objective TCS is to find Pareto optimal (or efficient) subsets of the test suite T to run for regression testing.

Yoo and Harman [29] introduced multi-objective variants of the greedy algorithms for the set cover problem. They also assessed the performances of MOEAs, and NSGA-II in particular. Epitropakis *et al.* [4] empirically showed that MOEAs produce more effective solutions (*i.e.*, detect more regression faults) than greedy approaches. Yoo *et al.* [32] successfully applied MOEAs to reduce the cost of regression testing within Google's test environment. We observe that the most commonly used MOEAs for TCS is NSGA-II (*e.g.*, [12, 29–31]).

2.1 Linkage Learning

Evolutionary Algorithm (EAs) with simple *variation operators* have been shown to perform poorly for combinatorial problems with a high number of variable problems [8, 11]. This is because the effectiveness of EAs strongly depends on their ability to mix and preserve good partial solutions [10]. Prior studies proposed more effective variation operators (*i.e.*, crossover and mutation) that exploit *linkage information* to improve the scalability of EAs [15, 18]. Linkage information can be inferred using different techniques, such as Bayesian Network [16], Dependency Structure Matrix [33], and hierarchical clustering [22, 23].

Gene-pool Optimal Mixing Evolutionary Algorithm (GOMEA) is one of the latest linkage-based evolutionary algorithm. GOMEA uses hierarchical clustering to learn linkage tree structures and uses the linkage information to create new solutions. In particular, GOMEA uses *gene optimal mixing* to improve existing solutions iteratively using local search and evaluating partial solutions. In each generation, GOMEA infers the linkage tree using the UPGMA algorithm [23]. UPGMA is a bottom-up approach that clusters genes (problem variables) based on their similarities. The similarity is computed using the normalized *mutual information*. The result of UPGMA is a linkage structure, called *Family Of Subsets* (FOS). A FOS is a set $\{F^0, F^1, \ldots, F^{|F|-1}\}$ where each F^i is a subset of the gene indexes. For example, the set $F^i = \{1, 2, 3\}$ indicates that the genes at index 1, 2, and 3 are linked together and should be considered a unique "block". The family of subsets (FOS) is a tree that contains N leaf nodes and $N - 1$ internal node, where N is the number of variable problems. The leaf nodes correspond individual variable problems (univariate subsets), while the internal nodes merge the child nodes into larger subsets.

Given the FOS, GOMEA creates new solution by iteratively applying each subset (linkage structure) into a parent individual and accepting only changes that strictly improve the fitness function. In other words, GOMEA applies an exhaustive local search on the linkage structures. Although GOMEA is very effective at achieving better convergence for problems with large numbers of decision variables, it is not designed for multi-objective problems such as TCS. In our context, we have multiple conflicting objectives (testing criteria) that must be optimized simultaneously. Another limitation of GOMEA is that it uses a computationally expensive local search heuristic to try all possible linkage structures through many fitness evaluations.

3   Approach

In this paper, we introduce a variant of NSGA-II that incorporates key elements of GOMEA, hereafter referred to as L2-NSGA. Algorithm 1 outlines the pseudo

---

Algorithm 1: L2-NSGA

```
 1  begin
 2  │   P ←── INITIAL-POPULATION()
 3  │   while not (end condition) do
 4  │   │   FOS ←── INFER-MODEL(P, 2)
 5  │   │   P' ←── ∅
 6  │   │   forall the i in 1..|P| do
 7  │   │   │   Parent ←── TOURNAMENT-SELECTION(P)
 8  │   │   │   Donor ←── TOURNAMENT-SELECTION(P)
 9  │   │   │   Child ←── L2-CROSSOVER(Parent, Donor, FOS)
10  │   │   │   Child ←── MUTATE(Child)
11  │   │   └   P' ←── P' ∪ {Child}
12  │   │   R ←── P' ∪ P
13  │   │   𝔽 ←── FAST-NONDOMINATED-SORT(R)
14  │   │   P ←── ∅
15  │   │   d ←── 1
16  │   │   while | P | + | 𝔽_d |≤ M do
17  │   │   │   CROWDING-DISTANCE-ASSIGNMENT(𝔽_d)
18  │   │   │   P ←── P ∪ 𝔽_d
19  │   │   └   d ←── d + 1
20  │   │   SORT-BY-CROWDING-DISTANCE(𝔽_d)
21  │   └   P ←── P ∪ 𝔽_d[1 : (M − | P |)]
22  └   return 𝔽_1
```

---

code of L2-NSGA. The algorithm starts with an initial pool of random solutions, *i.e.*, random subsets of test suites (line 2). The population then evolves through subsequent generations to find nearby non-dominated solutions (loop in 3–24). In line 4, the algorithm infers the linkage structures from the best individuals in the population P using UPGMA. The structures (FOS) are only inferred every other iteration to reduce the overhead of the inference process. To produce the population for the next generation, L2-NSGA first creates new individuals, using the L2-CROSSOVER, which uses the model inferred in line 4. We describe the crossover operator in detail in Sect. 3.1. In particular, the *binary tournament* selection is applied to select two individuals from the population: one parent (line 7) and one donor (line 8). In lines 9–10, the child solution is created by applying our new crossover operator (Sect. 3.1) and the *bit-flip mutation* operator. Once the offspring population P' is obtained, L2-NSGA uses the *fast non-dominated sorting algorithm* and *crowding distance* from NSGA-II to form the population for the next generation (*elitism*).

In line 13, the parent (P) and the offspring (P') populations are combined into one single pool R. The solutions in R are ranked in subsequent *non-dominated fronts* using the *fast non-dominated sorting* algorithm by Deb *et al.* [3]. The solutions in the first front $\mathbb{F}_1 \subseteq R$ are not dominated by any other solution in P; the solutions in the second front $\mathbb{F}_2$ are dominated by the solutions in $\mathbb{F}_1 \subset R$ but do not dominate one another; and so on.

The loop between lines 17 and 21 adds as many individuals to the next generation as possible, based on their non-dominance ranks, until reaching the population size. L2-NSGA first selects the non-dominated solutions from $\mathbb{F}_1$; if the number of selected solutions is lower than the population size, the loop selects the non-dominated solutions from $\mathbb{F}_2$, etc. The loop ends when adding the solutions of the current front F_d exceeds the maximum population size (the condition in line 17). In the latter case, the algorithm selects the remaining solutions from the front $\mathbb{F}_d$ according to the descending order of *crowding distance* in lines 22–23.

Notice that the *binary tournament selection* selects parent and donor solutions using the concept of Pareto optimality, which leads to selecting individuals with better (lower) dominance ranks. Further, the *crowding distance* increases the selection probability for the more diverse individuals within the same non-dominance front. The main loop in lines 3–24 terminates when the maximum number of generations is reached.

3.1 Linkage-Based Crossover

Given one *parent* solution and one *donor* solution, our goal is to copy genes from the donor to the parent using the linkage structures (FOS). Let FOS = $\{F^0, \ldots, F^n\}$ be the *family of subsets* produced the UPGMA on the population P. The new solution Child is obtained by cloning the parent solution and replicating K randomly selected subsets $F^j \in$ FOS from the donor solution. More formally, let $\text{FOS}_K \subset$ FOS be the set of K subsets randomly chosen from FOS; the new solution Child is formed as follows:

$$\text{Child}[i] = \begin{cases} \text{Parent}[i] & i \notin \text{one of the sets in FOS}_K \\ \text{Donor}[i] & i \in \text{one of the sets in FOS}_K \end{cases} \qquad (2)$$

where Child$[i]$ is the i-th gene of the child solution; Parent$[i]$ is the i-th gene the parent solution; and Donor$[i]$ is the i-th gene of the donor solutions.

The donor genes are replicated into the child altogether without applying the computationally expensive local search of GOMEA. Another important difference compared to GOMEA is that L2-NSGA always accepts the child solutions; parents and offsprings are selected for the next generation based on their dominance ranks and crowding distance values (lines 17–23 in Algorithm 1). Instead, GOMEA iteratively accepts partial changes only if they do not worsen the current single fitness value. Recall that GOMEA is a single-objective search algorithm.

In our preliminary experiments, we assessed different K values for the number of FOS to copy into the parent. We obtained good results for the systems used in our empirical study when setting K equal to 50 % of the linkage structures.

3.2 Similarity Function for Linkage Learning

UPGMA is a bottom-up iterative algorithm for hierarchical clustering, and it is used in both GOMEA and L2-NSGA to infer linkage tree structures. UPGMA requires to choose a distance function d to compute the linkage tree, *i.e.*, to decide which subsets to merge in each iteration. Various distance functions can be used, such as the *mutual information* [9], [23], *hamming distance*, and the *correlation coefficient*. L2-NSGA uses the *hamming distance* as it the classical distance function for binary vectors (*i.e.*, solution in our case) and has a much

Table 1. Programs used in the study.

Program	Versions	LOC	# Tests	Fault type	Language
bash	{v1, v2, v3}	44,991 – 46,294	1,061	Seeded	C
flex	{v1, v2, v3}	9,484 – 10,243	567	Seeded	C
grep	{v1, v2, v3}	9,400 – 10,066	806	Seeded	C
sed	{v1, v2, v3}	5,488 – 7,082	360	Seeded	C

lower computational complexity. The hamming distance between two problem variables X and Y corresponds to the number of substitutions to apply to X to obtain Y. The computational complexity of the hamming distance is $O(N \times M)$, with N being the population size, and M being the length of the chromosomes.

4 Empirical Study

We formulated the following research questions:

RQ1 *To what extent does* L2-NSGA *produce better Pareto efficient solutions compared to* NSGA-II?

RQ2 *What is the cost-effectiveness of the solution produced by* L2-NSGA *vs.* NSGA-II?

In particular, we assess the performance of L2-NSGA by comparing it with NSGA-II (the baseline). NSGA-II, which is the most frequently used MOEAs in regression testing [4,14,21,29,30]. NSGA-II is also a logical baseline since our approach extends it with linkage learning. RQ1 aims to assess to what extent L2-NSGA produces better solutions (subsets of test suites) than NSGA-II with regards to given test adequacy and cost criteria. RQ2 aims to understand how many faults can be detected by the solutions produced by the two MOEAs. This research question reflects practitioners' needs, interested in reducing the cost of regression testing without reducing the number of detected regression faults.

Benchmark. Our empirical study includes multiple versions of four real-world programs written in C: bash, flex, grep, and sed. Table 1 summarizes the main characteristics (*e.g.,* test suite size and version) of the programs in our benchmark. These programs are selected from the *Software-artifact Infrastructure Repository* (SIR) [6]. The four programs correspond to the well-known UNIX utilities obtained from the GNU website and are the largest programs written in C available in SIR. SIR provides multiple subsequent versions of the programs and their test suites. The test suite size varies from 360 to 1061 test cases, which have been created by applying both white-box (statement coverage) and black-box (category partition) test adequacy criteria [6]. SIR also includes faulty versions of these programs with seeded (artificial) faults. Similar to what has been done in the literature (*e.g.,* [29]), we considered non-trivial seeded faults that only few tests can detect. It is worth noting that these UNIX utilities have been widely used in the related literature on regression testing (*e.g.*, [4,7,29,30]).

Test Objectives. In our study, we considered three test criteria, which corresponds to the three objectives to optimize. In particular, we considered *statement coverage* (to maximize), *branch coverage* (to maximize), and *execution cost* (to minimize). For each available test case T, we stored the code branches and statements that T covers using gcov, which is a coverage tool from the C compiler in GNU. To have a reliable measure of test execution time, we counted the number of instructions executed by each test case T by using the gcov tool. This methodology of measuring the test execution cost has been widely used in the related literature to avoid biased measurements due to both the hardware and software environments used to run the test suites [29,30].

Experimental Protocol. We run the two MOEAs 20 times (each) to address their randomized nature. In each run, we stored the non-dominated front and the corresponding optimal solution set produce at the end of the search budget, *i.e.*, when reaching the maximum number of evaluated solutions.

To answer RQ1, we need to compare the non-dominated fronts produced by the MOEAs with regard to the optimal (true) Pareto front. Since the TCS problem is NP-complete [5], it is not possible to compute the true Pareto front in polynomial time for the programs in our benchmark. Hence, we build the so-called *reference front* [29,30] that combines the best parts of the non-dominated fronts produced by both NSGA-II and L2-NSGA across all 20 runs. More precisely, let $\{F_1, \ldots, F_k\}$ be all non-dominated fronts produced by L2-NSGA and NSGA-II; the reference front $\mathcal{R}$ is built as follows:

$$\mathcal{R} \subseteq \bigcup_{i=1}^{k} F_i, \forall p_1 \in \mathcal{R}, p_2 \in \mathcal{R} : p_2 \prec p_1 \tag{3}$$

Given the *reference front* $\mathcal{R}$, we then used the *inverted generational distance* (IGD) and the *hypervolume* (HV) as the *quality indicators* [34]. IGD measures both proximity of the non-dominated fronts produced by MOEAs to $\mathcal{R}$ as well as the solution diversity [34]. Therefore, smaller IGD values are preferable. In contrast, HV measures the area/volume that is dominated by a non-dominated front. Hence, larger HV values are preferable.

To answer RQ2, we analyze the fault detection capabilities of the subset of test suites produced by L2-NSGA and NSGA-II. To this aim, we analyze the number of regression faults that can be detected by each solution (sub-suite) in a given non-dominated front F_i. Hence, a non-dominated front F_i produced by a MOEA corresponds to a set of points with different cost values and different number of detected faults (cost-effective front). Non-dominated fronts that detects more faults with lower execution cost are preferable.

To quantify the *cost-effectiveness* into a single scalar value, we used the normalized Area Under the Curve (AUC) delimited by the cost-effective front (I_{CE} metric). This metric has been used to measure the average-fault detection capability of a non-dominated front for multi-objective TCS approaches [14]. I_{CE}

ranges within the interval $[0; 1]$. $I_{CE} = 1$ corresponds to the ideal (utopia) case where the front F_i detects all faults independently on the number of selected tests. $I_{CE} = 0$ indicates the worst-case scenario where no faults are detected. Hence, larger I_{CE} values are better.

To assess the significance of the differences among L2-NSGA and NSGA-II, we use the Wilcoxon rank-sum test with the threshold $\alpha=0.05$. A significant p-value indicates that L2-NSGA achieves better performance metric compared to NSGA-II across 20 runs. We further complement our statistical analysis with the Vargha-Delaney statistic ($\hat{A}_{12}$) to measure the effect size of the results. $\hat{A}_{12} > 0.5$ indicates a positive effect size for L2-NSGA.

Parameter Setting. For our experiments, we used the same parameter values used in the literature [29,30]. In particular, both NSGA-II and L2-NSGA use a *population* size of 100 solutions; and the *bit-flip mutation* operator with probability $p_m = 1/n$, with n being the test suite size (*i.e.*, chromosome length). For the recombination operators, NSGA-II uses the *scattered crossover* [14] with the probability $p_c = 0.8$. Instead, L2-NSGA uses the L2-CROSSOVER presented in Sect. 3 with the probability $p_c = 0.8$ as well. For both NSGA-II and L2-NSGA, we use the *binary tournament* selection. Finally, we used the stopping condition of 20 000 fitness evaluations, or equivalently 200 generations.

Implementation. We implemented L2-NSGA in Python using thepymoo library [1]. We use the implementation of linkage leaning and hierarchical clustering available in SciPy. The source code of L2-NSGA is publicly available as an artifact [13]. In our implementation, we pre-processed coverage data using the lossless *compaction algorithm* by Epitropakis *et al.* [4]. This algorithm has been proved to reduce the fitness evaluation cost drastically.

5   Results

In this section, we discuss the results achieved for each research question separately. Section 6 elaborates on the potential threats to the validity of our study.

Results for RQ1. Table 2 reports the median and IQR (interquartile range) of the IGD and HV values achieved by L2-NSGA and NSGA-II. The IGD metric has been computed using the *reference front* built as described in the study design. We observe that L2-NSGA achieves smaller (better) IGD values than the baseline. This means that the subset of test suites produced by L2-NSGA are much closer to the reference front and more well-distributed compared to NSGA-II. We further observe that the HV scores achieved by L2-NSGA are always larger than those obtained with NSGA-II. This means that the non-dominated fronts produced by our approach are closer to the reference fronts (IGD) and dominate a larger portion of the objective space (HV).

To provide a graphical interpretation of the results, Fig. 1 depicts the non-dominated fronts produced by the two MOEAs for sed version v1 when using two different numbers of generations. For the sake of this analysis, we selected the front achieving the median IGD value across the 20 independent runs. Figure 1a

Table 2. Median IGD and HV values (with IQR) achieved by the L2-NSGA and NSGA-II. Best performance is highlighted in grey color.

System	Version	IGD		HV	
		NSGA-II	L2-NSGA	NSGA-II	L2-NSGA
bash	v1	0.1987 (0.0192)	0.1046 (0.0224)	0.4165 (0.0276)	0.6418 (0.0483)
	v2	0.2059 (0.0238)	0.1136 (0.0201)	0.6223 (0.0215)	0.7710 (0.04242)
	v3	0.2839 (0.0333)	0.1221 (0.0300)	0.3638 (0.0252)	0.6110 (0.0435)
flex	v1	0.0300 (0.0068)	0.0265 (0.0058)	0.9924 (0.0014)	0.9937 (0.0016)
	v2	0.0324 (0.0144)	0.0230 (0.0086)	0.9810 (0.0038)	0.9853 (0.0060)
	v3	0.0519 (0.0333)	0.0350 (0.0159)	0.9808 (0.0053)	0.9857 (0.0028)
grep	v1	0.1872 (0.0881)	0.0995 (0.0467)	0.4623 (0.0908)	0.6327 (0.0983)
	v2	0.1702 (0.0573)	0.1301 (0.0865)	0.5246 (0.0782)	0.5991 (0.1575)
	v3	0.1920 (0.0835)	0.1428 (0.0389)	0.4310 (0.0851)	0.5540 (0.0968)
sed	v1	0.1123 (0.0834)	0.0544 (0.0570)	0.8863 (0.06489)	0.9580 (0.0552)
	v2	0.0546 (0.0141)	0.0158 (0.0258)	0.9508 (0.0393)	0.9900 (0.0209)
	v3	0.0752 (0.0617)	0.0253 (0.0143)	0.8919 (0.0805)	0.9761 (0.0433)

shows the front produced by the two MOEAs after 100 generations. L2-NSGA produced a better distributed front compared to NSGA-II. Besides, the solutions by L2-NSGA dominate all the solutions produced by the baseline. This means that developers can choose sub-suites from L2-NSGA that yield the same or larger coverage but incur a much smaller test execution cost. Figure 1b shows the front produced by the two MOEAs for the same system, but after 200 generations. Also in this case, L2-NSGA produced a better distributed front than NSGA-II.

Table 3 reports the statistical test results, namely the p-value of the Wilcoxon rank-sum test and the $\hat{A}_{12}$ statistic. According to these tests, the differences between the two MOEAs are statistically significant (p-value < 0.01) for all systems and all versions. The only exception to this rule is flex v1 for which the p-value is only marginally significant when considering the IGD metric. The effect size is always *large* for HV. These results suggest that L2-NSGA achieves better results independently of the size of the project and the test suites.

Results for RQ2. Table 4 reports the median and IQR of the I_{CE} values achieved by L2-NSGA and NSGA-II. Recall that I_{CE} measures the average number regression faults detected by MOEAs at different execution cost intervals (see Sect. 4 for more details). We observe that L2-NSGA achieves better (larger) I_{CE} values than NSGA-II in 10 out of 12 comparisons. Our approach achieves better results for all versions of bash, grep, and sed. The difference ranges from +19p.p. (percentage points) for bash v3 to +0.10p.p. for flex v3. Instead, for flex v1 and v2, the two approaches provide almost identical I_{CE} scores.

According to the Wilcoxon rank-sum tests and the Vargha-Delaney statistic (results also reported in Table 4), L2-NSGA statistically outperforms the baseline *w.r.t.* cost-effectiveness in all versions of bash, grep, and sed with a *large* effect size. For flex, the statistical significance only holds for version v3 with a *large*

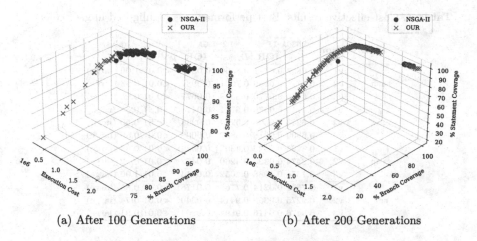

(a) After 100 Generations   (b) After 200 Generations

Fig. 1. Fronts produced by L2-NSGA and NSGA-II for sed version v1

Table 3. Results of the statistical tests

System	Version	IGD p-value	IGD $\hat{A}_{12}$	HV p-value	HV $\hat{A}_{12}$
bash	v1	<0.01	1.00 (large)	<0.01	1.00 (large)
	v2	<0.01	1.00 (large)	<0.01	1.00 (large)
	v3	<0.01	1.00 (large)	<0.01	1.00 (large)
flex	v1	0.06	0.64 (small)	<0.01	0.77 (large)
	v2	0.04	0.66 (small)	<0.01	0.80 (large)
	v3	<0.01	0.72 (med.)	<0.01	0.85 (large)
grep	v1	<0.01	0.88 (large)	<0.01	0.94 (large)
	v2	<0.01	0.76 (large)	<0.01	0.805 (large)
	v3	<0.01	0.81 (large)	<0.01	0.95 (large)
sed	v1	<0.01	0.76 (large)	<0.01	0.83 (large)
	v2	<0.01	0.91 (large)	<0.01	0.92 (large)
	v3	<0.01	0.87 (large)	<0.01	0.91 (large)

effect size. Lastly, there is no statistical difference between the two MOEAs for versions v1 and v2 (negligible effect size).

Running Time Analysis. Compared to NSGA-II, our approach applies linkage learning every two generations. The inference is based on UPGMA, which is a known fast algorithm for clustering. Nevertheless, this algorithm adds some extra overhead to the search process. Hence, it is important to quantify such overhead for practical purposes. To this aim, Fig. 2 reports the execution time spent by each algorithm to perform 200 generations on each program and independent run. The execution time was measured using a machine with Intel Core i7 processor running at 2.40GHz with 16GB RAM.

From Fig. 2, we observe that L2-NSGA is, on average, 30 % slower than NSGA-II for all programs (and versions) in our benchmark. For the two smallest programs (*i.e.*, flex and sed) the differences are between + 1 s and + 2s. Hence, the differences are very negligible in practice. A larger overhead is noticeable for bash and grep, which have the largest test suites. For the former system, the dif-

Table 4. Cost-effective results. Best performance is highlighted in grey color.

System Version		NSGA-II		L2-NSGA		Stat. Analysis	
		I_{CE}	IQR	I_{CE}	IQR	p-value	$\hat{A}_{12}$
bash	v1	0.6857	0.0171	0.8566	0.0395	<0.01	1.00 (large)
	v2	0.5711	0.0586	0.7031	0.0981	<0.01	0.98 (large)
	v3	0.6760	0.0770	0.8559	0.0677	<0.01	0.96 (large)
flex	v1	0.6718	0.0476	0.6721	0.0478	0.31	0.55 (negl.)
	v2	0.5243	0.0008	0.5244	0.0248	0.51	0.50 (negl.)
	v3	0.6809	0.0018	0.6827	0.0009	<0.01	0.89 (large)
grep	v1	0.3725	0.0323	0.43031	0.0586	<0.01	0.83 (large)
	v2	0.3474	0.0325	0.4260	0.0452	<0.01	0.92 (large)
	v3	0.1370	0.0088	0.2052	0.0214	<0.01	1.00 (large)
sed	v1	0.7552	0.0214	0.7760	0.0178	<0.01	0.85 (large)
	v2	0.9275	0.0350	0.9414	0.0340	<0.01	0.74 (large)
	v3	0.9476	0.0416	0.9894	0.0204	<0.01	0.91 (large)

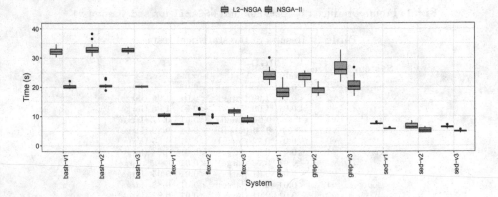

Fig. 2. Execution Time (in seconds) of NSGA-II and L2-NSGA

ferences in running time between L2-NSGA and NSGA-II are between +10 s and +15 s. For the latter, our approach requires between +5 s and +6 s compared to the baseline. However, we can conclude that a difference of a few seconds are very negligible in a practical setting.

Lastly, we note that running NSGA-II for longer will not improve its results (IGD, HV, and I_{CE}). For example, running NSGA-II on bash v1 for 600 generations (for 80 s on average) leads to HV= 0.35 (compared to 0.42 of L2-NSGA in Table 2 with 200 generations) and an $I_{CE} = 0.69$ (compared to 0.86 of L2-NSGA in Table 4 with 200 generations). These are the median values achieved over 20 independent runs.

6   Threats to Validity

The threats to *construct validity* are related to the metrics we used to assess the MOEAs. In our study, we used the *inverted generation distance* (IGD) and the *hyper-volume* (HV) to answer our RQ1. These metrics are well-established quality indicators for multi-objective algorithms [34]. This is also in line with the guidelines by Wang *et al.* [25] that recommended using IGD for problems (like TCS) with no known reference points beforehand. We combined the non-dominated fronts produced by all MOEAs and across all runs to build the reference front. This is a standard practice in regression testing [14,21,29,30,32]. Another potential threat is related to the test quality and cost metrics we optimize with the MOEAs. To collect the coverage and test execution cost data, we relied on the gcov profiling tool as done in the literature [4,30].

Threats to *internal validity* are related to the random nature of MOEAs and the L2-CROSSOVER operator. To address this threat, we run each MOEA 20 times on each program version. Then, we analyze the median results and rely on non-parametric statistical tests (*i.e.,* Wilcoxon test and the Vargha-Delaney statistics) to draw our conclusions.

Threats to *external validity* regard the generalizability of our results. We selected four medium to large size software systems written in C. These systems are well-known UNIX utilities from the SIR dataset [6] and have been widely used in prior studies in regression testing [14,21,28,30]. Furthermore, we considered three different versions of each program in the benchmark. Replicating our study with more programs, further releases, and more MOEAs is part of our future plan.

7   Conclusions and Future Work

In this paper, we have introduced a novel approach, called L2-NSGA, for multi-objective test case selection (TCS). L2-NSGA extends NSGA-II by incorporating linkage learning methods. Inspired by the latest advances in evolutionary computation, our approach replaces the fully-randomized crossover operator of NSGA-II with a new operator (L2-CROSSOVER) that identifies, preserves, and replicates patterns of genes (bits) that characterize the fittest solutions in a given population. These patterns (also called linkage structures) are inferred through agglomerative hierarchical clustering and UPGMA in particular.

We evaluated L2-NSGA on four real-world programs with large test suites and multiple versions. Our results showed that L2-NSGA produces better non-dominated fronts than its predecessor NSGA-II (the baseline), widely used in the literature. Furthermore, the test suites created with L2-NSGA can detect more regression faults than the solutions produced by the baseline.

As future work, we plan to consider alternative clustering algorithms to learn the linkage structures and different stochastic approaches for selecting the genes to replicate into new solutions during recombination. We aim to assess the usefulness of L2-NSGA for other regression testing techniques, such as test case prioritization. Finally, we would like to combine linkage learning with other MOEAs widely used in search-based software testing.

References

1. Blank, J., Deb, K.: Pymoo: multi-objective optimization in python. IEEE Access **8**, 89497–89509 (2020)
2. Chen, T.Y., Lau, M.F.: Dividing strategies for the optimization of a test suite. Inf. Process. Lett. **60**(3), 135–141 (1996)
3. Deb, K., Pratap, A., Agarwal, S., Meyarivan, T.: A fast elitist multi-objective genetic algorithm: NSGA-II. IEEE Trans. Evol. Comput. **6**, 182–197 (2000)
4. Epitropakis, M.G., Yoo, S., Harman, M., Burke, E.K.: Empirical evaluation of pareto efficient multi-objective regression test case prioritisation. In: Proceedings of the 2015 International Symposium on Software Testing and Analysis, pp. 234–245. ACM (2015)
5. Harrold, M.J., Gupta, R., Soffa, M.L.: A methodology for controlling the size of a test suite. ACM Trans. Softw. Eng. Methodol. (TOSEM) **2**(3), 270–285 (1993)
6. Do, H., Elbaum, S., Rothermel, G.: Supporting controlled experimentation with testing techniques: an infrastructure and its potential impact. Empir. Softw. Eng. **10**, 405–435 (2005). https://doi.org/10.1007/s10664-005-3861-2
7. Li, Z., Harman, M., Hierons, R.M.: Search algorithms for regression test case prioritization. IEEE Trans. Softw. Eng. **33**(4), 225–237 (2007)
8. Luong, N.H., Grond, M.O., La Poutré, H., Bosman, P.A.: Scalable and practical multi-objective distribution network expansion planning. In: IEEE Power & Energy Society General Meeting, pp. 1–5. IEEE (2015)
9. Luong, N.H., La Poutré, H., Bosman, P.A.: Multi-objective gene-pool optimal mixing evolutionary algorithms. In: Proceedings of the 2014 Annual Conference on Genetic and Evolutionary Computation, pp. 357–364 (2014)
10. Luong, N.H., La Poutré, H., Bosman, P.A.: Multi-objective gene-pool optimal mixing evolutionary algorithm with the interleaved multi-start scheme. Swarm Evol. Comput. **40**, 238–254 (2018)
11. Luong, N.H., Poutré, H.L., Bosman, P.A.: Exploiting linkage information and problem-specific knowledge in evolutionary distribution network expansion planning. Evol. Comput. **26**(3), 471–505 (2018)
12. Mondal, D., Hemmati, H., Durocher, S.: Exploring test suite diversification and code coverage in multi-objective test case selection. In: IEEE International Conference on Software Testing, Verification and Validation (ICST), pp. 1–10 (2015)
13. Olsthoorn, M., Panichella, A.: Replication package of "Multi-objective test case selection through linkage learning-based crossover (2021). https://doi.org/10.5281/zenodo.5105872
14. Panichella, A., Oliveto, R., Di Penta, M., De Lucia, A.: Improving multi-objective test case selection by injecting diversity in genetic algorithms. IEEE Trans. Softw. Eng (to appear). https://doi.org/10.1109/TSE.2014.2364175
15. Pelikan, M., Goldberg, D.E.: Escaping hierarchical traps with competent genetic algorithms. In: Proceedings of the 3rd Annual Conference on Genetic and Evolutionary Computation, pp. 511–518 (2001)
16. Pelikan, M., Goldberg, D.E., Cantú-Paz, E., et al.: BOA: The Bayesian optimization algorithm. In: Proceedings of the genetic and evolutionary computation conference GECCO-99, vol. 1, pp. 525–532. Citeseer (1999)

17. Pradhan, D., Wang, S., Ali, S., Yue, T., Liaaen, M.: CBGA-ES+: a cluster-based genetic algorithm with non-dominated elitist selection for supporting multi-objective test optimization. IEEE Trans. Softw. Eng. (2018)
18. Przewozniczek, M.W., Komarnicki, M.M.: Empirical linkage learning. IEEE Trans. Evol. Comput. **24**(6), 1097–1111 (2020)
19. Rothermel, G., Untch, R., Chu, C., Harrold, M.: Test case prioritization: an empirical study. In: IEEE International Conference on Software Maintenance, (ICSM 1999) Proceedings, pp. 179–188 (1999). https://doi.org/10.1109/ICSM. 1999.792604
20. Rothermel, G., Harrold, M.J., Ostrin, J., Hong, C.: An empirical study of the effects of minimization on the fault detection capabilities of test suites. In: Proceedings of the International Conference on Software Maintenance, pp. 34–44. IEEE CS Press (1998)
21. Saber, T., Delavernhe, F., Papadakis, M., O'Neill, M., Ventresque, A.: A hybrid algorithm for multi-objective test case selection. In: 2018 IEEE Congress on Evolutionary Computation (CEC), pp. 1–8. IEEE (2018)
22. Thierens, D.: The linkage tree genetic algorithm. In: Schaefer, R., Cotta, C., Kołodziej, J., Rudolph, G. (eds.) PPSN 2010. LNCS, vol. 6238, pp. 264–273. Springer, Heidelberg (2010). https://doi.org/10.1007/978-3-642-15844-5_27
23. Thierens, D., Bosman, P.A.: Optimal mixing evolutionary algorithms. In: Proceedings of the 13th Annual Conference on Genetic and Evolutionary Computation, pp. 617–624 (2011)
24. Verona, J.: Practical DevOps. Packt Publishing Ltd., Birmingham (2016)
25. Wang, S., Ali, S., Yue, T., Li, Y., Liaaen, M.: A practical guide to select quality indicators for assessing pareto-based search algorithms in search-based software engineering. In: Proceedings of the 38th International Conference on Software Engineering, pp. 631–642. ACM, New York (2016)
26. Watson, R.A., Hornby, G.S., Pollack, J.B.: Modeling building-block interdependency. In: Eiben, A.E., Bäck, T., Schoenauer, M., Schwefel, H.-P. (eds.) PPSN 1998. LNCS, vol. 1498, pp. 97–106. Springer, Heidelberg (1998). https://doi.org/ 10.1007/BFb0056853
27. Yoo, S., Harman, M.: Regression testing minimization, selection and prioritization: a survey. Softw. Test. Verif. Reliab. **22**(2), 67–120 (2012)
28. Yoo, S.: A novel mask-coding representation for set cover problems with applications in test suite minimisation. In: Proceedings of the 2nd International Symposium on Search-Based Software Engineering (SSBSE 2010). IEEE (2010)
29. Yoo, S., Harman, M.: Pareto efficient multi-objective test case selection. In: Proceedings of International Symposium on Software Testing and Analysis, pp. 140–150. ACM (2007)
30. Yoo, S., Harman, M.: Using hybrid algorithm for Pareto efficient multi objective test suite minimisation. J. Syst. Softw. **83**(4), 689–701 (2010)
31. Yoo, S., Harman, M., Ur, S.: Highly scalable multi objective test suite minimisation using graphics cards. In: Cohen, M.B., Ó Cinnéide, M. (eds.) SSBSE 2011. LNCS, vol. 6956, pp. 219–236. Springer, Heidelberg (2011). https://doi.org/10.1007/978-3-642-23716-4_20
32. Yoo, S., Nilsson, R., Harman, M.: Faster fault finding at google using multi objective regression test optimisation. In: 8th European Software Engineering Conference and the ACM SIGSOFT Symposium on the Foundations of Software Engineering (ESEC/FSE'11), Szeged, Hungary (2011)

33. Yu, T.L., Goldberg, D.E., Sastry, K., Lima, C.F., Pelikan, M.: Dependency structure matrix, genetic algorithms, and effective recombination. Evol. Comput. **17**(4),
595–626 (2009)
34. Zitzler, E., Thiele, L., Laumanns, M., Fonseca, C.M., Da Fonseca, V.G.: Performance assessment of multiobjective optimizers: an analysis and review. IEEE
Trans. Evol. Comput. **7**(2), 117–132 (2003)

Enhancing Resource-Based Test Case Generation for RESTful APIs with SQL Handling

Man Zhang[1]([✉])[iD] and Andrea Arcuri[1,2][iD]

[1] Kristiania University College, Oslo, Norway
[2] Oslo Metropolitan University, Oslo, Norway
{man.zhang,andrea.arcuri}@kristiania.no

Abstract. Nowadays, many companies use RESTful web services to develop their enterprise applications. These web services typically interact with databases. In REST, resource handling is a fundamental concept, where resources are manipulated by exposing HTTP endpoints. Rd-MIO* is an evolutionary algorithm which is specialized in test generation for such kind of services, i.e., RESTful APIs, via manipulating *resources* in various ways using HTTP actions (e.g., GET and POST). In this paper, we further extended Rd-MIO* by employing SQL commands to manipulate the resources for test generation, directly into the databases. We implemented our novel technique as an extension of the EVOMASTER tool. To evaluate our approach, we selected Rd-MIO* as a baseline technique and conducted an empirical study with five open source REST APIs. Results showed that our approach clearly outperforms the baseline over all of the five case studies.

Keywords: White-box test generation · SQL · REST API Testing · SBST

1 Introduction

REST is widely applied in developing web enterprise systems for providing services over the network, e.g., Google Drive[1] and Azure[2]. This kind of web services typically need communications over the network (e.g., with clients and external services), and interact with databases. Due to these interactions, it is challenging to test these systems, especially for system-level test case generation.

In REST, there exists a set of endpoints (e.g., POST and GET), which are exposed for providing services over HTTP. Dealing with *resources* is a fundamental concept, where the exposed endpoints enable manipulating these resources. Rd-MIO* [14,15] is a search-based testing approach which is developed by

---

[1] https://developers.google.com/drive/api/v3/reference.
[2] https://docs.microsoft.com/en-us/rest/api/azure/.

This work is supported by the Research Council of Norway (project on Evolutionary Enterprise Testing, grant agreement No 274385).

© Springer Nature Switzerland AG 2021
U.-M. O'Reilly and X. Devroey (Eds.): SSBSE 2021, LNCS 12914, pp. 103–117, 2021.
https://doi.org/10.1007/978-3-030-88106-1_8

handling resources for white-box test generations particularly for RESTful APIs. The approach defines a set of templates to structure HTTP calls in a test in terms of resources, and developed a set of novel strategies to sample and mutate the tests with such templates.

In this paper, we extended Rd-MIO* by employing Structured Query Language (SQL) to enhance resource handling, i.e., enable adding resources to be performed into database directly, and utilizing existing resources for the actions to be tested. We integrated our approach into EvoMaster [2] open-source tool, and conducted an empirical study with five open-source case studies (one artificial and four real-world). Results show that tests generated by our novel approach are capable of achieving on average 45.0% (up to 65.5%) line coverage and 20.5% (up to 27.3%) branch coverage, among the five case studies. Compared to the existing Rd-MIO* using the default setting, our novel approach demonstrates consistent and clear improvements on all of the five case studies. Relative improvements are up to 26.0% for target coverage, up to 26.2% for line coverage, 20.3% for branch coverage, and 40.6% for fault detection.

The rest of the paper is organized as: Background and Related work are described in Sect. 2. The proposed approach is presented in Sect. 3, followed by an empirical study on it (Sect. 4). We discuss the threats to validity in Sect. 5, and conclude the paper in Sect. 6.

2   Background and Related Work

2.1   Resource and Dependency Based MIO (Rd-MIO*)

The Many Independent Objective (MIO) [3] algorithm is an evolutionary algorithm inspired by the (1+1) Evolutionary Algorithm which only contains sampling and mutation. MIO is designed for generating system-level white-box tests, and Rd-MIO* [14,15] is an extension of it by handling test generation with an explicit consideration of resources and their dependencies in RESTful APIs. In Rd-MIO*, based on HTTP semantics, ten templates of structuring actions on manipulating resources in a test were developed [15], as follows:

  T1. GET is to retrieve resource(s);
  T2. PATCH is to partially update a resource which is likely nonexistent;
  T3. DELETE it to delete a resource which is likely nonexistent;
  T4. PUT is to replace a resource which is likely nonexistent;
  T5. POST is to create a resource;
  T6. POST/PUT-POST is to create a resource which likely exists;
  T7. POST/PUT-GET is to retrieve a resource which likely exists;
  T8. POST/PUT-PUT is to replace a resource which likely exists;
  T9. POST/PUT-PATCH is to partially update a resource which likely exists;
  T10. POST/PUT-DELETE is to delete a resource which likely exists.

Thus, a sequence of actions following the template can be regarded as a *resource-handling* with a specific purpose, and a test can be regarded as a sequence of such handlings. In addition, each of such templates has a property indicating that it is either *independent* (i.e., T1–T4) or *possibly-dependent* (i.e., T5–T10). With such definitions, an individual is defined as a sequence of *resource-handling*s which perform a sequence of actions (e.g., HTTP calls) on the resources. Moreover, Zhang et al. [15] defined *resource-based sampling* and *resource-based mutation* for producing and evolving the individual with such structure, i.e., *resource-handling*s. To investigate dependencies in REST APIs, Rd-MIO* is integrated with *resource dependency heuristic handling*, which is capable of identifying possible dependencies during the search [15]. Then the sampling and mutation in Rd-MIO* can further employ such identified dependencies to produce new individuals. In this paper, we extended the individual and *resource-handling* with direct SQL commands for enhancing such resource-based handling.

2.2 SQL Handling in EvoMaster

SQL is a widely used language for managing data in databases. To track all interactions with the database, in EvoMaster, SQL commands monitoring is implemented which is capable of tracing all executed SQL commands for accessing the SQL database of the SUT during the search [6]. Thus, when executing actions to be performed on a resource, we can know what tables are accessed with SQL. In Rd-MIO*, dependencies between resources and tables are also collected for identifying possible dependencies among the resources. For instance, if the same table is accessed by manipulations on resource A and resource B, then there might exist a dependency between A and B. For REST APIs, if a HTTP action triggers an access to tables, it is likely that the table is related to the resources to be manipulated. In addition, EvoMaster is integrated with a Domain Specific Language (DSL) (developed by [6]) which enables direct data insertions with SQL from the generated JUnit tests. With such existing support, we can employ SQL for manipulating the resources throughout the search.

2.3 REST API Testing

With a wide application of REST, there exists an increase research effort in test methods for REST APIs. To test RESTful API services, many methods [7–10,12, 13] have been developed with OpenAPI, which is a machine-readable schema that describes how to create requests for the services. The existing EvoMaster we extended in this work also uses such schemas to produce tests. In [7], Atlidakis *et al.* developed RESTler for generating a sequence of requests to test REST APIs. The sequence is decided by an inference on dependencies among the endpoints based on the OpenAPI (at the beginning) and an analysis on runtime responses. Godefroid *et al.* [9] also employs the OpenAPI schema to generate test data for REST APIs using fuzzing techniques. In [10], the schema is applied for studying differences among different versions of RESTful API services with differential testing technique. However, most of the approaches on REST APIs are in the context of black-box testing [8,13].

To our best knowledge, the only approaches for handling white-box test generation for REST APIs are from our work on EvoMaster [3,4,6,15]. In this paper, we extended the approach which is for handling test generation with resource-based methods (as described in Sect. 2.1) on EvoMaster, and further selected the approach as our baseline in the empirical study.

3   Resource Handling with SQL

Resource-based technique (i.e., Rd-MIO*) has demonstrated its effectiveness in white-box test generation for RESTful APIs [15]. In Rd-MIO*, the *resource-handling* is based on the templates which only rely on HTTP actions. However, it might not be always feasible to apply HTTP calls on manipulating resources, e.g., the dependent resources might require different levels of authorizations, or the creation of the resource is not clearly defined in the schema. In these cases, the state of the resources can not be changed with the Rd-MIO* templates during search, and that could limit the effectiveness of resource-based techniques for maximizing code coverage and faults finding in the context of white-box testing. To manipulate such states, instead of using HTTP actions, it is also applicable to directly modify data in the database, if any is used. In addition, this is typically true in RESTful web services which interact with databases for persisting *resources*.

Considering an example, where a REST API which interacts with a database has two resources, *foo* (with POST and GET) and *bar* (only with GET). *foo* is required to refer to an existing *bar*, but there does not exist a clear creation action for *bar* in the schema as shown in Fig. 1. In this case, without an existing *bar*, this issue limits the achievable line coverage on all of the endpoints. However,

```
1  "/foo/{id}": {
2    "get": {..},
3    "post": {
4      "parameters": [
5      {
6        "name": "id",
7        "in": "path",
8        "required": true,
9        "type": "integer",
10       "format": "int32"
11     },{
12       "name": "barId",
13       "in": "query",
14       "required": true,
15       "type": "string"
16     }],
17     "responses": {
18       "200": {..},"201": {..},"401": {..},"403": {..},"404": {..}
19     },
20     "deprecated": false
21   }
22 },
23 "/bar/{id}": {
24   "get": {..}
25 }
```

Fig. 1. Snippet code of a schema with OpenAPI

Table 1. Resource-based sampling templates with SQL commands

#	Template	Description	Independent?
11	*SQL*-POST	To create an existing resource	No
12	*SQL*-GET	To retrieve an existing resource	No
13	*SQL*-PUT	To replace an existing resource	No
14	*SQL*-PATCH(-PATCH)	To (partially) update an existing resource	No
15	*SQL*-DELETE	To delete an existing resource	No

Note that *SQL* refers to INSERT and SELECT commands, and the template is only applicable to the resources which has identified possibly-related tables.

based on the *SQL commands monitoring* (see Sect. 2.2), the accessed table can be known when executing GET on *bar*. Thus, we could possibly add a resource for the *bar* by using INSERT on the accessed tables.

To enable the application of SQL in *resource-handling*, we firstly extend the templates by involving SQL to manipulate resources. Based on semantics of HTTP actions, we further develop five templates with SQL (as shown in Table 1). The templates share similar testing purposes on the endpoints of the SUT with T6–T10 templates in Rd-MIO* (see Sect. 2.1). However, we extend them for resource preparation by using SQL (i.e., SELECT and INSERT) commands. As the resource handled by the proposed templates is possible to have an impact to following actions in the test, then we identify them as *possibly-dependent* templates, i.e., the *independent* property is False in Table 1. With SQL, SELECT can be applied to the situation whereby there exist resources in the SUT (e.g., seeded data), then endpoints can be tested with such existing resources, i.e., link the endpoints with existing ones. For INSERT, it is to create new resources directly into the database, then further employ the newly created ones to test the endpoints. In addition, we also provide a further extension for T6–T10 templates with SQL, e.g., an extension would be *SQL*-POST/PUT-GET for T7 that is applicable when the POST/PUT cannot function properly to create required resources. For instance, to test a retrieve operation of an existing *foo*, it requires a preparation of the *foo* resource. But POST *foo* could not be created due to lack of dependent resources, i.e., *bar*. In this case, we can either employ *SQL*-GET instead of POST-GET or create the *bar* for the POST. Such dependency could be identified with dependency handling in Rd-MIO* [15]. Here, we can employ

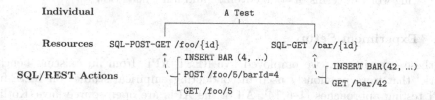

Fig. 2. An example to illustrate a representation of resource-based individual with SQL handling

such information for resource creation with SQL. Figure 2 illustrates a test with a representation of resource-based individual employing the proposed templates. The test comprises two resource handlings: one is to retrieve an existing *foo* with an extended POST-GET template, and the other is to retrieve an existing *bar* with *SQL*-GET template.

To ensure that SQL actions and REST actions perform on the same resource, we need to further handle value binding among the actions during sampling. The binding is implemented based on name matching using the Trigram Algorithm [11] (which has been applied in [15]) for calculating a degree of similarity between a column name of a table and a gene name in REST actions. Note that for a SQL action, its genes are typically flatten, while for a REST action, its genes might be structured (e.g., when representing JSON body payloads). In this case, we need to go through every genes in the REST action in order to find the most matched one (but the similarity degree must be more than 0.6 [15]), then bind the SQL gene and the REST gene. The SQL gene and the REST gene might have different types, e.g., a *id* of a resource might be `Long` in SQL but `String` in the REST action. In this case, we handle a type conversion for genes to be bound with different types. The binding direction depends on the type of the SQL, i.e., we bind the rest gene based on when SQL is `SELECT`, and bind the SQL gene based on the REST gene when SQL is `INSERT`. For a resource handling, values on the binding genes might be modified, then we need to further synchronize such binding genes after the mutation. Notice, genes for a `SELECT` and REST genes binding with `SELECT` are not mutable. Based on such binding, SQL actions and REST actions could be restrained for performing on the same resource, as shown in Fig. 2, e.g., `barId` is bound with `id` of the INSERT on the table `BAR`, and so when one is mutated, then the value of the other is automatically updated.

4   Empirical Study

To assess our novel proposed approach, we have carried out an empirical study which aims at answering two research questions:

RQ1: How does resource-based MIO with SQL perform? Among the different settings, which one performs best?

RQ2: How much improvement does our approach achieve compared to the existing work in terms of code coverage and fault detection?

4.1   Experiment Setup

In these experiments, we employed five REST APIs from an existing benchmark[3] that were previously used in conducting empirical studies on RESTful API testing approaches [4–6,14]. All of the APIs are open-source Java/Kotlin projects that interact with a database. Table 2 reports descriptive statistics of the case studies with the number of classes (#Classes), lines of codes (LOCs),

---

[3] https://github.com/EMResearch/EMB.

Table 2. Descriptive statistics of the case studies

Name	#Classes	LOCs	#Endpoints	Resource #R (#Indep.)	Database (#Tables, #Columns)
rest-news	10	718	7	4 (1)	(1, 5)
catwatch	69	5442	13	13 (11)	(5, 45)
features-service	23	2347	18	11 (1)	(6, 20)
proxyprint	68	7534	74	56 (26)	(15, 92)
scout-api	75	7479	49	21 (2)	(14, 70)
Total	245	23520	161	105 (41)	(41, 232)

#R: a number of resources; #Indep: a number of independent resources out of #R

number of endpoints (#Endpoints), number of resources (#R), number of independent resources (#Indep) out of #R, number of tables (#Tables) and number of columns (#Columns). Regarding the case studies, *rest-news* is an artificial API which was applied in a university course of enterprise development, and the remaining four (i.e., *catwatch, features-service, proxyprint, scout-api*) are real open-source projects searched from GitHub (https://github.com/).

We implemented our approach (denoted as Rd-MIO*$_{sql}$) by extending Rd-MIO* in EvoMaster with SQL handling on the resources. To assess its performance, we firstly studied the probability of employing SQL to handle resources with three settings, i.e., $P_{sql} \in \{0.1, 0.3, 0.5\}$. Note that, in the context of REST API testing, the endpoints should have a higher priority to be involved in a test. Therefore, we set the maximum value of the setting as 0.5, i.e., SQL and POST/PUT have an (at most) equal probability to be involved in a resource-handling for preparing resources. Then we selected Rd-MIO* with its best configuration [15] as the baseline technique to compare with. The performance of the techniques are compared with three coverage metrics: the number of covered targets (#Targets), line coverage (%Lines) and branch coverage (%Branches). #Targets is a coverage criterion used in EvoMaster for test generation which comprises status code coverage, code coverage and fault finding (i.e., the aggregation of all other coverage criteria). More details about the target coverage can be found in [3]. %Lines and %Branches are metrics typically used in evaluating white-box testing techniques. To compare with the baseline, we also employ the number of potential faults (#Faults) as a metric for fault detection In those experiments, considering the stochastic nature of the search algorithm, we repeated our experiments 30 times, following common guidelines on conducting SBSE experiments [1]. All of the techniques were executed with the same search budget (i.e., 100k HTTP calls), on the same machine.

4.2 Experiment Results

Results for RQ1. In Table 3, we report the average #Targets, %Lines and %Branches achieved by our approach combined with all settings (i.e., $P_{sql} =$

$\{0.1, 0.3, 0.5\}$) for all of the case studies. Results show that our approach enables covering on average 45.0% (up to 65.5%) of lines and 20.5%(up to 27.3%) of branches among the five case studies.

Table 3. Average #Targets, %Lines, %Branches obtained by Rd-MIO*$_{sql}$.

SUT	#Targets	%Lines	%Branches
rest-news	341.44	52.9%	**27.3%**
catwatch	1238.01	33.1%	17.8%
features-service	723.02	**65.5%**	21.2%
proxyprint	2522.48	32.7%	14.5%
scout-api	1967.17	40.8%	21.9%
Average		45.0%	20.5%

Table 4 represents further results for each of the settings with a rank among the settings. The setting with the maximum value (i.e., $P_{sql} = 0.5$) achieves the best results on *rest-news*, *proxyprint*, *scout-api*. This might indicate that, in these case studies, there might exist some difficulties by using endpoints (i.e., POST or PUT) to create resources. Thus, a relatively higher probability (such as 0.5) of applying SQL has a high chance to obtain better results. Compared with *features-service* and *catwatch*, the preference on applying SQL is relatively lower, i.e., 0.1 for *features-service* and 0.3 for *catwatch*. In total, based on average rank among the case studies, we selected 0.5 (i.e., 50%) as the default configuration for P_{sql}.

> *RQ1: Among the five REST APIs, our approach is capable of automatically generating tests that cover 45.0% of lines (up to 65.5%) and 20.5% of branches (up to 27.3%) on average. We recommend to apply SQL for handling resource with a 50% probability.*

Table 4. Average #Targets, %Lines, %Branches by different configurations of $P_{sql} \in \{0.1, 0.3, 0.5\}$. We also report ranks of the configurations for each SUT (value **1** indicates the best), and p-value and χ^2 of the Friedman test based on the ranks.

SUT	#Targets			%Lines			%Branches		
	0.1	0.3	0.5	0.1	0.3	0.5	0.1	0.3	0.5
rest-news	337.29(3)	342.08(2)	**345.20(1)**	52.6%(3)	53.0%(2)	**53.3%(1)**	26.7%(3)	27.4%(2)	**27.9%(1)**
catwatch	1240.03(2)	**1241.00(1)**	1233.15(3)	33.1%(2)	**33.2%(1)**	33.0%(3)	17.8%(2)	**17.9%(1)**	17.6%(3)
features-service	**724.34(1)**	723.65(2)	721.09(3)	**65.7%(1)**	65.6%(2)	65.4%(3)	**21.4%(1)**	21.1%(2)	21.0%(3)
proxyprint	2520.97(2)	2509.59(3)	**2536.91(1)**	32.7%(2)	32.6%(3)	**32.9%(1)**	14.4%(2)	14.3%(3)	**14.7%(1)**
scout-api	1955.09(3)	1966.76(2)	**1979.67(1)**	40.6%(3)	40.8%(2)	**41.1%(1)**	21.6%(3)	22.0%(2)	**22.2%(1)**
Average Rank	2.20	2.00	**1.80**	2.20	2.00	**1.80**	2.20	2.00	**1.80**
Friedman Test		(0.400,	0.819)		(0.400,	0.819)		(0.400,	0.819)

Results for RQ2. To compare with the baseline technique, Table 5 reports the average of #Targets, %Lines, %Branches and #Faults, and their results of pair comparison analysis by Mann-Whitney-Wilcoxon U-tests (p-value) and Vargha-Delaney effect sizes ($\hat{A}_{xy}$). For coverage metrics, based on the average results, our approach performs consistently better than the baseline for all of the metrics. Regarding the pair comparison results, in four out of the five case studies (i.e., *rest-news*, *catwatch features-service* and *proxyprint*), our approach achieves clearly significant improvement which can be demonstrated by the low p-value (i.e., < 0.01) and the high effect size (i.e., > 0.86). For *scout-api*, there exists modest improvement, and the improvements on #Targets and %Lines are statistically significant (i.e., p-value < 0.05 and $\hat{A}_{xy} > 0.5$).

To assess the fault detection by our approach, we also report the number of "potential" faults (#Faults) detected by our proposed approach and the baseline in Table 5. Note that faults can be detected with the HTTP status code (i.e., 500 in RESTful APIs). Regarding the #Faults metric, our approach achieves significant improvements over all of the case studies.

In Fig. 3, we also analyze the average number of covered targets (i.e., a metric combined several coverage metrics) using line plots over time, i.e., at every 5% of the used budget, during the search. Based on these results, for all of the case studies, our approach shows a clear margin throughout the search compared with the baseline. This demonstrates the advantage of our approach on both exploration and exploitation phases with SBST on RESTful APIs.

Table 5. Results by comparing with the baseline technique

SUT	Metrics	A	B	$hatA_{ba}$	p-value	relative$_{(b-a)/a}$
				A(Base) B(Rd-MIO*$_{sql}$)		
rest-news	#Targets	273.91	345.20	1.00	<0.01	+26.0%
	%Lines	42.2%	53.3%	1.00	<0.01	+26.2%
	%Branches	23.2%	27.9%	1.00	<0.01	+20.3%
	#Faults	4.72	6.63	1.00	<0.01	+40.6%
catwatch	#Targets	1055.03	1233.15	1.00	<0.01	+16.9%
	%Lines	27.4%	33.0%	1.00	<0.01	+20.5%
	%Branches	14.8%	17.6%	1.00	<0.01	+19.1%
	#Faults	16.70	20.76	0.97	<0.01	+24.3%
features-service	#Targets	707.52	721.09	0.94	<0.01	+1.9%
	%Lines	64.3%	65.4%	0.86	<0.01	+1.7%
	%Branches	18.5%	21.0%	0.95	<0.01	+14.0%
	#Faults	37.55	39.57	0.92	<0.01	+5.4%
proxyprint	#Targets	2342.90	2536.91	0.90	<0.01	+8.0%
	%Lines	30.7%	32.9%	0.86	<0.01	+7.3%
	%Branches	13.5%	14.7%	0.92	<0.01	+9.1%
	#Faults	90.19	100.74	0.99	<0.01	+11.7%
scout-api	#Targets	1944.03	1979.67	0.69	0.003	+1.8%
	%Lines	40.4%	41.1%	0.68	0.004	+1.7%
	%Branches	21.9%	22.2%	0.61	0.069	+1.4%
	#Faults	111.47	113.42	0.71	<0.01	+1.8%

Thus, we can conclude that

> **RQ2:** *Rd-MIO* enhanced with our SQL handling (with a 50% probability of its application) consistently outperforms the baseline technique in all of the five REST APIs in terms of target coverage, line coverage, branch coverage and fault detection.*

Discussion. Regarding the coverage improvement on the case studies, we found that our approach is the most effective to *rest-news*. By checking this case study, we found that there exist some difficulties when creating *news* resource with POST endpoint, because a *news* need to refer to a valid country specified with `String`, i.e., one of pre-defined list restored in a textual file (i.e., `.txt`). With the search, it is difficult to get a valid `String` within the limited budget, especially when there exist many objectives to be optimized in our context. Since the *news* resource cannot be created, it would have an impact on testing related actions on this resource, e.g., GET, UPDATE. For instance, Fig. 4 shows a snippet code of the GET endpoint (see `NewsRestApi.kt`[5]) on this resource (i.e., `GET /news/{id}`) with coverage information achieved by tests generated by our approach (i.e., all lines are covered). Note that lines with green color indicate the line covered by tests. Regarding the line coverage on this endpoint, we found that the line 161 is not solved by tests generated by the baseline (denoted with × in the figure) with $100k$ search budget, and a precondition to reach the line

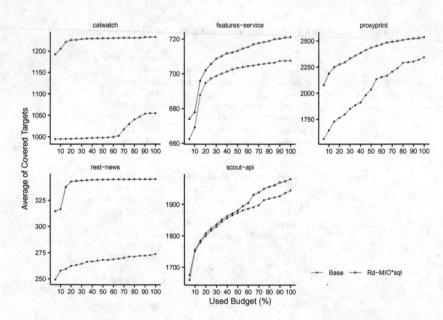

Fig. 3. Average covered targets (*y-axis*) with Base and Rd-MIO*$_{sql}$ throughout the search, reported at 5% intervals of the used budget allocated for the search (*x-axis*).

```
141     @ApiOperation("Get a single news specified by id")
142     @GetMapping(path = arrayOf("/{id}"))
143     fun getNews(@ApiParam(ID_PARAM)
144             @PathVariable("id")
145             pathId: String?)
146         : ResponseEntity<NewsDto> {
147
148         val id: Long
149         try {
150             id = pathId!!.toLong()
151         } catch (e: Exception) {
152             /*
153                 invalid id. But here we return 404 instead of 400,
154                 as in the API we defined the id as string instead of long
155             */
156             return ResponseEntity.status(404).build()
157         }
158
159         val dto = crud.findById(id).orElse(null) ?: return ResponseEntity.status(404).build()
160
161  X      return ResponseEntity.ok(NewsConverter.transform(dto))
162     }
```

Fig. 4. An example of coverage of GET /news/{id} endpoint in *rest-news* achieved by our technique

```
1  @Test
2  public void test_5() throws Exception {
3      List<InsertionDto> insertions0 = sql().insertInto("NEWS_ENTITY", 275L)
4          .d("ID", "862")
5          .d("AUTHOR_ID", "\"xxuxEf_0uLPFbIX\"")
6          .d("COUNTRY", "\"8ih8sWF\"")
7          .d("CREATION_TIME", "\"2042-10-16 10:29:25\"")
8          .d("TEXT", "\"B1zjmtfSzgzi\"")
9        .dtos();
10     controller.execInsertionsIntoDatabase(insertions0);
11     given().accept("application/vnd.tsdes.news+json;charset=UTF-8;version=2"
         )
12         .get(baseUrlOfSut + "/news/862")
13         .then()
14         .statusCode(200)
15         .assertThat()
16         .contentType("application/vnd.tsdes.news+json")
17         .body("'newsId'", containsString("862"))
18         .body("'authorId'", containsString("xxuxEf_0uLPFbIX"))
19         .body("'text'", containsString("B1zjmtfSzgzi"))
20         .body("'country'", containsString("8ih8sWF"))
21         .body("'creationTime'", containsString("2042-10-16T"));
22 }
```

Fig. 5. A test automatically generated by our approach which is able to cover the lines 159 and 161 in Fig. 4

is related to an existing *news* resource with the specified id. However, with the proposed approach, the problem can be easily addressed by directly inserting a *news* resource, despite that the country might not be valid (as the check is carried out only when a new country entry is created). A test to handle the problem is shown in Fig. 5.

Regarding *catwatch* case study, it also obtains a noticeable improvement with our approach. As its statistics shown in Table 2, 11 out of 13 endpoints are *independent*, i.e., GET actions. The remaining two are endpoints such as /import and /export that do not refer to any specific resources. Thus, it is unlikely to manipulate the resources in this REST API (e.g., *language, contributor*) using

HTTP actions with the default Rd-MIO*. An alternative solution such as SQL handling would show its effectiveness to this situation. For instance, regarding `LanguageService.java` related to *language* resource, the line coverage by Rd-MIO* and Rd-MIO*$_{sql}$ are 56.2% *vs.* 96.9%. Due to space limitation, complete coverage report can be found with a link[4] that are conducted by Intellij coverage report[5].

Regarding *features-service*, most of the resources have a reference to a POST action for their creation. In addition, its schema clearly shows their hierarchical relationships among the resources, which further makes required resources complete (i.e., prepare corresponding ancestor's resources) with a high probability. This could explain the modest improvement and the effectiveness with a relatively low ($P_{sql} = 0.1$) application probability (as shown in Table 4) on this case study. However, our approach still demonstrates its effectiveness compared with the baseline, i.e., the significant improvement shown for all of the metrics. This indicates that SQL handling is possibly required for resource handling for testing REST API despite that POST/PUT endpoints for the resources have been clearly defined.

Regarding *proxyprint*, there exist various resources (i.e., 56 #R in Table 2) and their relationships are not clearly identified with the schema. For instance, `POST /request/accept/{id}` is to accept a request to add a new printshop, and the request can be registered via `POST /request/register`. POST uses to create a resource, and its dependent resources if exist are typically specified with a hierarchical form, e.g., `/products/{productName}/features/{featureName}` and `/products/{productName}` in *features-service*. But in this case, the dependency between the two endpoints are not obvious with their URIs, (i.e., `/request/register` and `/request/accept`) that might limit an effectiveness of HTTP actions on manipulating such resources. However, for `POST /request/accept/{id}`, the accessed table can be identified (as described in Sect. 2.2) that allow SQL to prepare such resource for the POST. The effectiveness of our approaches can be shown with 95.2% line coverage on `RegisterRequestController.java` (See footnote 3) for handling the request, compared with 35.7% by Rd-MIO*. In addition, in this case study, there exists an endpoint `/admin/seed` for initializing data into the service (see `AdminController.java` (See footnote 3)). To test the system, we seed such data by requesting the endpoint before each test as shown in Fig. 6a. An effective test to `POST /request/accept/{id}` (shown in Fig. 6b) is just employed such seeded data, i.e., `id=2` at line 6 refers to a seeded request (see line 119 in `AdminController.java` (See footnote 3)).

Regarding *scout-api*, its schema is similar with *features-service*, i.e., *resources* are connected and have a POST for its creations. By further identifying the source code, we found that there exist some difficulties in handling *media_file* resources. For instance, `POST /v1/media_files` is to "Add a media file to the system. Specify URL of media file or use 'data URI' to upload base64-encoded file". Currently, it is not effective to generate such data with the search, i.e., a

---

[4] https://doi.org/10.5281/zenodo.5059928.
[5] https://www.jetbrains.com/help/idea/code-coverage.html.

```
1  @Override
2  public void resetStateOfSUT() {
3    DbCleaner.clearDatabase_H2(connection);
4    deleteDir(new File("./target/temp"));
5    try {
6      URL url = new URL("http://localhost:" + getSutPort() + "/admin/seed");
7      HttpURLConnection con = (HttpURLConnection) url.openConnection();
8      con.setRequestMethod("POST");
9      con.setDoOutput(true);
10     con.connect();
11     ...
12   } catch (Exception e) {...}
13 }
```

(a) snippet code for seeding data for each test using an endpoint of SUT

```
1  @Test
2  public void test_74() throws Exception {
3    try{
4      given().accept("*/*")
5      .header("Authorization", "Basic bWFzdGVyOjEyMzQ=") // admin
6      .post(baseUrlOfSut + "/request/accept/2")
7      .then()
8      .assertThat()
9      .contentType("text/plain")
10     .body(containsString("{\"success\":true}"));
11   } catch(Exception e){
12   }
13 }
```

(b) a test generated by our approach which refers to an existing data

Fig. 6. A test automatically generated by our approach which employs the existing data for preparing a resource for /request/accept/{id}

valid URI referring to a media file (e.g., image). But we could employ SQL to add data into the database for making the resource exists. Besides, in this case study, most of data retrieves are implemented with a query parameter named attrs which indicates "The attributes to include in the response. Comma-separated list". However, with $100k$ HTTP calls, currently EVOMASTER cannot handle such constraints (e.g., specified with textual language) properly. This might be a reason for the modest improvements on this case study, but they are still statistically significant.

Significant improvements on fault detection could be a result of such improvement on coverage. Thus, by carefully analyzing results on the five case studies, we summarize that:

> Our proposed technique significantly enhances the handling on resources which is capable of generating more effective tests against REST APIs, particularly effective on the SUTs whose creation actions are restricted or unclear.

5   Threats to Validity

Conclusion Validity. Our applied technique is in the context of search-based testing. To handle its randomness nature, we repeated our experiments 30 times, which is recommended by standard guidelines [1] in search-based software engineering for conducting experiments. To properly draw the conclusions based on the results, we employed a set of statistical tools, i.e., Friedman test (p-value and χ^2) for variance analysis of performances of different settings among case studies, Mann-Whitney U-test (p-value) and Vargha-Delaney ($\hat{A}_{12}$) for reporting comparison results with the baseline technique.

Construct Validity. In these experiments, outputs are obtained from search-based techniques. To avoid any potential bias in such outputs, we first used the same stopping criterion (i.e., $100k$ HTTP calls) for baseline and proposed techniques. In addition, all the experiments were executed on the same machine for further dealing with this validity threat.

Internal Validity. The approach is implemented on the EVOMASTER tool that is open-source, and the experiments were conducted with case studies which are available online as well. We cannot guarantee that our implementation is free of bugs, but the implementation and experiments can be examined by anyone, as we made them open-source (www.evomaster.org).

External Validity. The approach was evaluated with five REST APIs which interact with SQL databases, taken from a benchmark for REST API testing. More case studies would help to generalize results of our approach. REST is widely applied in industry, however, most of them are not open-source, which limits our experiments with more case studies.

6   Conclusions and Future Work

Testing REST APIs is challenging, especially for system-level test generation, due to their possible complex interactions with SQL databases. In REST, exposed endpoints are typically defined based on resources and actions that can be performed on them. Thus, via the endpoints, manipulating resources with different states can help obtaining better code coverage in the context of white-box testing. Rd-MIO* is such approach for automatically generating tests using search-based techniques. In this paper, we further extended it by enhancing the resource manipulation with direct SQL handling. We implemented our approach in the EVOMASTER open-source tool, and conducted an empirical study with five open-source case studies. Experimental results show that our approach significantly outperforms the existing Rd-MIO*, in terms of code coverage and fault detection. Our novel technique demonstrates its advantages on all of the five case studies, particularly on the SUTs whose creation actions are restricted or too complex.

In future, we plan to 1) conduct more studies with various types of databases, and 2) investigate solutions for handling constraints specified with textual language. For more information, visit our webpage at www.evomaster.org.

References

1. Arcuri, A., Briand, L.: A hitchhiker's guide to statistical tests for assessing randomized algorithms in software engineering. Softw. Test. Verif. Reliab. (STVR) **24**(3), 219–250 (2014)
2. Arcuri, A.: EvoTaster: evolutionary multi-context automated system test generation. In: IEEE International Conference on Software Testing, Verification and Validation (ICST). IEEE (2018)
3. Arcuri, A.: Test suite generation with the many independent objective (MIO) algorithm. Inf. Softw. Technol. (IST) **104**, 195–206 (2018)
4. Arcuri, A.: Restful API automated test case generation with EvoMaster. ACM Trans. Softw. Eng. Methodol. (TOSEM) **28**(1), 3 (2019)
5. Arcuri, A.: Automated blackbox and whitebox testing of RESTful APIs with EvoMaster. IEEE Softw. **38**, 72–78 (2020)
6. Arcuri, A., Galeotti, J.P.: Handling SQL databases in automated system test generation. ACM Trans. Softw. Eng. Methodol. (TOSEM) **29**(4), 1–31 (2020)
7. Atlidakis, V., Godefroid, P., Polishchuk, M.: Restler: stateful rest API fuzzing. In: Proceedings of the 41st International Conference on Software Engineering, ICSE 2019, pp. 748–758. IEEE Press (2019). https://doi.org/10.1109/ICSE.2019.00083
8. Ed-douibi, H., Cánovas Izquierdo, J.L., Cabot, J.: Automatic generation of test cases for rest APIs: a specification-based approach. In: 2018 IEEE 22nd International Enterprise Distributed Object Computing Conference (EDOC), pp. 181–190 (2018)
9. Godefroid, P., Huang, B.Y., Polishchuk, M.: Intelligent rest API data fuzzing. In: Proceedings of the 28th ACM Joint Meeting on European Software Engineering Conference and Symposium on the Foundations of Software Engineering, ESEC/FSE 2020, pp. 725–736. Association for Computing Machinery, New York (2020). https://doi.org/10.1145/3368089.3409719
10. Godefroid, P., Lehmann, D., Polishchuk, M.: Differential regression testing for rest APIs. In: Proceedings of the 29th ACM SIGSOFT International Symposium on Software Testing and Analysis, ISSTA 2020, pp. 312–323. Association for Computing Machinery, New York (2020). https://doi.org/10.1145/3395363.3397374
11. Martin, S., Liermann, J., Ney, H.: Algorithms for bigram and trigram word clustering. Speech Commun. **24**(1), 19–37 (1998)
12. Martin-Lopez, A., Segura, S., Ruiz-Cortés, A.: RESTest: black-box constraint-based testing of RESTful web APIs. In: Kafeza, E., Benatallah, B., Martinelli, F., Hacid, H., Bouguettaya, A., Motahari, H. (eds.) ICSOC 2020. LNCS, vol. 12571, pp. 459–475. Springer, Cham (2020). https://doi.org/10.1007/978-3-030-65310-1_33
13. Viglianisi, E., Dallago, M., Ceccato, M.: RESTTESTGEN: automated black-box testing of restful APIs. In: IEEE International Conference on Software Testing, Verification and Validation (ICST). IEEE (2020)
14. Zhang, M., Marculescu, B., Arcuri, A.: Resource-based test case generation for restful web services. In: Proceedings of the Genetic and Evolutionary Computation Conference, pp. 1426–1434 (2019)
15. Zhang, M., Marculescu, B., Arcuri, A.: Resource and dependency based test case generation for RESTful Web services. Empir. Softw. Eng. **26**(4), 1–61 (2021). https://doi.org/10.1007/s10664-020-09937-1

Replications and Negative Results

Empirical Study of Effectiveness of EvoSuite on the SBST 2020 Tool Competition Benchmark

Robert Sebastian Herlim[1(✉)], Shin Hong[2], Yunho Kim[3], and Moonzoo Kim[1]

[1] KAIST, Daejeon, South Korea
robert.herlim@kaist.ac.kr, moonzoo@cs.kaist.ac.kr
[2] Handong Global University, Pohang, South Korea
hongshin@handong.edu
[3] Hanyang University, Seoul, South Korea
yunhokim@hanyang.ac.kr

Abstract. EvoSuite is a state-of-the-art search-based software testing tool for Java programs and many researchers have applied EvoSuite to achieve high test coverage. However, due to high complexity of object-oriented programs, EvoSuite still suffers several limitations in terms of test coverage achievement. In this paper, to improve the effectiveness of EvoSuite by analyzing EvoSuite's limitations, we conducted an empirical study to identify the limitations of EvoSuite on the most recent SBST 2020 Tool Competition benchmark that consists of 70 classes selected from real-world Java projects. We have manually classified the branches of the target programs that EvoSuite could not cover and reported corresponding limitations of EvoSuite with concrete examples.

Keywords: Empirical study · EvoSuite · SBST tool competition

1 Introduction

Automated test case generation has been a prominent research topic for the past decade [2,5,7–9]. Among several automated test generation techniques, search-based software testing attracts researchers for its high scalability and high test coverage. EvoSuite [5] is a state-of-the-art search-based software testing tool for Java programs and many researchers have used EvoSuite to detect faults in real-world industrial cases [1,13] and achieve high test coverage [6,12].

In this paper, to improve the effectiveness (i.e., test coverage achievement) of EvoSuite by analyzing the EvoSuite's limitations, we conducted an empirical study by applying EvoSuite to the SBST 2020 Tool Competition [4] benchmark (calling it the SBST 2020 benchmark).[1] We replicated the contest setting used by

---

[1] SBST 2020 Tool Competition benchmark was the latest available dataset in the annual SBST Tool Competition series by the time we performed this study. The SBST 2020 benchmark consists of 70 classes selected from real-world open-source Java projects. The contest infrastructure for replicating the SBST competition series is available at https://github.com/JUnitContest/JUGE.

© Springer Nature Switzerland AG 2021
U.-M. O'Reilly and X. Devroey (Eds.): SSBSE 2021, LNCS 12914, pp. 121–135, 2021.
https://doi.org/10.1007/978-3-030-88106-1_9

Table 1. Target subjects & EvoSuite's achieved coverage

Subject	#Classes	#Branches				Br. Coverage (%)	
		Total	Mean	Median	Stdev	Mean	Stdev
FESCAR	20	490	24.5	11	27.3	66.9	42.9
GUAVA	20	926	46.3	19	61.5	67.5	32.4
PDFBOX	20	1,070	53.5	24	75.6	54.7	36.1
SPOON	10	1,072	107.2	45	12.9	28.0	24.5

EvoSuite during the competition to obtain its coverage report. From the report, we manually analyzed each branch that EvoSuite could not cover and grouped them into a few categories.

There have been several attempts to study the limitations of EvoSuite in previous works, such as categorizing the kinds of hard-to-detect faults [1] and bad quality tests [11]. To the best of our knowledge, this is the first attempt to identify the limitations of EvoSuite exclusively for categorizing reasons of not-covered branches in the SBST 2020 benchmark. Compared with the original EvoSuite's post-mortem report [10], this paper shows a clearer picture of the challenges of EvoSuite on the SBST 2020 benchmark by reporting the limitations with concrete examples. The main contributions of this paper are as follows:

1. We performed an empirical study by applying EvoSuite to the recent SBST 2020 benchmark, from which we identified several limitations that EvoSuite struggles with.
2. We extensively analyzed the branches that EvoSuite could not cover in the benchmark and classified the corresponding reasons for those branches, which have not been done previously by other empirical study papers!

The remaining sections are organized as follows: Sect. 2 describes the study questions and the empirical study setup. Section 3 reports the answers to the study questions. Finally, Sect. 4 concludes this paper with future work.

2   Empirical Study Setup

2.1   Benchmark Overview

The SBST 2020 Tool Competition [4] benchmark contains 70 different classes selected from the following four real-world open-source projects:

- **FESCAR:** an open-source distributed transaction library to support transactions in microservice.
- **GUAVA:** a common Java library developed by Google which provides collection classes.
- **PDFBOX:** a PDF processing library which provides PDF manipulation utilities, such as text extraction, splitting, merging, and document signing.
- **SPOON:** a library for Java source code analysis and transformation.

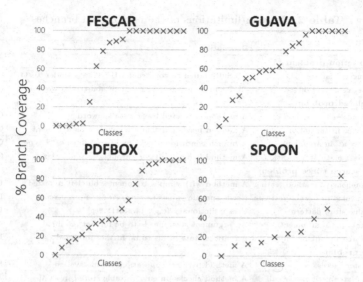

Fig. 1. EvoSuite's achieved branch coverage per class. Each data point represents the average score of EvoSuite's achieved branch coverage in a class of the respective subject.

Table 1 describes the benchmark subjects and the branch coverage on each subject achieved by EvoSuite following the analysis procedure (see Sect. 2.2). For example, FESCAR (see the second row of the table) has 20 classes that contain total 490 branches and EvoSuite achieved 66.9% branch coverage on FESCAR on average in the experiment. Note that the benchmark does not provide any detail of fault existence in the target classes, so fault detection is beyond the scope of our study.

Figure 1 shows the scatter plot of class coverage on each subject. For example, GUAVA has four classes on which EvoSuite achieved around 60% branch coverage (see the four data points in the middle part of the GUAVA graph) and six classes on which EvoSuite achieved 100% branch coverage (see the rightmost six data points in the GUAVA graph).

2.2 Analysis Procedure

The experiments were conducted on one machine equipped with octa-core AMD Ryzen 7 1700 (up to 3.7 GHz) and 16 GB RAM, running a 64-bit version of Ubuntu 16.04. We used OpenJDK v1.8.0 for the Java SE and Maven v3.3.9 for the project build tool. We used the official Docker infrastructure in the version with commit hash 2ed9d22. Except the post-processing part[2], we followed the EvoSuite's contest configurations to use EvoSuite's default configurations. Three minutes was set for the time budget, consisting 50% for the search and 50% for other remaining part. JaCoCo was used to measure the branch coverage, and by which we generated coverage report (using HTML format) to analyze the

---

[2] For this independent replication study, we disabled the test suite minimization step to reduce the risk of coverage loss caused by unintended test case reduction.

Table 2. Reasons/limitations of the not-covered branches

	Category	Description	Mnemonic
1	**Construction problem**		
1A	Construction failure	EvoSuite failed to construct CUT (Class Under Test)	C-CF
1B	Complex construction	CUT can be instantiated, but in non-trivial ways	C-CC
2	**OO-related problem**		
2A	Private access on method	A method protected by private keyword	O-PAM
2B	Inheritance instantiation	A method needs particular subclasses as argument	O-IIP
2C	Class<?> as an argument	A branch condition checks on special Class<?> type	O-CLA
2D	Inner class method invocation	A method is only callable through its inner classes	O-ICM
3	**Large search space problem**		
3A	Incomprehensive method testing	A method with simple arguments, but left untested	L-IMT
3B	Specific value in iterable/stream	Needs specific values in byte/string/input stream	L-ISV
3C	Key-value store pattern	Uses a dictionary (e.g., java.util.Map)	L-KVS
3D	Obj. state in an argument	An argument state needs to be further modified	L-OSA
3E	Obj. state in invoking object	An object state needs to be further modified	L-OSI
4	**Other problem**		
4A	File system access	A method performs operations on file system	FSA
4B	JVM's System.getProperty call	A method checks on env. variable stored in JVM	JSC
4C	Branch unreachable	Unfeasible branches by program executions	UBR

Listing 1.1. Example of *reached but not covered* branch

```
L1:void f(int x,int y) {
L2:    ...
L3:    if ( x>0 ) { /* br1 */
L4:    } else {      /* br2 */
L5:      if ( y>0 ) { /* br3 */}}}
```

not-covered branches. To limit the random variance, we performed six repeated experiment runs on each subject. We counted a branch b as not-covered if b was not covered by any of the six experiment runs.

Note that we investigated the *reached but not covered* branches only. For Listing 1.1, with an input (x,y)=(1,1) for f(), the branch br1 in L3 is reached and covered, br2 in L4 is reached but not covered, and br3 in L5 is not reached (and, thus, not covered). In other words, we did not analyze the branches that were not reached by any test input because the reason for not covering such unreached branches can be complex to classify. For example, the reason of why br3 was not covered with (x,y)=(1,1) does not only depend on L5, but its all predecessor conditions such as L2 and so on. We could hypothesize that the br3 coverage failure was caused by "argument x was always >0" (the same cause as failure in br2), but it may not be true because another input where (x,y)=(0,0) would neither make br3 to be covered.

From now on, we use the term *not-covered* to represent *reached but not covered* branches in this paper. We manually analyzed total 359 not-covered branches in the SBST 2020 benchmark. The raw data is accessible through https://bit.ly/evoStudySSBSE2021RENE.

2.3   Study Questions

After manually analyzing *reached but not covered* branches by EvoSuite, we classified the limitations of EvoSuite on the SBST 2020 benchmark into four groups (i.e., construction problem, OO-related problem, large search space problem, and other problem) of the 14 categories as shown in Table 2. For the empirical study, we made the following four study questions:

SQ 1. Object Construction Problem. How much do the object construction problems impact EvoSuite's branch coverage?

SQ 2. OO-related Problem. How much do the OO-related problems impact EvoSuite's branch coverage?

SQ 3. Large Search Space Problem. How much do the large search space problems impact EvoSuite's branch coverage?

SQ 4. Other Problem. How much do the environment-related problem and unreachable branches impact EvoSuite's branch coverage?

Second, we tried to identify *common major* limitations of EvoSuite on the SBST 2020 benchmark. The term *common* is used on the limitations that are observed on all four target subjects of the benchmark. Such common problems are particularly interesting because they may be general limitations that apply to not only SBST 2020 benchmark but also other programs. We define *common* and *major* limitations as follows:

- A category becomes a *common* problem if its occurrences can be found across all four subjects in the benchmark.
- A category becomes a *major* problem (in one subject) if it appears in at least 25% of the classes with not-covered branches (i.e., classes with <100% branch coverage).

SQ 5. Common Major Problems. By running EvoSuite on the SBST 2020 Tool Competition benchmark, is there any common major problem found across all target subjects?

3   Empirical Study Results

Figure 2 shows the distribution of the limitation categories of the branches that EvoSuite could not cover (see Table 2). For example, the 11 branches of FES-CAR and the 20 branches of GUAVA were not covered by EvoSuite due to the construction failure (C-CF) and the complex construction (C-CC) respectively (see the bar of light blue color (FESCAR) and the bar of green color (GUAVA) of the two leftmost bars (C-CF and C-CC) in Fig. 2).

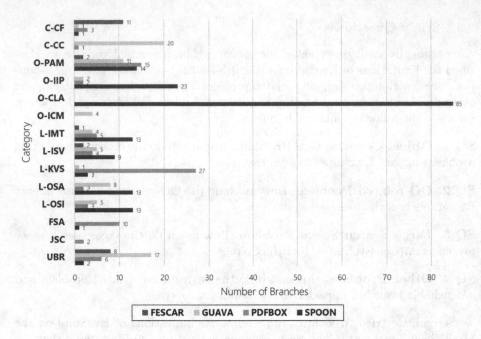

Fig. 2. Distribution of the limitation categories of not-covered branches

3.1 SQ1: Object Construction Problem

1A Construction Failure (C-CF). The C-CF category indicates that Evo-Suite fails to instantiate an instance of CUT (class under test). Several interesting causes of C-CF in the benchmark are as follows:

1. **Constructor needs complex arguments:**
   For example, consider a constructor[3] of PDVisibleSignDesigner (PDFBOX–130) shown in Listing 1.2. The constructor needs: (1) a PDDocument-typed document with p pages ($p > 0$); (2) an InputStream-typed imageStream transformed from any valid BufferedImage; and (3) an integer page where page $\in (0, p]$. Violating any of the constraints (e.g., page = 0, null imageStream or empty InputStream such as returned by new ByteArray InputStream(new byte[5])) would result an exception raised during the execution. Due to these constraints, we found EvoSuite could not construct a PDVisibleSignDesigner instance during the runs.
   Another example is FilteredEntryMultimap (GUAVA–47), where its constructor needs a Predicate-typed instance. We found in eight out of 12 test cases where EvoSuite used a BloomFilter instance as an argument of a Predicate-typed instance, in which six out of the eight test cases failed (i.e., raising exceptions) during the BloomFilter construction. This indicates that generating a valid Predicate instance is highly complex for EvoSuite. We observed that such failures in constructing BloomFilter induced failure constructions

---

[3] We observed that other six PDVisibleSignDesigner constructors have a similar construction failure problem as described in this paper.

Listing 1.2. Construction failure in PDFBOX-130

```
L1:  public PDVisibleSignDesigner(PDDocument document,
L2:    InputStream imageStream, int page) throws IOException {
L3:    readImageStream(imageStream);
L4:    calculatePageSize(document, page); }
```

of `FilteredEntryMultimap`, which causes testing could not reach any other member methods that needs at least one `FilteredEntryMultimap` instance as target object.

2. **Dependency on another C-CF class:**
   For example, the constructor of `FilteredMultimapValues` (`GUAVA-240`) needs a `FilteredMultimap`-typed argument. Every subclass of `FilteredMultimap` needs a `Predicate` instance (a complex object as described above), causing EvoSuite to fail at constructing a `FilteredMultimapValues` instance. As a result, all seven related member methods were not covered.

3. **Accessibility conflict on constructor's arguments:**
   For example, the constructor of `PDTrueTypeFontEmbedder` (`PDFBOX-235`) receives a `TrueTypeFont`-typed instance as a parameter. EvoSuite could not generate a `PDTrueTypeFontEmbedder` instance since `TrueTypeFont` is package-private and located in a different package.

4. **Missing class from the classloader:**
   The classloader could not find a constructor parameter type (e.g., `FESCAR-6`, `FESCAR-8`, `FESCAR-15`, `FESCAR-41`, `SPOON-155`), which induced an exception (i.e., `NoClassDefFoundError`).[4]

1B Complex Construction (C-CC). Compared to the C-CF category where object creation entirely fails, this C-CC category applies to the CUTs with successful instantiation, but of only *simple* objects. Several interesting causes of C-CC in the benchmark are as follows:

1. **Implicit object construction convention:**
   For example, the only way to construct `ImmutableEnumSet` (`GUAVA-206`) is by invoking the *static factory* method `asImmutable` as shown in Listing 1.3. However, `asImmutable` may not generate a `ImmutableEnumSet` instance (but `ImmutableSet`-typed instead) if the given `set` argument's size is ≤ 1 (L3–L5). To mitigate this case, EvoSuite should infer how to obtain the correct `ImmutableEnumSet` instance by invoking `asImmutable` with an `EnumSet` instance of >1 elements (L6).

2. **Dependency to other unknown class:**
   Another example is `Graphs` (`GUAVA-22`), whose methods perform graph operations (e.g., transposing, finding reachable nodes) on `Graph` instances. For this case, we found EvoSuite generated method call sequences using *empty* `Graph` instances. That is because the standard construction (i.e., through

---

[4] We suspect that these limitations were caused by a bug in EvoSuite since those missing classes had been correctly placed in the same directory and package as the CUT.

Listing 1.3. Complex construction problem in GUAVA-206

```
L1: static ImmutableSet asImmutable(EnumSet set) {
L2:     switch (set.size()) {
L3:         case 0: return ImmutableSet.of();
L4:         case 1: return ImmutableSet.of(
L5:             Iterables.getOnlyElement(set));
L6:         default: return new ImmutableEnumSet(set); } }
```

Listing 1.4. Inheritance instantiation problem in SPOON-105

```
L1: // To cover: pass a CtCatch instance to the first argument
L2: SourcePosition buildPositionCtElement(CtElement e, ...) {
L3:   if (e instanceof CtCatch) { // then branch was not covered
L4:     return SourcePosition.NOPOSITION;
L5:   } ... }
```

available constructors) produces empty `Graph` objects by default. To construct more diverse `Graph` objects (e.g., adding nodes/edges, cyclic/acyclic, directed/undirected), EvoSuite has to use a builder class. Since the relationship between the builder class and CUT to construct more complex `Graph` instances is unknown to EvoSuite, EvoSuite failed to cover branches relevant to diverse `Graph` instances.

3.2 SQ2: OO-Related Problem

2A Private Access on Method (O-PAM)

We observed that 42 methods (from 13 different classes) could not be tested due to the private access issue. For example, almost 50% (nine out of 20) of the `PositionBuilder`'s (`SPOON-105`) private methods were not covered.

2B Inheritance Instantiation Problem (O-IIP)

The O-IIP category is mostly encountered in the form of inheritance-checking conditions, caused by the `instanceof` operator in Java. An example of O-IIP category is shown in Listing 1.4. In the example, the return statement at L4 was not covered because EvoSuite could not satisfy the condition at L3. For example, SPOON suffered from O-IIP severely (i.e., 23 branches in five out of the ten SPOON classes were affected).

2C Class<?> as a Method Argument (O-CLA)

Java provides `java.lang.Class` to represent any class or interface in the application, which is commonly utilized by the factory classes. Having a `Class<?>` parameter enlarges the search space because all classes in the classpath become candidates for the method's arguments. For example, `DefaultCoreFactory` (`SPOON-65`) creates a `CtElement` instance based on the supplied argument `klass`, as shown in Listing 1.5. We found that EvoSuite failed to cover any of the 83 (= $3 + 80$) *then* branches that can be taken if the corresponding *equality* checking branch passes (e.g., L2, L4, L6).

Listing 1.5. Class<?> as method argument in SPOON-65

```
L1: public CtElement create(Class<? extends CtElement> klass) {
L2:     if (klass.equals(CtAnnotationFieldAccess.class))
L3:         return createAnnotationFieldAccess();
L4:     if (klass.equals(CtArrayRead.class))
L5:         return createArrayRead();
L6:     if (klass.equals(CtArrayWrite.class))
L7:         return createArrayWrite();
L8: /* ... 80 more similar if-statments */ }
```

Listing 1.6. Inner class method invocation requirement in GUAVA-102

```
L1:  // To cover: use NodeIterator's remove API
L2:  public class LinkedListMultimap<K, V> {
L3:      private void removeNode(Node<K, V> node) {
L4:          if (node.previous != null) { /* not covered */ } ... }
L5:      ...
L6:      // NodeIterator is an inner class of LinkedListMultimap
L7:      private class NodeIterator {
L8:          public void remove() { ...
L9:              removeNode(current);
L10:         ... }
L11:     } ... }
```

2D Inner Class Method Invocation Requirement (O-ICM)

Although inner classes are located inside the CUT, EvoSuite did not generate a method call sequence using methods from the inner classes. However, some of the CUT's methods can only be invocable though the inner classes of the CUT.[5] Listing 1.6 shows an example of O-ICM category in LinkedListMultimap (GUAVA-102). In LinkedListMultimap, a private method removeNode (L3) was never invoked because it was invocable only through the remove API (L8) of LinkedListMultimap's iterator inner classes, such as NodeIterator (L7). Our coverage report showed that although EvoSuite had constructed NodeIterator instances (e.g., by generating valueIterator call), no further method invocation was performed on the resulted iterator instances. Therefore, removeNode was not covered.

3.3   SQ3: Large Search Space Problem

3A Incomprehensive Method Testing (L-IMT)

For example, EvoSuite did *not* generate a call sequence for a member method createSerializedForm in SparseImmutableTable (GUAVA-129), although the method is declared as public and takes *no* argument. We observed L-IMT also occurred in the *caching* pattern, whose example is shown in Listing 1.7. This is a common pattern to prevent multiple creations of expensive objects (L5)

---

[5] We guess that EvoSuite may consider that generating method call sequences using the methods of the CUT's inner classes would not increase the coverage of CUT since the CUT's inner classes are separate classes from the CUT.

Listing 1.7. Caching pattern inside class in GUAVA-212

```
L1:  // To cover: invoke toString() twice.
L2:  public String toString() {
L3:      String result = toString;
L4:      if (result == null) {
L5:          result = computeToString();
L6:          toString = result;
L7:      } // The else branch was not covered
L8:      return result; }
```

by keeping previously-created reference in the class' field (L6). Through this pattern, the next invocation of `toString` does not invoke `computeToString` if the result has been stored in the `toString` member field. The benchmark contains several methods adopting this caching pattern, such as in `MediaType` (GUAVA-212), `Graphs` (GUAVA-22), and `PDType3Font` (PDFBOX-265). EvoSuite rarely performed repeated invocations on such methods, which left the *else* branches (L4 in Listing 1.7) not covered.

3B Specific Value in Iterable/Stream (L-ISV)

The L-ISV category requires some specific input byte sequences to satisfy the branch condition. Several L-ISV examples are as follows:

- The `decode` of `JPXFilter` (PDFBOX-220) needs a valid JPEG2000-formatted `InputStream` as an argument. The `decode` calls another method `readJPX`, where `readJPX` will throw an `IOException` if the given `InputStream` in the method argument is not JPEG2000-formatted. In this case, EvoSuite failed to supply the valid `InputStream`, leaving other seven branches in `readJPX` method not reached.
- The `getEndOfComment` of `PositionBuilder` (SPOON-105) needs a `char[]` buffer as an argument. The method searches the end-of-comment token (i.e., `'*/'`) in the `char[]` buffer. EvoSuite failed to generate a valid test case to cover the equality checking branch within the `getEndOfComment` method.

3C Key-Value Store Pattern (L-KVS)

The L-KVS category is related to the use of key-value data structure (e.g., `Map`) in branch conditions. Such conditions increase the complexity as they require a correct guess in three dimensions: *key*, *value*, and the *key-value* pair combination. For example, consider `Predictor` (PDFBOX-117) as shown in Listing 1.8. In this example, branch in L6 was not covered because `decodeParams` never had an entry for key = `COSName.PREDICTOR` as requested at L5-L6. Note that, to put an item to `COSDictionary`, EvoSuite has to select a key from 517 available `COSName`. We found that L-KVS majorly impacted PDFBOX (i.e., 10 out of 20 classes (50%) suffered L-KVS as shown in Fig. 3)

3D Object State Problem in Argument (L-OSA)

The L-OSA category requires further alteration of the state of the object passed as a method argument. L-OSA examples are as follows:

Listing 1.8. Key-value store problem in PDFBOX-117

```
L1:  // To cover: pass decodeParams argument containing entry
L2:  //     { key = COSName.PREDICTOR , value = COSNumber > 1 }
L3:  static OutputStream wrapPredictor(OutputStream out,
L4:      COSDictionary decodeParams) {
L5:      int predictor = decodeParams.getInt(COSName.PREDICTOR);
L6:      if (predictor > 1) { /* not covered*/ }
L7:      else { return out; } }
```

Listing 1.9. Argument state problem in SPOON-169

```
L1:  // To cover: invoke ctClass.setTypeMembers()
L2:  public <T> void visitCtClass(CtClass<T> ctClass) {
L3:      addClassImport(ctClass.getReference());
L4:      for (CtTypeMember t : ctClass.getTypeMembers()) {
L5:          ... // This block was not covered
L6:      } super.visitCtClass(ctClass); }
```

- The `visitCtClass` of `ImportScannerImpl` (SPOON-169):
  As illustrated in Listing 1.9, the body statement in L5 was not covered because `getTypeMembers` (L4) called only returned empty iterables. To cover the not-covered branch, `setTypeMembers` invocation on `ctClass` argument was necessary prior to the `visitCtClass` method call (to set the `typeMembers` field of `ctClass` argument). However, EvoSuite did not invoke a such call.
- The `setCount` of `TreeMultiset` (GUAVA-39):
  As illustrated in Listing 1.10, the `setCount` method has a *then* branch (L7) which was not covered because EvoSuite did not pass an integer value greater than 0 as an argument to `setCount` to satisfy the branch condition.

3E Object State Problem in Invoking Object (L-OSI)

The L-OSI category requires to alter the CUT's object state further for not-covered branches. Several L-OSI examples are as follows:

- The `addClassImport` of `ImportScannerImpl` (SPOON-169) as shown in Listing 1.11. The `addClassImport` has three `if` statements (L4, L5, L6) whose conditions check whether the member field `targetType` is not equal to `null`. All three conditions were not satisfied because the `targetType` field was never got assigned to non-`null` value by EvoSuite. To assign the `targetType` field with non-`null` value, EvoSuite should invoke the `computeImports` prior to the `addClassImport` method call since the `targetType` initialization happens only in the `computeImport` call.
- The `isEmpty` of `LinkedListMultimap` (GUAVA-102) checks whether the linked list is empty by the `head == null` conditional expression. We found EvoSuite applied only empty lists to the `isEmpty` method in all attempts, which caused the negated branch of `head == null` (i.e., `head != null`) remain not covered.

Listing 1.10. Argument state problem in GUAVA-39

```
L1:  // To cover: argument newCount > 0
L2:  public boolean setCount(@Nullable E element, int oldCount,
L3:      int newCount) { ...
L4:      AvlNode<E> root = rootReference.get();
L5:      if (root == null) {
L6:          if (oldCount == 0) {
L7:              if (newCount > 0) { /* not covered block */ }
L8:              return true;
L9:          } else { return false; } } ... }
```

Listing 1.11. Invoking object state problem in SPOON-169

```
L1:  // To cover: invoke computeImports prior to addClassImport
L2:  protected boolean addClassImport(CtTypeReference<?> ref) {
L3:      ...
L4:      if (targetType != null && ...) { /* not covered */ } ...
L5:      if (targetType != null && ...) { /* not covered */ } ...
L6:      if (targetType != null) { ... /* not covered */ } ... }
L7:
L8:  public void computeImports(CtElement element) { ...
L9:      targetType = ... /* targetType was set to non-null here */
L10: ... }
```

3.4   SQ4: Other Problem

4A File System Access (FSA)

The FSA category relates to attempts to access files in the file system. EvoSuite already provides a Virtual File System (VFS) [3] to handle such file accesses during testing. However, there are still cases where VFS itself is insufficient, for example when the target program expects files with certain extension, file format, or possibly existing OS-related files.   Several FSA examples in the benchmark are as follows:

- `FileSystemFontProvider` (PDFBOX-8) as shown in Listing 1.12. During its construction, `FileSystemFontProvider` performs a scan (L3) for existing font files in the file system. The test failed to find font files in the file system, causing `files` (L1) and `fonts` (L3) became empty lists. Thus, the `for` loop in L4 and other six branches within the same class became not covered.
- `MavenLauncher` (SPOON-32) requires to read a valid Maven's `pom.xml` file, whose path specified in its constructor's argument. If a valid `pom.xml` file does not exist in the file system, the execution will raise an `SpoonException` so the test will not cover certain branches.

4B JVM's System.getProperty Call (JSC)

JRE allows JVM to store values through `System.setProperty`. However, Evo-Suite provides *no* mechanism to update those values. For an example of `FileSystemFontProvider` (PDFBOX-8) in Listing 1.13, the program queried the `"pdfbox.fontcache"` (L2) and `"user.home"` (L4) property. But the values of `path` in L3 and L5 were always `null` since EvoSuite did not update those values.

Listing 1.12. File system access in PDFBOX-8

```
L1: List<File> files = new ArrayList<File>();
L2: FontFileFinder fontFileFinder = new FontFileFinder();
L3: List<URI> fonts = fontFileFinder.find();
L4: for (URI font : fonts) {
L5:     files.add(new File(font)); // not covered
L6: } ...
```

Listing 1.13. JVM's `System.getProperty` problem in PDFBOX-8

```
L1: private File getDiskCacheFile() {
L2:     String path = System.getProperty("pdfbox.fontcache");
L3:     if (path == null || ...) { // else was not covered
L4:         path = System.getProperty("user.home");
L5:         if (path == null || ...) { // else was not covered
L6:             path = System.getProperty("java.io.tmpdir"); } }
L7:     return new File(path, ".pdfbox.cache"); }
```

4C Branch Unreachable (UBR)

The UBR category captures all branches that are infeasible to cover by any execution paths. We found that 33 not-covered branches belonged to UBR, which corresponded to around 9% of the not-covered branches that we manually analyzed. For an example in the Listing 1.14, `getDeclaration` in `CtLocalVariable- ReferenceImpl` (SPOON-20) has a null-checking branch (L3) on the return value of `getFactory` (L2). The `getFactory` (L5–L7) never returns a `null` value, causing the *then* branch in L3 not to be covered.

3.5   SQ5: Common Major Problems

Figure 3 shows the distribution of the limitation categories (described in Table 2) of the not-covered branches per subject in the SBST 2020 benchmark. Note that Fig. 3 shows data aggregated per class (i.e., multiple branches with the same category within the same class is counted as one) to find a common major problem in SQ 5.

We found that EvoSuite has *no* common major problem across all four target subjects. However, each subject has its own major problem (see the number of the classes of each subject (Table 1) and Fig. 3). For example, the *key-value store pattern* (L-KVS) was a major problem in PDFBOX only (i.e., 10 out of 20 classes of PDFBOX suffered L-KVS. But, only one class of GUAVA (and SPOON) suffered L-KVS and FESCAR had no class that suffered L-KVS). Similarly, *construction failure* (C-CF) was a major problem in FESCAR only.

Listing 1.14. Unreachable branch in SPOON-20

```
L1:  public CtLocalVariable<T> getDeclaration() {
L2:      final Factory factory = getFactory();
L3:      if (factory == null) { return null; /* not covered */ }
L4:  ... }
L5:  public Factory getFactory() {
L6:      if (this.factory == null) { return DEFAULT_FACTORY; }
L7:      return factory; }
```

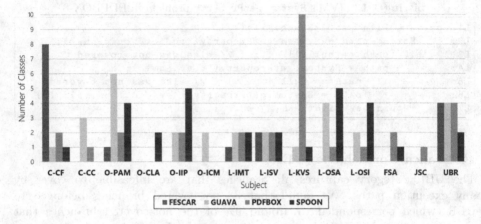

Fig. 3. Limitation category distribution aggregated per class

4   Conclusion and Future Work

To improve the effectiveness of EvoSuite by analyzing the EvoSuite's limitations, this paper presents the limitations of EvoSuite through an empirical study on the latest SBST 2020 benchmark. Through the manual analysis of the 359 reached-but-not-covered branches, we classified the four groups of the limitations of Evo-Suite (i.e., construction problems, OO-related problems, large search space problems, and so on (Table 2)). We reported all observed limitations of EvoSuite on the SBST 2020 benchmark with concrete examples so that researchers and practitioners can address such limitations more clearly. For future work, we plan to apply EvoSuite to more target benchmarks and study the effect of allocating higher search budget and using different fitness functions towards coverage attainment.

Acknowledgments. We would like to thank Ahcheong Lee for his effort to discuss the experiment results. This research work is supported by Basic Research Program (NRF-2020R1C1C1013512, NRF-2020R1C1C1013996, NRF-2021R1A2C2009384) of National Research Foundation (NRF) of South Korea and NRF grant funded by the Korea government (MSIT) (2021R1A5A1021944).

References

1. Almasi, M.M., Hemmati, H., Fraser, G., Arcuri, A., Benefelds, J.: An industrial evaluation of unit test generation: finding real faults in a financial application.

In: 2017 IEEE/ACM 39th International Conference on Software Engineering: Software Engineering in Practice Track (ICSE-SEIP), pp. 263–272 (2017). https://doi.org/10.1109/ICSE-SEIP.2017.27

2. Arcuri, A.: Restful API automated test case generation. In: 2017 IEEE International Conference on Software Quality, Reliability and Security (QRS), pp. 9–20 (2017). https://doi.org/10.1109/QRS.2017.11

3. Arcuri, A., Fraser, G., Galeotti, J.P.: Automated unit test generation for classes with environment dependencies. In: Proceedings of the 29th ACM/IEEE International Conference on Automated Software Engineering, ASE 2014, New York, NY, USA, pp. 79–90. Association for Computing Machinery (2014). https://doi.org/10.1145/2642937.2642986

4. Devroey, X., Panichella, S., Gambi, A.: Java unit testing tool competition: eighth round. In: Proceedings of the IEEE/ACM 42nd International Conference on Software Engineering Workshops, ICSEW 2020, New York, NY, USA, pp. 545–548. Association for Computing Machinery (2020). https://doi.org/10.1145/3387940.3392265

5. Fraser, G., Arcuri, A.: EvoSuite: automatic test suite generation for object-oriented software. In: Proceedings of the 19th ACM SIGSOFT Symposium and the 13th European Conference on Foundations of Software Engineering, pp. 416–419, New York, NY, USA. ACM (2011)

6. Fraser, G., Arcuri, A.: 1600 faults in 100 projects: automatically finding faults while achieving high coverage with EvoSuite. Empir. Softw. Eng. 20(3), 611–639 (2015). https://doi.org/10.1007/s10664-013-9288-2

7. Fraser, G., Staats, M., McMinn, P., Arcuri, A., Padberg, F.: Does automated unit test generation really help software testers? A controlled empirical study. ACM Trans. Softw. Eng. Methodol. 24(4) (2015). https://doi.org/10.1145/2699688

8. Pacheco, C., Lahiri, S.K., Ernst, M.D., Ball, T.: Feedback-directed random test generation. In: 29th International Conference on Software Engineering (ICSE 2007), pp. 75–84 (2007). https://doi.org/10.1109/ICSE.2007.37

9. Panichella, A., Kifetew, F.M., Tonella, P.: Automated test case generation as a many-objective optimisation problem with dynamic selection of the targets. IEEE Trans. Softw. Eng. 44(2), 122–158 (2018). https://doi.org/10.1109/TSE.2017.2663435

10. Panichella, A., Campos, J., Fraser, G.: EvoSuite at the SBST 2020 tool competition. In: Proceedings of the IEEE/ACM 42nd International Conference on Software Engineering Workshops, ICSEW 2020, New York, NY, USA, pp. 549–552. Association for Computing Machinery (2020). https://doi.org/10.1145/3387940.3392266

11. Panichella, A., Panichella, S., Fraser, G., Sawant, A.A., Hellendoorn, V.J.: Revisiting test smells in automatically generated tests: limitations, pitfalls, and opportunities. In: 2020 IEEE International Conference on Software Maintenance and Evolution (ICSME), pp. 523–533 (2020). https://doi.org/10.1109/ICSME46990.2020.00056

12. Rojas, J.M., Fraser, G., Arcuri, A.: Seeding strategies in search-based unit test generation. Softw. Test. Verif. Reliab. 26, 366–401 (2016). https://doi.org/10.1002/stvr.1601

13. Shamshiri, S., Just, R., Rojas, J.M., Fraser, G., McMinn, P., Arcuri, A.: Do automatically generated unit tests find real faults? An empirical study of effectiveness and challenges (T). In: 2015 30th IEEE/ACM International Conference on Automated Software Engineering (ASE), pp. 201–211 (2015). https://doi.org/10.1109/ASE.2015.86

Improving Android App Responsiveness Through Automated Frame Rate Reduction

James Callan[✉] and Justyna Petke

University College London (UCL), London, UK
{james.callan.19,j.petke}@ucl.ac.uk

Abstract. Responsiveness is one of the most important properties of Android applications to both developers and users. Recent survey on automated improvement of non-functional properties of Android applications shows there is a gap in the application of search-based techniques to improve responsiveness. Therefore, we explore the use of genetic improvement (GI) to achieve this task. We extend Gin, an open source GI framework, to work with Android applications. Next, we apply GI to four open source Android applications, measuring frame rate as proxy for responsiveness. We find that while there are improvements to be found in UI-implementing code (up to 43%), often applications' test suites are not strong enough to safely perform GI, leading to generation of many invalid patches. We also apply GI to areas of code which have highest test-suite coverage, but find no patches leading to consistent frame rate reductions. This shows that although GI could be successful in improvement of Android apps' responsiveness, any such test-based technique is currently hindered by availability of test suites covering UI elements.

Keywords: Genetic improvement · Search-based software engineering · Responsiveness · Android · Mobile applications

1 Introduction

Responsiveness is one of the most important qualities of Android applications to their users. Inukollu et al. found that 59% of users would give a bad review to an unresponsive app [17]. Khalid et al. [19] found that unresponsiveness was one of the most frequent reasons that users left bad reviews on mobile applications. Lim et al. [23] found that unresponsiveness was to blame 1/3 of the times when users abandoned applications.

Despite the importance of app responsiveness, there is not much research on its automated improvement. Given that the first Android version appeared only in 2008, the discrepancy between the number of approaches for software improvement for desktop vs. mobile applications is, perhaps, unsurprising. Recently Hort et al. [16] conducted a survey on Android performance optimization. It reveals

© Springer Nature Switzerland AG 2021
U.-M. O'Reilly and X. Devroey (Eds.): SSBSE 2021, LNCS 12914, pp. 136–150, 2021.
https://doi.org/10.1007/978-3-030-88106-1_10

that most approaches for responsiveness improvement focus on problem detection, rather than automated improvement. Among the most common techniques in the second category are: offloading and refactoring. Offloading [29], however, requires external infrastructure, while refactoring-based approaches tend to focus on very specific improvements, like introducing concurrency to long running processes [9] or combining HTTP requests [22]. Although these transformations could indeed help improve responsiveness, we believe that the search space of mutations could be combined and extended. With increase of the space of possible code refactorings, the search space for finding improvements will inadvertently increase. That's why search-based approaches would be a good fit to explore it. Notably, Hort et al. [16] do not report any search-based approaches for automated responsiveness improvement. With this work we intend to fill this gap.

In the desktop domain, Genetic Improvement (GI) has recently shown success in improvement of various functional (e.g., bug fixing [3]) and non-functional (e.g., runtime [21] or energy consumption [7]) properties. GI uses search-based algorithms to navigate the space of patches to existing software. It uses a fitness function that guides the search. Fitness could be based on test case failures, to check whether the program behaves correctly, and/or other measure, such as runtime to measure improvement of program's execution time.

In order to apply GI to improvement of responsiveness, we must first define the fitness function. Responsiveness, however, can be difficult to quantify. Moreover, measurements such as runtime are inherently noisy. Inspired by previous work [14], we propose using the frame rate of an application as a metric for responsiveness.

In this work we apply genetic improvement to improve Android app responsiveness. In particular, we extend an existing GI framework, Gin, to work on the Android domain. Next, we use it to improve frame rate of four Android applications. We find improvement of up to 50%, though closer inspection reveals many of the patches to be invalid, due to weak test suites—used as proxies for correct program behaviour, as is common in GI work. Nevertheless, we found a valid mutation that reduced frame rate by 43%. Subsequently, we apply GI on code with high test-suite coverage. However, in this case, no consistent improvements were found.

In summary, this work provides the following contributions:

- extension of an open source GI framework for the Android domain;
- first open source framework for automated frame rate reduction of Android applications[1];
- feasibility study for application of genetic improvement for the purpose of automated improvement of Android app responsiveness.

Our results show that although GI could be successful in improvement of Android apps' responsiveness, any such test-based technique is currently hindered by availability of test suites covering UI elements.

---

[1] Available: https://github.com/AndroidGI/AndroidGI.

The rest of the paper is divided as follows: Sect. 2 presents a short introduction to genetic improvement; Sect. 3 outlines our proposed framework for improving Android app responsiveness; Sect. 4 presents our methodology for the empirical study; with results in Sect. 5; Sect. 6 notes threats to validity of our work; Sect. 7 shows related work on automated improvement of responsiveness of Android apps; while Sect. 8 concludes the paper.

2   Background

Genetic improvement uses automated search to improve existing software [27]. Typically it operates at the level of source code, though mutations to the binary, assembly, and others have been tried. GI takes existing software, mutates it, generating sometimes thousands of software variants. Each variant is represented as a list of edits to the original code. Typical mutations involve copying, deleting, or replacing a code fragment, that being either a statement (most often), line or other (e.g., a binary operator). The search space of the evolved programs is navigated using a search strategy. Although historically genetic programming has been used, recent work show that local search can be equally effective [6]. Although the technique is simple, it has already been incorporated in the industry, during development process [13].

Work on Android software improvement using GI is scarce—so far only one work on GI exists in the Android domain [7], in which 'deep parameters' (constants not exposed to developers) were modified in order to find transformations which reduce the energy consumption of an application. The framework, however, is not open source, and source code was re-factored so that the search was conducted on an external file with parameters, causing upfront cost, and limiting mutations that could be automatically applied.

In this work we investigate the power of more traditional GI to improve another non-functional property of Android applications, namely their responsiveness.

3   Improvement of Android App Responsiveness Using GI

The main challenge of applying GI in the Android domain to improve responsiveness lies in defining and evaluating the fitness function. In the past, responsiveness has been measured using the execution time [12,20,28] of test cases. Whilst this may capture responsiveness, it will be negatively impacted by long running background processes which do not impact the actual responsiveness of the application. Gordon et al. [11] measured the "user-perceived latency" of interactions with applications, which is the time between a user input the completion of the action it triggers. This metric requires user scenarios to be manually defined, including start and end points, and does not allow us to utilise developer defined UI tests. However, we chose to use frame rate as a proxy for responsiveness, as it is both easily measured and directly captures delays in updates to the UI. An

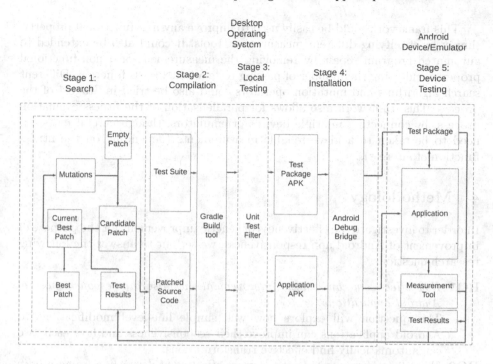

Fig. 1. Genetic improvement framework for Android applications.

application whose frames are not rendered in a timely manner will be unresponsive. Therefore, fixing these delays will result in a more responsive application. We believe that frame rate, and thus responsiveness, can be improved through source code transformations.

To measure an applications' frame rate, we must exercise the application's UI on a device or emulator, so we cannot rely solely on local unit tests. This means that applications must be packaged and installed on a device or emulator, which is a costly process. It also removes our ability to use optimisation techniques such as in-memory compilation.

Therefore, we propose the general framework shown in Fig. 1. The improvement process takes place across two devices: desktop and an emulator or mobile device. All communication between the desktop device is performed by the Android debug bridge, running on the desktop device.

In the desktop environment, new patches are generated, through mutation and selection (Stage 1), patches are applied, applications are built and packaged (Stage 2). Finally, local unit tests are run to determine whether or not a patch should be installed on the actual device (Stage 3). This step is important to vastly increase GI efficiency, as it reduces the number of program variants that need to be packaged and installed on a device or emulator, in order to measure their fitness. Patched applications which pass unit testing are then installed (Stage 4). On the Android device, modified versions of the application are exercised by the test package, and fitness measurements can be taken (Stage 5).

This framework could be easily used to improve any non-functional property, simply by specifying different measurement tools. It could also be extended to automated program repair by removing the measurement of a non-functional property and using the number of passing tests as the fitness function. Different search algorithms and mutation operators could also be tried in Stage 1 of the process. This framework also allows for parallelisation of the fitness evaluation process, by connecting multiple devices or emulators, though careful measures need to be taken to achieve reliable measurements (depending on the fitness function of interest).

4 Methodology

In order to investigate the effectiveness of genetic improvement for the purpose of improvement of Android app responsiveness, we set out to answer the following research questions:

RQ1 *How effectively can genetic improvement optimise the responsiveness of Android applications?*
This question will explore how well simple line-level modifications to Android applications can improve their responsiveness and how easily we can automatically find effective transformations.

RQ2 *What type of source code changes are effective at decreasing frame rate in Android applications?*
The changes that we find to have the largest impact on frame rate could be used to inform developers of ways in which they can improve the responsiveness of their apps. They could also be useful in inspiring future automated techniques for improving the responsiveness of Android applications.

RQ3 *How expensive is it to improve the frame rate of Android applications using genetic improvement?*
This question will allow us to quantify whether it is worth it to run GI in this manner. We will be able to present the balance of cost running vs the improvement to allow developers to make an informed decision about applying GI. We will also explore how the cost varies between applications and what impacts the cost of running GI.

In order to answer our research questions we implemented the framework presented in Fig. 1, and run it on a selection of Android applications.

4.1 Framework

We realise the abstract framework presented in Fig. 1 in the Gin GI tool [8]. We chose it as among non-functional property improvement GI tooling, Gin is scalable to large real-world software and is optimised for Java—a popular choice for Android software. We utilise the pre-existing functionality from Gin which allows the generation and modification of source code files with line-level changes. We also use the existing local search algorithm from Gin. By default, local search is run for 100 steps, at each step either copying, deleting or replacing a randomly selected line of code. We elected to run it for 400 steps to try to increase the chances of finding effective changes.

In order to run on Android and gather data for fitness evaluation, we have modified the components which compile the projects being improved and run their tests. We also added the functionality to install applications on Android devices and measure their frame rendering statistics.

Fitness. There are a number of different metrics which can be used to measure frame rate. They include the frames per second (FPS), average time taken to render a frame, and the number of delayed frames. In order to measure the frame rate of an application, we first need to run it, exercising its UI. We use UI tests for this purpose and use the built-in *dumpsys gfxinfo* tool to gather various measures. The tool gives detailed statistics about the render times of frames of a particular process. These statistics include the number of janky frames (those that take longer than 1/60th of a second to render), the median and, various percentiles (50th, 75th, 90th, 95th, 99th) of frame render time are given. We ran the whole test suite of our selected applications 100 times, measuring all these metrics, and found that the 95th percentile of frame render time to be least noisy, thus we use it as our frame rate measurement. Improving this metric will mean that the largest delays in responsiveness have been fixed.

Testing. Patch evaluation consisted of running all test cases which covered the area of code being modified to ensure that the functionality of the project had been preserved. UI tests also had to be run to measure the frame rate of the application. To improve efficiency of the GI process, we identify test cases that cover the given class for improvement, using *jacoco* [2]. Next, we use *espresso* [1] to identify UI tests. Finally, we split the UI tests into two, based on 60% delayed frame rate measure. The reason for this split is two-fold: first, running tests on the emulator or device is expensive, so we want to avoid unnecessary runs; second, we want to have a held-out test suite to check generalisability of improvements found. Therefore, for Stage 3 and Stage 5 of our GI process presented in Fig. 1 we use UI tests causing largest frame delays (over 60% frame delays), as well as all non-UI tests covering a given class. If all tests pass at Stage 3, we keep this program variant, and evaluate it's improvement in Stage 5, where each test is run 10 times, and median 95th percentile frame render time recorded. Due to the measurement of frame rate sometimes missing the test execution and not capturing the full execution of the test, small 3 s delays were added to the end of each UI test. This allowed the frame rate measurement to be consistently captured. Each performance test suite was then run until 200 frame measurements had been recorded. Before this the measurement could experience noise, leading to false positive improvements. Once 200 frames have been recorded we can see if the patch is in fact an improvement by comparing the median proportion of delayed frames in each test to that of the current best solution.

Search. Before we used the default local search implemented in Gin, we conducted a pre-study, to see if genetic programming (also implemented in Gin) might have been a better choice. Local search showed more promising results than GP as it was able to find optimised solutions faster. This is in line with the findings of Blot et al. [6]. We performed 20 runs on each of the selected classes in each of the projects. This allows us to collect a large amount of data and be confident about the efficacy of our setup, despite the non-deterministic nature of GI. We perform statistical tests on our results in order to quantify the effectiveness of GI at finding improvements.

4.2   Validation

For each final patch from each GI run, we use all tests covering a given class for validation purposes. We ran each 10 times and record median frame rate improvement. This allowed us to run statistical test on the results and see which patches offered significant improvements. The number of delayed frames was measured in the same way as during the GI runs. We performed this evaluation on a real device rather than an emulator, to ensure that improvements were valid in a real-world environment and test for device overfitting. We also conducted manual analysis of the patches to confirm their validity.

4.3   Benchmarks: Mobile Application Selection

We aim to improve real-world software and, therefore, choose to use real open source applications. Since we are using the Gin improvement tool, our modifications are limited to Java source code. Android applications may consist of mixtures of Kotlin and Java source code, but only the part of the application being modified needs to be written in Java. In our GI framework each patch is validated using the test suite of the application. This limits us to improving open source applications with areas of code which are well-tested. Moreover, we need UI tests to measure frame rate. Therefore, a number of criteria had to be met by applications used in this study:

- The application must be open source and at least partly written in Java.
- The application must be able to be compiled and deployed on an Android Emulator.
- The application must have sufficient areas of code covered by a test suite (at least one class with 40% line coverage).
- The application must contain at least one test that exercises it's UI.
- The application must contain at least one non-trivial UI class.[2]

Checking these criteria for a given app is costly (particularly test coverage). The application must be downloaded, compiled, installed and tested. The coverage of the unit tests and the instrumented tests must be measured separately.

---

[2] Based on manual judgement we decided to select applications with at least one UI class with at least 100 lines of code.

Fortunately, Pecorelli et al. [26] performed an analysis of all applications from FDroid, documenting both the number of tests and the coverage of those tests.

In order to curate a set of applications to evaluate our approach on, we checked applications analysed in [26] in descending order of line coverage. We then discarded applications which were not written in Java, those that could not be compiled, those whose tests could not be run successfully, and those which were too small for meaningful improvement to be found. If an application was not discarded, the areas of the application covered by its test suite had to be checked.

The first step in this process was to remove flaky tests - for two reasons. Firstly, the *jacoco* test coverage plugin [2] requires all tests to pass so flaky tests could disrupt the coverage measurement. Secondly, flaky tests may produce false negatives in patch validation. If a test fails due to flakiness, rather than due to the applied patch, it will make valid patch appear invalid. Thus, they must be excluded from the experiments and, therefore, should be excluded from coverage measurements. In some cases, build files had to be modified to remove conflicting dependencies or enable test coverage measurement. No source code was modified in this process.

When running GI on a desktop application, automated test generation tools such as EvoSuite [10], can be used to supplement test suites and increase code coverage. Sadly there are limited tools available for automated test generation for Android applications and none that can automatically generate regression tests were found. We found 3 tools which could generate automatic UI test input, however none worked on the recent versions of Android we ran our experiments on. Even if they did work they generated no assertions so could not be used to confirm patch validity. Therefore, the existing test suite of the application had to be relied on to validate patches.

Due to the large cost of validating a suitable application and the rarity of these applications, this process was repeated until 4 applications were found. Beyond this point line coverage was less than 15% so it was unlikely that more suitable applications would be found. Overall, we examined 192 applications, and 188 were discarded.

Profiling. Next, we profile each application we want to improve to identify code where changes influencing frame rate are most likely to be found. We thus focused on the UI implementing classes, the activity, view, and fragment classes. For each application we select the class which is most covered by the jankiest UI tests, that has at least 100 lines of code. We added the second condition, as classes with few lines of code are unlikely to hold improvements.

However, UI tests often contain very few assertions, relative to the amount of code which they exercise, and unit test for UI classes are very uncommon. Our proposed GI approach uses testing as a proxy for correctness. Because of this, while targeting UI-related classes may find the strongest improvements, it may also find invalid improvements due to the weaknesses of the test oracle.

Therefore, for each application, we select a class for improvement which is best covered by the whole test suite, and covered by at least one UI test, so we could measure frame rate usage.

Table 1. The number of tests cases and % line coverage for each of the selected classes

App name	Class name	No. tests	Line Cov.(%)
AntennaPod	PreferenceActivity (Exp1)	8	43
	MainPreferencesFragment (Exp2)	37	68
Gnu Cash	AccountsListFragment (Exp1)	11	64
	GnuCashApplication (Exp2)	37	76
MicroPinner	MainDialog (Exp1)	10	44
	MainPresenterImpl (Exp2)	14	75
WikimediaCommons	AboutActivity (Exp1)	9	45
	RecentSearchesContentProvider (Exp2)	18	63

In order to identify covered classes we used the *jacoco* Android coverage tool on each of the selected test cases Firstly, as *jacoco* only runs on whole test suites, we added JUnit's `@Ignore` decorators to all tests but the test case being investigated. We then ran *jacoco* on the modified test suite and extracted the coverage information, this process was repeated for each test. The classes which were most commonly exercised were then manually analysed to check for suitability, as described above.

Table 1 shows the final set of applications we found using our selection procedure, including the classes we identified using our profiling procedure and their test coverage.

4.4   Physical Setup

Our experiments were run on a research cluster, with 16 GB of RAM and an Intel Xeon e5 CPU, with an emulator using Android version 7. The evaluation of improvements was performed on a NOKIA 9 running Android version 10.

5   Results

Below we present the results of our experiments. In our first set of experiments (Exp1) we ran GI 20 times on the class in each of the four projects which was most covered by janky UI tests. In our second experiment, for each project, (Exp2) we ran GI on the class with the highest line coverage, that was also covered by at least one UI test.

5.1   RQ1: Improvements to Responsiveness

In order to answer RQ1, we present the improvement of frame rate before and after our patches are applied. Improvement is presented as the percentage decrease in the 95th percentile of frame render time. We also performed the Mann-Whitney U statistical test with the null hypothesis: *"There is no difference between the frame rate of the unpatched application and the patched*

Table 2. Improvements achieved in poorly tested UI classes

Project	No. improvements found	Max. % dec in 95th per. render time
AntennaPod	0	0.0
Gnu Cache	1	11.11
MicroPinner	1	5.56
Wikimedia commons	8	50.00

Table 3. Improvements achieved in well tested classes

Project	No. improvements found	Max. % dec in 95th per. render time
AntennaPod	0	0.00
Gnu Cache	0	0.00
MicroPinner	1	5.26
Wikimedia commons	0	0.00

application." for each patch discovered. This is to determine whether or not the improvements were statistically significant at the 95% confidence level. We treat those improvements as which are not statistically significant as 0% improvements. Tables 2 and 3 show our results.

We find that only 11 out of 160 of the GI runs performed found statistically significant improvements and 8 of those were in one application. In the vast majority of cases no improvements were found and the GI execution simply returned an empty patch. In 7 cases in the first experiment, patches were found which suggested improvements during search, however, validation resulted in them being found not to offer statistically significant improvements.

We also measure the execution time and memory usage of the patches where statistically significant improvements to frame rate were found, in order to quantify the way frame rate improvements affect other metrics for responsiveness. However, we find that where improvements are found, there is very little effect on either memory consumption or execution time. These measurements are noisy and may not be sensitive to the types of improvements which we found.

There is also the chance that the applications simply are not unresponsive enough to find significant improvements. Visual observation of UI tests does show noticeable improvements, though not significant. This shows that indeed frame rate measurements we take are more sensitive to UI changes, and have real, albeit small, impact. If tests were deliberately made to expose the unresponsive areas of applications, we may have an even better chance of finding improvements.

5.2   RQ2: Types of Improvements

To understand the types of improvement which can improve the frame rate of an application, we undertook a manual investigation of patches. We investigated the edits of the patch which was found to offer the most improvement in each project in order to find the most effective changes.

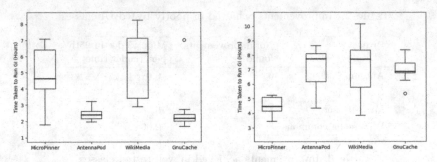

(a) Times taken for experiments on UI classes (b) Times taken for experiments on well covered classes

Fig. 2. Boxplots of the time taken for each run on each project in hours

One patch in particular offered significantly better improvements than any other. A patch to the WikiMedia Commons application offered improvements of 50% to frame render time. This patch contained 3 edits, 1 more than any other patch found. 2 of these edits remove text from the screen, making the whole patch invalid. However, one of the changes removes a line setting the gravity of a drop down menu's animation. Running this single change alone still produces a 43% improvement to frame render time, showing that it is the most important change. When deploying the modified version of the app we can see that opening and closing the drop down menus is significantly smoother and there is no obvious visual impairment to the animation. This improvement will not have large effects on the execution time or memory consumption of the test suite, however, it does make the application run more smoothly from a users perspective, fixing a stuttering animation.

It is possible that there are other opportunities for this kind of change available. However, the majority of open source applications have no tests and those that do have very poor coverage [26].

In the cases were improvements found turned out to be invalid, again the classes being improved did not have adequate coverage and the test which did cover were not very robust. Some patches removed lines of text which were meant to be displayed or prevented a dialog box from being displayed. In some cases the lines which were removed were covered but there were no assertions to check that the text was being displayed correctly. Much stronger regression testing would be needed to remove the risk of invalid patches being produced. This issue was not found for the single improving patch produced for well-covered classes, only on the UI classes with lower coverage.

5.3 RQ3: Cost of Improving Responsiveness

In order to answer RQ3, to evaluate the cost of improvement, we timed the execution of each GI run. The results of this evaluation can be found in Fig. 2.

The runs took between 2 and 16 h to complete. All of the experiments took a total of 883 h of compute time.

The execution time varied greatly between projects and the runs on particular projects. This variance comes from differing lengths of test suites and the number of patches which could be built, and therefore tested, that were found. Trying to target classes which are covered by small, fast test suites would help to reduce the cost of GI.

Running tests on the emulator is very expensive, and almost certainly responsible for the long runtimes. When analysing the Wikimedia commons setup used for the About Activity class we find that running the unit test filter only requires a median of 5 s over 10 runs. Whereas compiling, installing, and running the UI tests once takes a median of 2 min and 12 s over 10 runs. When running GI on Android in the future, it may be significantly faster to target properties that can be measured exclusively using local tests, removing the need for an emulator or real device.

6   Threats to Validity

There are a number of threats to the validity of this work. Below we present these threats and the actions taken to mitigate them.

Noise in Measurements. Whilst the fitness measurement only showed a small amount of noise when tested, these small deviations could still produce false positives for improvements. In order to mitigate this threat, we conduct repeated measurements and statistical tests on all improvements, in order to verify that the improvements are real.

Stochastic Search. Using randomised search may result in us 'getting lucky', and finding improvements that would not be likely to be found in subsequent runs. In order to show how our approach works generally, we perform 20 runs for each experimental setup (160 runs total).

Overfitting. As our patches are generated on a single emulator there is a chance that they will not translate to other, real world hardware. In order to test this, we validate all improvements that are found on a real device. Improvements may also be overfitted to the set of tests used during fitness evaluations. To test for this overfitting, a larger set of tests is used to validate the patches that are found, checking if any of them fail, along with how much of an impact the improvements have on other test cases.

7   Related Work

A recent survey [16] revealed several approaches for improving Android app responsiveness.

Offloading is a popular technique for improving the responsiveness of applications [5,11,12,18,20,28]. When offloading, expensive computation is performed

on an external server, saving both computational effort and energy usage on the
actual device. The main challenge of offloading is dynamically deciding what
should be offloaded. Offloading requires developers to create an external infrastructure, e.g., using cloud computing, to perform computation. This could be
complex and costly for developers. In this work, we propose finding purely local
changes to applications which do not require the set up of external hardware.

Pre-fetching is another technique used to improve responsiveness [4,15,30].
Online resources are asynchronously fetched before they are needed so that the
user does not have to wait for the request to be executed. Pre-fetching is limited
to improving a limited number of operations, and is not applicable to many
applications.

Local transformations for improving responsiveness of applications have also
been considered. Hecht et al. [14] tested the impact of repairing Android code
smells on frame rate. Lin et al. [24] developed a tool to automatically refactor
code into asynchronous tasks. Yijung et al. [25] automatically refactored inefficient local database writes for applications in order to improve responsiveness.

None of the discovered related work considers utilising a larger set of refactorings and using search-based approaches to navigate this space.

8   Conclusions and Future Work

In this work we present a genetic improvement approach for improvement of
responsiveness of Android applications. Even though we report negative results,
our research also revealed several avenues for future research.

Whilst genetic improvement is capable of finding improvements to the frame
rate of Android applications it is greatly limited by the number of and distribution of available tests. In order for genetic improvement to be applied successfully,
applications need more UI tests to allow janky areas of code to be exposed and
more unit testing of UI elements increasing the code coverage.

In future work we plan to extend the traditional set of operators with refactorings specialised for responsiveness. We also plan to expand our research to
investigate the power of GI to improve other properties of Android applications.
We also plan to use multi-objective search, as naturally improvements to responsiveness might negatively influence other software properties, such as memory
consumption. We would also aim to speed up GI for Android, if we can successfully find improvements using only local tests, we can avoid having to package
and install the application, greatly speeding up fitness evaluations. We believe
that despite current obstacles related to testing, future automated improvement
tooling for Android will benefit from search-based approaches, such as genetic
improvement.

Acknowledgements. This work was funded by the EPSRC fellowship EP/
P023991/1.

References

1. Espresso for UI testing. https://developer.android.com/training/testing/espresso/
2. Jacoco. https://docs.gradle.org/current/userguide/jacoco_plugin.html
3. Arcuri, A., Yao, X.: A novel co-evolutionary approach to automatic software bug fixing, pp. 162–168, July 2008
4. Baumann, P., Santini, S.: Every byte counts: selective prefetching for mobile applications. In: Proceedings of ACM on Interactive, Mobile, Wearable and Ubiquitous Technologies, vol. 1, no. 2, June 2017. https://doi.org/10.1145/3090052
5. Berg, F., Dürr, F., Rothermel, K.: Increasing the efficiency and responsiveness of mobile applications with preemptable code offloading. In: 2014 IEEE International Conference on Mobile Services, pp. 76–83 (2014). https://doi.org/10.1109/MobServ.2014.20
6. Blot, A., Petke, J.: Empirical comparison of search heuristics for genetic improvement of software. IEEE Trans. Evol. Comput. 1 (2021). https://doi.org/10.1109/TEVC.2021.3070271
7. Bokhari, M.A., Bruce, B.R., Alexander, B., Wagner, M.: Deep parameter optimisation on android smartphones for energy minimisation: a tale of woe and a proof-of-concept. In: GECCO (Companion), pp. 1501–1508. ACM (2017)
8. Brownlee, A.E.I., Petke, J., Alexander, B., Barr, E.T., Wagner, M., White, D.R.: Gin: genetic improvement research made easy. In: Proceedings of the Genetic and Evolutionary Computation Conference, GECCO 2019, pp. 985–993. Association for Computing Machinery (2019). https://doi.org/10.1145/3321707.3321841
9. Feng, R., Meng, G., Xie, X., Su, T., Liu, Y., Lin, S.: Learning performance optimization from code changes for android apps. In: 2019 IEEE International Conference on Software Testing, Verification and Validation Workshops (ICSTW), pp. 285–290 (2019). https://doi.org/10.1109/ICSTW.2019.00067
10. Fraser, G., Arcuri, A.: EvoSuite: automatic test suite generation for object-oriented software. In: SIGSOFT FSE, pp. 416–419. ACM (2011)
11. Gordon, M.S., Hong, D.K., Chen, P.M., Flinn, J., Mahlke, S., Mao, Z.M.: Accelerating mobile applications through flip-flop replication. In: Proceedings of the 13th Annual International Conference on Mobile Systems, Applications, and Services, MobiSys 2015, New York, NY, USA, pp. 137–150. Association for Computing Machinery (2015). https://doi.org/10.1145/2742647.2742649
12. Gordon, M.S., Jamshidi, D.A., Mahlke, S., Mao, Z.M., Chen, X.: COMET: code offload by migrating execution transparently. In: Proceedings of the 10th USENIX Conference on Operating Systems Design and Implementation, OSDI 2012, pp. 93–106. USENIX Association, USA (2012)
13. Haraldsson, S.O., Woodward, J.R., Brownlee, A.E.I., Siggeirsdottir, K.: Fixing bugs in your sleep: how genetic improvement became an overnight success. In: Bosman, P.A.N. (ed.) Genetic and Evolutionary Computation Conference, Berlin, Germany, 15–19 July 2017. Companion Material Proceedings, pp. 1513–1520. ACM (2017). https://doi.org/10.1145/3067695.3082517
14. Hecht, G., Moha, N., Rouvoy, R.: An empirical study of the performance impacts of android code smells. In: 2016 IEEE/ACM International Conference on Mobile Software Engineering and Systems (MOBILESoft), pp. 59–69 (2016). https://doi.org/10.1109/MobileSoft.2016.030
15. Higgins, B.D., Flinn, J., Giuli, T.J., Noble, B., Peplin, C., Watson, D.: Informed mobile prefetching. In: Proceedings of the 10th International Conference on Mobile Systems, Applications, and Services, MobiSys 2012, New York, NY, USA, pp.

155–168. Association for Computing Machinery (2012). https://doi.org/10.1145/2307636.2307651

16. Hort, M., Kechagia, M., Sarro, F., Harman, M.: A survey of performance optimization for mobile applications. IEEE Trans. Softw. Eng. (TSE) (2021)

17. Inukollu, V., Keshamoni, D., Kang, T., Inukollu, M.: Factors influencing quality of mobile apps: role of mobile app development life cycle. Int. J. Softw. Eng. Appl. **5** (2014)

18. Kemp, R., Palmer, N., Kielmann, T., Bal, H.: Cuckoo: a computation offloading framework for smartphones. In: Gris, M., Yang, G. (eds.) MobiCASE 2010. LNICST, vol. 76, pp. 59–79. Springer, Heidelberg (2012). https://doi.org/10.1007/978-3-642-29336-8_4

19. Khalid, H., Shihab, E., Nagappan, M., Hassan, A.E.: What do mobile app users complain about? IEEE Softw. **32**(3), 70–77 (2014)

20. Kosta, S., Aucinas, A., Hui, P., Mortier, R., Zhang, X.: ThinkAir: dynamic resource allocation and parallel execution in the cloud for mobile code offloading. In: Proceedings of the IEEE INFOCOM, pp. 945–953, March 2012. https://doi.org/10.1109/INFCOM.2012.6195845

21. Langdon, W.B.: Performance of genetic programming optimised Bowtie2 on genome comparison and analytic testing (GCAT) benchmarks. BioData Min. **8**, 1 (2015)

22. Li, D., Lyu, Y., Gui, J., Halfond, W.G.J.: Automated energy optimization of HTTP requests for mobile applications. In: Proceedings of the 38th International Conference on Software Engineering, ICSE 2016, New York, NY, USA, pp. 249–260. Association for Computing Machinery (2016)

23. Lim, S.L., Bentley, P., Kanakam, N., Ishikawa, F., Honiden, S.: Investigating country differences in mobile app user behavior and challenges for software engineering. IEEE Trans. Softw. Eng. **41**, 40–64 (2014). https://doi.org/10.1109/TSE.2014.2360674

24. Lin, Y., Okur, S., Dig, D.: Study and refactoring of android asynchronous programming (T). In: 2015 30th IEEE/ACM International Conference on Automated Software Engineering (ASE), pp. 224–235 (2015). https://doi.org/10.1109/ASE.2015.50

25. Lyu, Y., Li, D., Halfond, W.G.J.: Remove rats from your code: automated optimization of resource inefficient database writes for mobile applications. In: Proceedings of the 27th ACM SIGSOFT International Symposium on Software Testing and Analysis, ISSTA 2018, New York, NY, USA, pp. 310–321. Association for Computing Machinery (2018). https://doi.org/10.1145/3213846.3213865

26. Pecorelli, F., Catolino, G., Ferrucci, F., De Lucia, A., Palomba, F.: Testing of mobile applications in the wild: a large-scale empirical study on android apps. In: ICPC 2020, New York, NY, USA. Association for Computing Machinery (2020). https://doi.org/10.1145/3387904.3389256

27. Petke, J., Haraldsson, S.O., Harman, M., Langdon, W.B., White, D.R., Woodward, J.R.: Genetic improvement of software: a comprehensive survey. IEEE Trans. Evol. Comput. **22**(3), 415–432 (2018)

28. Ra, M., Sheth, A., Mummert, L., Pillai, P., Wetherall, D., Govindan, R.: Odessa: enabling interactive perception applications on mobile devices. In: MobiSys 2011 (2011)

29. Saarinen, A., Siekkinen, M., Xiao, Y., Nurminen, J., Kemppainen, M., Hui, P.: Can offloading save energy for popular apps?, August 2012

30. Yang, Y., Cao, G.: Prefetch-based energy optimization on smartphones. IEEE Trans. Wirel. Commun. **17**(1), 693–706 (2017)

Challenge Solutions

Searching for Multi-fault Programs in Defects4J

Gabin An[ID], Juyeon Yoon[ID], and Shin Yoo[✉][ID]

KAIST, Daejeon, Republic of Korea
{agb94,juyeon.yoon,shin.yoo}@kaist.ac.kr

Abstract. Defects4J has enabled numerous software testing and debugging research work since its introduction. A large part of its contribution, and the resulting popularity, lies in the clear separation and distillation of the root cause of each individual test failure based on careful manual analysis, which in turn allowed researchers to easily study individual faults in isolation. However, in a realistic debugging scenario, multiple faults can coexist and affect test results collectively. Study of automated debugging techniques for these situations, such as failure clustering or fault localisation for multiple faults, would significantly benefit from a reliable benchmark of multiple, coexisting faults. We search for versions of Defects4J subjects that contain multiple faults, by iteratively transplanting fault-revealing test cases across Defects4J versions. Out of 326 studied versions of Defects4J subjects, we report that over 95% (311 versions) actually contain from two to 24 faults. We hope that the extended, multi-fault Defects4J can provide a platform for future research of testing and debugging techniques for multi-fault programs.

Keywords: Software faults · Multiple faults · Bug database

1 Introduction

Defects4J [9] is one of the most popular real-world Java fault datasets in the field of software engineering, with over 650 citations as of June 2021 since its publication in 2014. Defects4J provides a number of software faults, along with a clearly separated and isolated set of test cases that can reveal each fault, making it easier for researchers to study individual faults in isolation. Due to both the ease of use and the realism of the curated faults, it has been broadly adopted in the empirical validation of numerous automated debugging work such as Fault Localisation (FL) [2,13,17] and Automated Program Repair (APR) [4,11,15].

However, in realistic debugging scenarios, multiple faults can coexist in software and affect the test results together. For example, a Continuous Integration (CI) process of large-scale industry software can produce hundreds of failing test cases that are caused by distinct root causes [7]. The isolation of individual faults that made Defects4J compatible with the Single Fault Assumption (SFA) ironically prevents it from being used to study the debugging of multiple faults.

© Springer Nature Switzerland AG 2021
U.-M. O'Reilly and X. Devroey (Eds.): SSBSE 2021, LNCS 12914, pp. 153–158, 2021.
https://doi.org/10.1007/978-3-030-88106-1_11

According to a systematic literature review of multiple faults localisation [19], the majority (33) of the 55 selected studies used only C faults for the evaluation. Only ten studies are reported to consider Java programs, five out of which employ Defects4J [12,14,18,20,21]. Only Zheng et al. [21] combined separate multiple Defects4J faults; since the procedure of creating the multiple faults was manual, only 46 have been created. The remaining work either concern multi-hunk faults, i.e., a single fault that can only be fixed by changing multiple locations [16] and consequently use Defects4J as it is [18,20], or actually concern neither multiple faults nor multi-hunk faults [12,14]. Note that, in this paper, we use the term *multiple faults* to denote the faults that can be fixed independently of each other.

Given the contributions to the automated debugging research made by Defects4J under SFA, we believe that the study of automated multi-fault debugging techniques [19], such as failure clustering [5,7,8] or fault localisation for multiple faults [1,6,21], would significantly benefit from the construction of a reliable dataset of realistic multi-fault Java programs. In this paper, we build a **real-world** Java **multi-fault** dataset by extending Defects4J. Instead of artificially injecting mutation or manually grafting faults, we use iterative search to systematically detect the existence of multiple faults in each version via fully automated transplantation and execution of the fault-revealing test cases. We report that 311 out of 326 studied faulty versions (95.4%) contain multiple faults, ranging from two to 24. The result data and replication package are publicly available[1].

2 Proposed Approach

The faults in Defects4J are extracted from the actual development history of various projects. Since every fault has a different life span [3,10], even a fault that was recently fixed may have existed in the project for a long time. In this work, we check if a specific fault N in version P of a Defects4J subject exists in an older version P' containing another fault M. If N exists in P', we regard P' as a multi fault program that includes both N and M. Note that we modify neither P nor P': the check is performed by test transplantation, and therefore we only reveal what already exists in P'. The following sections present the motivating example and our proposed method to search for multi-fault programs.

2.1 A Motivating Example

Listing 1.1 shows the fault Math-5 in Defects4J and its developer patch changing the return value from NaN to INF.[2] This fault is revealed by the test case testReciprocalZero (Listing 1.2) that checks if the return value is equal to INF. Each Defects4J fault is similarly provided with a set of fault-revealing test cases that reveals a single fault.

---

[1] https://github.com/coinse/Defects4J-multifault.
[2] http://program-repair.org/defects4j-dissection/#!/bug/Math/5.

```
1  --- a/src/main/java/org/apache/commons/math3/complex/Complex.java
2  +++ b/src/main/java/org/apache/commons/math3/complex/Complex.java
3  @@ -304,7 +304,7 @@ @@ public Complex reciprocal() {
4          if (real == 0.0 && imaginary == 0.0) {
5  -           return NaN;
6  +           return INF;
7          }
```

Listing 1.1. The developer patch for Math-5

```
1  public void testReciprocalZero() {
2      Assert.assertEquals(Complex.ZERO.reciprocal(), Complex.INF);
3      // Error message: junit.framework.AssertionFailedError: expected:<(NaN,
              NaN)> but was:<(Infinity, Infinity)>
4  }
```

Listing 1.2. The fault-revealing test case of Math-5

We note that, with few exceptions of recently added subjects and versions, the majority of faulty versions in Defects4J are indexed chronologically based on their revision dates, so that a lower ID refers to a more recently fixed fault: for instance, Math-5 was fixed later than Math-6. Therefore, the faulty source code version of Math-6 (referred to as Math-6b) may also contain the fault Math-5. Listing 1.3 confirms that Math-5 does exist in Math-6b, but is simply not revealed due to the absence of the fault-revealing test case, `testReciprocalZero`. When transplanted to Math-6b, the test fails with the same error message as in Math-5b, showing that Math-6b contains at least two faults, Math-5 and Math-6.

2.2 Searching for Multiple Fault Versions

Let B_M be the Defects4J faulty source code version that corresponds to the fault M.[3] As shown in our motivating example, if a fault N is fixed after a fault M, the fault N may *already exist* in B_M. Consequently, to build a multi-fault dataset, we check which faults exist in which preceding faulty versions.

Search Strategy. For each fault N in a project, we sequentially check whether the fault exists in each previous faulty version B_M, such that $M.id > N.id$, from the latest version to the older version. The search stops once N is not revealed in B_M. For example, the fault Lang-3 is revealed in Lang-[4,16]b, but not in Lang-17b. In this case, the search immediately stops and moves to the next iteration with a new N (Lang-4). This is because if B_M does not contain the fault N, it is likely that versions older than B_M do not include N either.

Existence Check. To determine the presence of a fault N in B_M, we *transplant* all fault-revealing tests of N to B_M. We confirm that N exists in B_M if and only if (1) all target test class files to where test case methods are transplanted exist in B_M, (2) all transplanted test cases are successfully compiled and fail against B_M, and (3) the error messages in B_M are the same as those in B_N. If

---

[3] `defects4j checkout -p Math -v 6b -w <dir>` checks out B_{Math-6} into `<dir>`.

```
304            if (real == 0.0 && imaginary == 0.0) {
305                return NaN; // Math-5b
306            }
```

Listing 1.3. In Math-6b, `Complex.java` (line 305) contains the fault Math-5

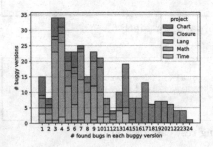

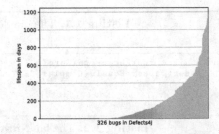

(a) The number of faulty versions in Defects4J with each number of faults

(b) The sorted life span of faults in days (average=154, standard deviation=246)

Fig. 1. The summary of search results

the fault-revealing test cases of the faults N and M overlap with each other, we further execute the fault-revealing tests of N on the fixed version of M to ensure that the overlapped test cases still fail due to N without the presence of M.

Building Multi-fault Subjects. When the above search is done, we obtain the set of pairs E such that $(N, M) \in E$ if and only if N exists in B_M. For every fault M in Defects4J, the set of *found faults* in B_M, $F(B_M)$, is defined as $F(B_M) = \{M\} \cup \{N | (N, M) \in E\}$. If $|F(B_M)| > 1$, B_M is a multi-fault subject.

2.3 Implementation Details

The process in Sect. 2.2 is dockerised and automated. We use `javaparser`[4] to detect the line range of the target test methods during transplantation. In the docker container, one can simply checkout to the multi-fault version by invoking `python3.6 checkout.py Math-1-2-3 -w /tmp/Math-1-2-3`, after which the *same* source code with Math-3b, augmented with the fault-revealing test cases of Math-1 and Math-2, is checked out.

3 Results

Multiple Fault Subjects. Figure 1a shows how many faults are contained in the faulty versions of five projects[5]. The x-axis shows the number of faults found

---

[4] https://github.com/javaparser/javaparser.

[5] Defects4J Bug IDs: Lang 1-65, Chart 1-26, Math 1-106, Time 1-27, and Closure 1-106. Note that Lang-2, Time-21, Closure-63 and -93 are excluded since they are either no longer reproducible under Java 8 or the duplicate bugs.

in each faulty version, and the y-axis shows the number of faulty versions. Out of 326 faulty programs, 95.4% (=311/326) of them contain multiple faults (i.e., # found faults >1). Furthermore, 126 and 22 faulty versions have ≥ 10 and ≥ 20 faults, respectively. For example, Closure-90b contains 24 faults. Our repository contains the full results of the found multi-fault versions.

Lifespan of Faults. To confirm whether lifespans of Defects4J faults vary similarly to existing findings [3,10], we calculate the lifespan of each fault. Let us define the *lifespan* of fault N as the number of days between the date of the oldest previous faulty version where fault N is detected and the revision date of N when the patch is applied. If there is no preceding version where the fault N is revealed, the lifespan is zero. Figure 1b shows that lifespans of faults range from 0 days up to longer than three years (e.g., Lang-41 has the lifespan of 1,187 days). The variance in lifespan suggests that the probability of having multiple faults at any given time can be nontrivial.

4   Conclusion

The paper presents a multi-fault Java dataset based on Defects4J, for which subjects with multiple real faults are constructed by transplanting tests without modifying the source code. Exploiting the chronological indexing of Defects4J, we propose a systematic search strategy to find co-existing faults that have not yet been revealed by failing tests. The results show that 311 out of 326 versions in Defects4J actually contain multiple faults. We hope that our extension of Defects4J can aid future research on search-based automated debugging under the existence of multiple faults.

Acknowledgement. This work is supported by National Research Foundation of Korea (NRF) Grant (NRF-2020R1A2C1013629), Institute for Information & communications Technology Promotion grant funded by the Korean government (MSIT) (No.2021-0-01001), and Samsung Electronics (Grant No. IO201210-07969-01).

References

1. Abreu, R., Zoeteweij, P., Van Gemund, A.J.: Spectrum-based multiple fault localization. In: 2009 IEEE/ACM International Conference on Automated Software Engineering, pp. 88–99. IEEE (2000)
2. Le, T.D.B., Lo, D., Le Goues, C., Grunske, L.: A learning-to-rank based fault localization approach using likely invariants. In: Proceedings of the 25th International Symposium on Software Testing and Analysis, pp. 177–188 (2016)
3. Canfora, G., Ceccarelli, M., Cerulo, L., Di Penta, M.: How long does a bug survive? An empirical study. In: Proceedings of Working Conference on Reverse Engineering, pp. 191–200. IEEE (2011)
4. Chen, Z., Kommrusch, S.J., Tufano, M., Pouchet, L.N., Poshyvanyk, D., Monperrus, M.: Sequencer: sequence-to-sequence learning for end-to-end program repair. IEEE Trans. Softw. Eng. (2019)

5. Dang, Y., Wu, R., Zhang, H., Zhang, D., Nobel, P.: ReBucket: a method for clustering duplicate crash reports based on call stack similarity. In: 2012 34th International Conference on Software Engineering (ICSE), pp. 1084–1093. IEEE (2012)
6. Ghosh, D., Singh, J.: Spectrum-based multi-fault localization using chaotic genetic algorithm. Inf. Softw. Technol. **133**, 106512 (2021)
7. Golagha, M., Lehnhoff, C., Pretschner, A., Ilmberger, H.: Failure clustering without coverage. In: Proceedings of the 28th ACM SIGSOFT International Symposium on Software Testing and Analysis, pp. 134–145 (2019)
8. Jones, J.A., Bowring, J.F., Harrold, M.J.: Debugging in parallel. In: Proceedings of the International Symposium on Software Testing and Analysis, pp. 16–26 (2007)
9. Just, R., Jalali, D., Ernst, M.D.: Defects4J: a database of existing faults to enable controlled testing studies for Java programs. In: Proceedings of the 2014 International Symposium on Software Testing and Analysis, pp. 437–440 (2014)
10. Kim, S., Whitehead Jr., E.J.: How long did it take to fix bugs? In: Proceedings of the International Workshop on Mining Software Repositories, pp. 173–174 (2006)
11. Koyuncu, A., et al.: FixMiner: mining relevant fix patterns for automated program repair. Empirical Softw. Eng. **25**, 1–45 (2020)
12. Laghari, G., Murgia, A., Demeyer, S.: Fine-tuning spectrum based fault localisation with frequent method item sets. In: Proceedings of the 31st IEEE/ACM International Conference on Automated Software Engineering, pp. 274–285 (2016)
13. Li, X., Li, W., Zhang, Y., Zhang, L.: DeepFL: integrating multiple fault diagnosis dimensions for deep fault localization. In: Proceedings of the 28th ACM SIGSOFT International Symposium on Software Testing and Analysis, pp. 169–180 (2019)
14. Li, X., d'Amorim, M., Orso, A.: Iterative user-driven fault localization. In: Bloem, R., Arbel, E. (eds.) HVC 2016. LNCS, vol. 10028, pp. 82–98. Springer, Cham (2016). https://doi.org/10.1007/978-3-319-49052-6_6
15. Liu, K., Koyuncu, A., Kim, D., Bissyandé, T.F.: TBar: revisiting template-based automated program repair. In: Proceedings of the 28th ACM SIGSOFT International Symposium on Software Testing and Analysis, pp. 31–42 (2019)
16. Saha, S., et al.: Harnessing evolution for multi-hunk program repair. In: International Conference on Software Engineering, pp. 13–24 (2019)
17. Sohn, J., Yoo, S.: FLUCCS: using code and change metrics to improve fault localization. In: Proceedings of the 26th ACM SIGSOFT International Symposium on Software Testing and Analysis, pp. 273–283 (2017)
18. Xia, X., Bao, L., Lo, D., Li, S.: "Automated debugging considered harmful" considered harmful: a user study revisiting the usefulness of spectra-based fault localization techniques with professionals using real bugs from large systems. In: International Conference on Software Maintenance and Evolution, pp. 267–278 (2016)
19. Zakari, A., Lee, S.P., Abreu, R., Ahmed, B.H., Rasheed, R.A.: Multiple fault localization of software programs: a systematic literature review. Inf. Softw. Technol. **124**, 106312 (2020)
20. Zhang, M., Li, X., Zhang, L., Khurshid, S.: Boosting spectrum-based fault localization using pagerank. In: Proceedings of the 26th ACM SIGSOFT International Symposium on Software Testing and Analysis, pp. 261–272 (2017)
21. Zheng, Y., Wang, Z., Fan, X., Chen, X., Yang, Z.: Localizing multiple software faults based on evolution algorithm. J. Syst. Softw. **139**, 107–123 (2018)

Refining Fitness Functions for Search-Based Automated Program Repair
A Case Study with ARJA and ARJA-e

Giovani Guizzo[✉], Aymeric Blot, James Callan, Justyna Petke, and Federica Sarro

University College London (UCL), London, UK
{g.guizzo,a.blot,james.callan.19,j.petke,f.sarro}@ucl.ac.uk

Abstract. Automated Program Repair (APR) strives to automatically fix faulty software without human-intervention. Search-based APR iteratively generates possible patches for a buggy software, guided by the execution of the patched program on a test suite (i.e., a set of test cases). Search-based approaches have generally only used Boolean test case results (i.e., pass or fail), but recently more fined-grained fitness evaluations have been investigated with promising yet unsettled results. Using the most recent extension of the very popular Defects4J bug dataset, we conduct an empirical study using ARJA and ARJA-e, two state-of-the-art search-based APR systems using a Boolean and a non-Boolean fitness function, respectively. We aim to both extend previous results using new bugs from Defects4J v2.0 and to settle whether refining the fitness function helps fixing bugs present in large software.

In our experiments using 151 non-deprecated and not previously evaluated bugs from Defects4J v2.0, ARJA was able to find patches for 6.6% ($\frac{10}{151}$) of bugs, whereas ARJA-e found patches for 8% ($\frac{12}{151}$) of bugs. We thus observe only a small advantage in using the refined fitness function. This contrasts with the previous work using Defects4J v1.0.1 where ARJA was able to find adequate patches for 26.3% ($\frac{59}{224}$) of the bugs and ARJA-e for 47.3% ($\frac{106}{224}$). These results may indicate a potential overfitting of the tools towards the previous version of the Defects4J dataset.

Keywords: Search-based automated program repair · Empirical study · Software engineering

1 Introduction

Automated Program Repair (APR) [6], as the name suggests, tries to automatically derive software patches, in order to fix bugs with none (or little) human intervention. Various approaches, based on symbolic execution, machine learning and search-based algorithms, have been proposed for APR [2,6]. In this work we focus on search-based APR.

© Springer Nature Switzerland AG 2021
U.-M. O'Reilly and X. Devroey (Eds.): SSBSE 2021, LNCS 12914, pp. 159–165, 2021.
https://doi.org/10.1007/978-3-030-88106-1_12

Given a buggy program and related test suite, search-based APR approaches iteratively generate candidate patches by mutating the program. A fitness function compiles and tests each candidate patch to assess whether it produces expected outputs for all inputs in the test suite. If the test suite passes, then it is an indication that the generated patch was successful and it is deemed "adequate". This type of *Boolean* fitness function has been the approach most used so far, and only recently a more fine-grained fitness evaluation (i.e., non-Boolean), which uses not only the binary result of test cases but also their output in case of a failure, has been proposed [1,12].

Yuan and Banzhaf [12] have been the first to propose a more refined fitness function and included it in the ARJA-e tool. Their empirical evaluation, conducted on 224 real-world Java bugs from Defects4J [3] v1.0.1, showed that ARJA-e correctly fixed 39 bugs, achieving substantial performance improvements over the more traditional search-based APR tools using fitness functions based on Boolean test results. On the other hand, a more recent study conducted by Bian et al. [1] did not reveal any major significant difference when comparing the effectiveness and efficiency of such traditional vs. refined fitness functions.

In this challenge paper, we aim at unveiling whether there is indeed any difference in using traditional vs. refined fitness functions. We use a corpus of real-world software projects with potentially harder-to-fix bugs that has not been used in previous studies. This corpus consists of 151 non-deprecated bugs from 13 software programs from Defects4J v.2, which were not contained in earlier versions of this dataset. We evaluate and compare two well-known state-of-the-art search-based APR software: ARJA [11] and its extension, ARJA-e [12]. Both use Multi-Objective Evolutionary Algorithms (MOEAs) and differ in the implemented fitness functions. While ARJA uses the more traditional fitness function, based on number of failing test cases; ARJA-e uses the "smooth" non-Boolean fitness to gradually guide the APR process towards a passing test suite.

Our results show that there is little benefit in using refined fitness functions, with ARJA producing 10 patches vs. 12 produced by ARJA-e. Moreover, the fix rates are much lower than those reported in the literature, pointing to overfitting to the previous Defects4J dataset.

2   Background

A handful of approaches has been proposed to refine fitness functions in search-based program repair, to not rely on just Boolean test case results. We present all of them below.

ARJA-e. Unlike most other APR tools in the literature, ARJA, ARJA-e's predecessor, uses multi-objective optimisation search, considering both *patch size* (f_1) and *weighted failure rate* (f_2). Whilst the patch size simply is the number of edits in a given patch x, the weighted failure rate is defined by Eq. 1, with T_{pos} and T_{neg} the sets of negative and positive sets and $w \in [0,1]$ the weight parameter introducing bias against the latter.

$$f_2(x) = \frac{|\{t \in T_{pos} : x \text{ fails } t\}|}{|T_{pos}|} + w * \frac{|\{t \in T_{neg} : x \text{ fails } t\}|}{|T_{neg}|} \qquad (1)$$

ARJA-e further extends ARJA with a more fine-grained fitness function, given by Eq. 2. Instead of simply counting the number of failed test cases, the *error ratio* (h) of each executed test is calculated. This ratio is the mean *assertion distance* $(d(e))$ of each assertion executed by the test $(e \in E(x,t))$ for a particular patch. A specific normalised distance metric is used for each type of assertion, e.g., the Levenshtein distance for string objects, or absolute distance for numbers.

$$f_2(x) = \frac{\sum_{t \in T_{pos}} h(x,t)}{|T_{pos}|} + w * \frac{\sum_{t \in T_{neg}} h(x,t)}{|T_{pos}|} ; \quad h(x,t) = \frac{\sum_{e \in E(x,t)} d(e)}{|E(x,t)|} \quad (2)$$

2Phase. 2Phase's [1] fitness function takes a hybrid approach between ARJA and ARJA-e. When two patches produce differing numbers of passing and failing tests, the one with the least failing/most passing will be considered better. Otherwise, the sum of their assertion distances on failing tests will determine which patch is preferred.

GenProgNS. GenProgNS [10] is an implementation of GenProg [5] which replaces fitness evaluation based on the number of passing tests with the novelty of the solution. A Boolean vector b represents the outcome of each test case for a particular variant. For test case i, b_i is assigned 1 if the test case passes and 0 if it fails. The Hamming distance of these vectors is then used to calculate novelty and the most novel solutions are preferred. This approach prioritises exploration of the large search space over exploitation of the improvements found so far.

Checkpoints. Checkpoints [9] implements a fitness function in which the values of variables that are present in test cases are tracked throughout execution. These variables' values are compared with those from the original test executions of the buggy program, and fitness is assigned based on their comparison. For failing test cases on a particular variant, the variant is considered more fit if it maintains the values of variables in tests which originally passed and changes variable values in the tests which originally failed.

3   Experimental Design

In this work we want to answer the following question:

How effective is search-based APR if refined fitness functions are used when compared with traditional fitness evaluation, which considers only Boolean test case results?

With this in mind we focus on comparing effectiveness and efficiency of ARJA and ARJA-e. ARJA is a mature tool and ARJA-e provides an extension with the fitness function change, thus making fitness comparison fair for our purposes.

Table 1. Detail of Dejects4J between v1.0.1, v2.0, and depreciated bugs.

Project	# Bugs				Project	# Bugs			
	v1.0.1	v2.0	Dep.	Total		v1.0.1	v2.0	Dep.	Total
Chart	26	0	0	26	JacksonDatabind	0	112	0	112
Cli	0	39	1	39	JacksonXml	0	6	0	6
Closure	131	43	2	174	Jsoup	0	93	0	93
Codec	0	18	0	18	JxPath	0	22	0	22
Collections	0	4	24	4	Lang	64	0	1	64
Compress	0	47	0	47	Math	106	0	0	106
Csv	0	16	0	16	Mockito	0	38	0	38
Gson	0	18	0	18	Time	26	0	1	26
JacksonCore	0	26	0	26					
Total	391	444	29	835		←	←	←	←

Dataset. Defects4J [3] is a prevalent and extremely widespread dataset of real Java bugs. Recently Defects4J has been updated with many new bugs for which very little is known in comparison. We use these new bugs to drive our investigation. To our knowledge, the new bugs introduced in Defects4J v2.0 have only been tackled with non-search-based approaches [7,13]. Table 1 shows the set of bugs in both versions Defects4J v1.0.1 and v2.0. Although there are 444 non-deprecated new bugs in the dataset, we ended up using a subset of 151 buggy project versions due to a few technical challenges. The list of all bugs and results of our experiments can be found at https://figshare.com/s/35ea3fd819e737ed806b.

Technical Challenges. ARJA has a few undocumented requirements. ARJA is divided into two modules: the core module contains all the classes for the execution of the algorithms and generation of patches; the external module is used by the core module to instrument the code, run test cases, and capture code coverage. The default location of the external module is hard-coded into ARJA's source code, thus executing the tool within a working directory different from ARJA's root directory results in failures. This can be fixed by providing the path to the external module as an argument, but this is undocumented. This problem is aggravated because ARJA neither fails/crashes when it does not find the external project, nor does it output errors. Hence, it executes normally with missing functionalities, but the results seem to be successful with no generated patches. The second and most crucial challenge regards the resource files/scripts provided by Defects4J to checkout, compile, and to export metadata of projects. The supporting scripts sometimes fail due to various reasons. For example, we could not compile the Compress projects using Defects4J because using Java 8 (required by Defects4J) in combination with the Maven and Ant compilation scripts provided by Defects4J results in failures due to unsupported compilation of Java 1.4 sources (version of the project). Other examples of fail-

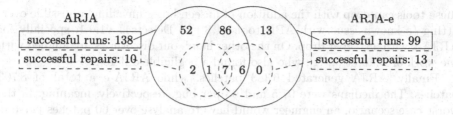

Fig. 1. Set of bugs with successful runs and repairs for ARJA and ARJA-e.

ures include: inclusion of nonexistent files and missing items in the classpaths, missing configuration files during checkout, and failure to replace placeholders (e.g. ${*project.root.dir*}) with actual paths. These problems can be fixed by manually (and laboriously) inspecting each of the 444 subjects' resource files. Finally, even with working projects, correct set-ups, and correct metadata, ARJA sometimes failed to instrument the code, localise faults, or it simply hanged. The 151 projects used in this paper are the only ones we could execute without any issues.

Experimental Setup. We used the latest commits of ARJA[1] and ARJA-e[2]. Both tools were run to completion using their default recommended configuration without a specific time limit. Experiments were repeated ten times using independent random seeds, using a Sun Grid Engine cluster running CentOS Linux 7 nodes with Java v1.8.0_131, Perl v5.16, SVN v1.8.19, and Git v2.9.5.

4   Results and Discussion

Figure 1 shows the summary of our results. The solid circles represent bugs for which the tools were able to successfully run, whereas the dashed lines represent the subset of bugs for which the tools found test-suite adequate patches.

> Our results show that ARJA is able to find adequate patches for **6.62%** ($\frac{10}{151}$) of the subjects, or 10 out of 138 of the bugs if we consider only successful runs. ARJA-e is able to find adequate patches for **7.95%** ($\frac{12}{151}$) of the subjects, or 12 out of 99 of the bugs if we consider only successful runs.

According to the original work of ARJA and ARJA-e using Defects4J v1.0.1, the tools found adequate patches for 26.33% ($\frac{59}{224}$) and 47.32% ($\frac{106}{224}$) of the bugs, respectively. The dissimilarity between our findings and the results of previous work [11,12] is striking: the differences between both tools is rather small (6.62% vs 7.95%) when compared to the difference found in their original papers (26.33% vs 47.32%). Furthermore, the low fixing rate suggests that the effectiveness of

[1] https://github.com/yyxhdy/arja/tree/e7950328c05e3f7eb38e1af11efc31055af09d05.

[2] https://github.com/yyxhdy/arja/tree/f24b777a7c53a390ff97ecfd66fbbdedd8f8b6b3.

these tools can drop with the addition of unseen bugs, unveiling a possible over-fitting (a known issue with APR tools [4,8]) to Defects4J v1.0.1, specially for ARJA-e with a steeper drop. On the other hand, our discoveries are aligned with the work of Bian et al. [1], who also found a negligible difference.

Finally, ARJA generated 6 383 patches, while ARJA-e a total of 8 703 patches. The medians were 97.5 and 63 per bug, respectively, meaning, in the worst case scenario, an engineer would have to analyse over 60 patches per bug to check for semantic correctness. This hinders the feasibility of both tools in practice due to the great amount of manual effort needed.

5   Conclusions

Search-based APR has been successfully used to generate test-suite adequate patches. The search over mutated program variants is guided by a fitness function that usually only considers Boolean test case results. In order to improve it's effectiveness, more refined fitness functions were proposed, that take *types of failures* into account. However, previous work is not unanimous on whether this more sophisticated fitness function actually is more effective.

In this work we ran two state-of-the-art tools, ARJA and ARJA-e, that differ in their fitness implementation, to compare whether the more refined fitness version in ARJA-e indeed helps the search. We ran our experiments on the newly added 151 bugs in the famous Defects4J set. Our results show that neither fitness is significantly better than another. Moreover, we also reveal that the two ARJA variants struggle to find test-suite adequate patches on the new dataset, having found significantly more on older benchmarks.

Acknowledgments. Funded by ERC 741278 and EPSRC EP/P023991/1.

References

1. Bian, Z., Blot, A., Petke, J.: Refining fitness functions for search-based program repair. In: ICSE Workshops (2021)
2. Gazzola, L., Micucci, D., Mariani, L.: Automatic software repair: a survey. IEEE Trans. Softw. Eng. **45**(1), 34–67 (2019)
3. Just, R., Jalali, D., Ernst, M.D.: Defects4J: a database of existing faults to enable controlled testing studies for Java programs. In: ISSTA, pp. 437–440 (2014)
4. Kechagia, M., Mechtaev, S., Sarro, F., Harman, M.: Evaluating automatic program repair capabilities to repair API misuses. IEEE Trans. Softw. Eng. (2021)
5. Le Goues, C., Nguyen, T., Forrest, S., Weimer, W.: GenProg: a generic method for automatic software repair. IEEE Trans. Softw. Eng. **38**(1), 54–72 (2012)
6. Monperrus, M.: The living review on automated program repair. Technical report, hal-01956501, HAL (2018)
7. Motwani, M., Brun, Y.: Automatically repairing programs using both tests and bug reports. CoRR abs/2011.08340 (2020)
8. Smith, E.K., Barr, E.T., Goues, C.L., Brun, Y.: Is the cure worse than the disease? Overfitting in automated program repair. In: SIGSOFT FSE, pp. 532–543 (2015)

9. de Souza, E.F., Le Goues, C., Camilo-Junior, C.G.: A novel fitness function for automated program repair based on source code checkpoints. In: GECCO, pp. 1443–1450 (2018)
10. Trujillo, L., Villanueva, O.M., Hernandez, D.E.: A novel approach for search-based program repair. IEEE Softw. **38**(4), 36–42 (2021)
11. Yuan, Y., Banzhaf, W.: ARJA: automated repair of java programs via multi-objective genetic programming. IEEE Trans. Softw. Eng. **46**(10), 1040–1067 (2020)
12. Yuan, Y., Banzhaf, W.: Toward better evolutionary program repair: an integrated approach. ACM Trans. Softw. Eng. Methodol. **29**(1), 5:1–5:53 (2020)
13. Zhu, Q., et al.: A syntax-guided edit decoder for neural program repair. In: ESEC/FSE (2021)

Author Index

Printed in the United States
by Baker & Taylor Publisher Services